THE ENDING OF MARK AND THE ENDS OF GOD

Essays in Memory of Donald Harrisville Juel

Beverly Roberts Gaventa and Patrick D. Miller, editors

WJK WESTMINSTER
JOHN KNOX PRESS
LOUISVILLE · KENTUCKY

© 2005 Westminster John Knox Press

Chapter 1, "A Disquieting Silence: The Matter of the Ending," was previously published in *A Master of Surprise* by Donald Harrisville Juel, published by Fortress Press, 1994. Used with permission.

Book design by Sharon Adams
Cover design by Night and Day Design

First edition
Published by Westminster John Knox Press
Louisville, Kentucky

This book is printed on acid-free paper that meets the American National Standards Institute Z39.48 standard. ♾

PRINTED IN THE UNITED STATES OF AMERICA

05 06 07 08 09 10 11 12 13 14 — 10 9 8 7 6 5 4 3 2 1

Library of Congress Cataloging-in-Publication Data

The ending of Mark and the ends of God : essays in memory of Donald Harrisville Juel / Beverly Roberts Gaventa and Patrick D. Miller, editors.— 1st ed.
    p. cm.
    Includes bibliographical references.
    ISBN 0-664-22739-2 (alk. paper)
    1. Bible. N.T. Mark XVI, 1–8—Criticism, interpretation, etc. 2. Bible—Criticism, interpretation, etc. I. Juel, Donald. II. Gaventa, Beverly Roberts. III. Miller, Patrick D.

BS2585.52.E54 2005
226.3'06—dc22

                                                    2004057153

Contents

Introduction

The ending of a story is never entirely satisfying. Sometimes the ending does not seem appropriate to the story that has preceded it. This problem can send authors into rounds of revisions and generate reams of criticism. In other cases, readers simply are not ready to be done with the story, in which case they join in the lament of small children, "But I don't want it to be over yet!" Or perhaps they simply read the last few pages again and again, hoping somehow to extend the story's grasp.

The ending of Mark's Gospel has produced much speculation and interpretation, but few biblical scholars have treated Mark's ending as provocatively as did the late Donald Harrisville Juel, whose most mature treatment of that text appears as the first chapter of this volume. Impatient with any attempt to convert Mark's abrupt ending into something mild and mellow, Don argued against interpreters who seek to force closure onto a text that so vehemently resists it. For him, Mark's Jesus is "on the loose," which means that the ending of the Gospel can neither be tamed nor confined. As a tribute to Don, we invited some of his close friends and colleagues to reflect on the intersections between Don's interpretation of Mark 16:1–8 and their own work, either with other biblical texts or with issues in systematic or practical theology.

We begin with those essays that directly address Mark's Gospel (Blount, Black, Murchison). These are followed by studies of other biblical texts and issues provoked by Don Juel's work, beginning with several essays on New Testament texts (Thompson, Gaventa, Gillespie, Welker), and continuing with three treatments of Old Testament texts (Miller, Olson, Lapsley). The final section addresses larger questions of discipleship and theological education (Charry, Keifert).

This arrangement should not obscure the issues and questions that cut across the various contributions. Some essays in this volume explore the endings of other biblical texts. Jacqueline Lapsley studies the ending of the book of Ezekiel, an ending that aims toward exactly the kind of closure missing in Mark's Gospel. Yet Lapsley shows that the vision of God now securely restored in the temple stands unresolved alongside the relentless depiction of human sin earlier in the book. Patrick Miller's examination of Genesis 50 reflects on the ending of Jacob's life and thereby the end of the era of Israel's ancestors, which is simultaneously the beginning of the story of the multiplication of Abraham's offspring and the exodus from Egypt. Dennis Olson explores the death of Moses at the end of Deuteronomy, an event that both tragically leaves Moses outside the land of Canaan and makes possible the fulfillment of the promise to the next generation. Thomas W. Gillespie takes up Romans 9–11, which he categorizes as an instance of early Christian prophecy, one that entails the sort of startling ending Juel found in Mark 16.

Other essays in this volume address theological issues present in Juel's treatment of Mark's ending, whether implicitly or explicitly. Marianne Meye Thompson takes up the role of God in Johannine eschatology, contending that the clear dualism in John's treatment of human beings cannot be employed to predict the final status of any human being, since the resurrection is God's own act, and only God can determine the future of anyone. Beginning with Juel's characterization of God in Mark's Gospel as no longer safely contained in heaven, C. Clifton Black explores the complementary notion of God's elusiveness. Attempts to fix Jesus, whether in a shrine or on a cross, will inevitably fail. Beverly Roberts Gaventa considers the portrait of God in Paul's Letter to the Romans, finding that Romans shares with Mark's Gospel the understanding that God is "on the loose," not to be contained either by Paul's argumentation or by crafty interpreters of Paul's letter.

A third set of essays considers Juel's interpretation of Mark's ending as it concerns disciples and discipleship. Resisting Juel's finding that "everyone" is shut out of Mark's Gospel except God alone, Blount emphasizes the readers Mark is hoping to create, readers who will follow Jesus. From the Gospel's beginning, Mark hopes to motivate readers to follow—whether or not they manage to do it well. Ellen T. Charry shares this concern about following by asking the very difficult question of what exactly it means for faithful followers to follow a God whose ways must be acknowledged to be "unfollowable," not in Mark's Gospel alone but in much of human life. D. Cameron Murchison begins with the disappointment and promise Juel finds in the Markan ending and explores those same themes in connection with an American Christianity deeply shaped by a culturally distorted sense of the material conditions needed for human well-being. Michael Welker begins with Juel's treatment of Jesus' baptism and reflects on baptism both in Mark and elsewhere in the New Testament as a change of lordship. He finds in Juel's insistence on the shock and surprise of Mark's Gospel a theological antidote to the domestication of baptism in much of the church's practice.

All of these threads come together in the essay of Patrick R. Keifert on the Bible and theological education. Keifert reflects on his extended collaboration with Don Juel on matters of pedagogy and their urgency for the church's life. Observing the paralyzing silence regarding the Bible in much ecclesial debate and discourse, Keifert and Juel undertook to rethink theological education in ways that would enhance the ability of pastors to seek the truth of biblical texts with and for believing communities.

The ending of a story is never entirely satisfying. That is, for us, especially true of the ending of Don Juel's story. It is evident, however, not only in these pages but in the work of many others, that this particular story of a marvelous teacher, a perceptive scholar, and a dear friend has not ended. It will go on in the teaching, preaching, and writing of countless persons whom Don Juel taught and still teaches.

Chapter 1

A Disquieting Silence:
The Matter of the Ending
Donald Harrisville Juel

No point in a story is as significant for appreciation and interpretation as its ending. That is surely the case in Mark's Gospel. The abrupt and unsatisfying conclusion has not surprisingly spawned a massive secondary literature—most of recent vintage, however. Interest in the ending became possible only with the publication of editions that relegated verses 9–20 to the footnotes. Until the great Alexandrian codices were known, few paid attention to the scattered references to a Gospel of Mark that lacked a proper conclusion. Further, only after a scholarly consensus had determined that Mark could no longer be read as Matthew's epitomizer could readers become fascinated—and troubled—by the mysterious anti-climax that forms the end of our Gospel: "So they went out and fled from the tomb, for terror and amazement had seized them; and they said nothing to anyone, for they were afraid" (Mark 16:8).

There are perhaps additional factors in the current fascination with the Markan ending. One is the willingness to read Mark as a narrative. When the text is broken down into component parts that are the focus of investigation, as among form critics, the strange conclusion can be explained more easily. The episode at the empty tomb may be read as an effort to explain why the story appeared so late in the tradition (the women never told anyone) or as an effort to put distance between the apostolic testimony and the resurrection from the empty tomb. Such explanations require detaching the verses from their narrative setting and proposing another, hypothetical *Sitz im Leben* in the context of which the snippet is to be understood. The verses sound rather different as the conclusion of a narrative. Any who have been present at one of David Rhoads's "presentations" of Mark can testify to the uneasiness in the audience when the last words are spoken—even in an audience of sophisticates who know in advance how the narrative will end.[1]

There is much ground to cover in any study of Mark's ending. Fortunately the whole field need not be replowed. Andrew Lincoln's fine piece in the Journal of Biblical Literature has made it unnecessary to review all of the research.[2] His analysis of current studies, his examination of words for "terror" and "amazement" in Mark, his brief review of evidence for ending a sentence with *gar*—such matters require little additional comment. I prefer to confine my study to the experience of the ending and to ask if criticism has any role at all to play in commending a particular experience of the Gospel's ending—and thus of the narrative as a whole.

While we might speak of a scholarly consensus regarding the ending of Mark, there is surely no consensus regarding its interpretation. In fact, there is still reluctance among interpreters to settle with 16:8 as the conclusion of the Gospel. That reluctance gives evidence of a feature of public imagination well analyzed by Frank Kermode in his *The Sense of an Ending*:[3] people do not tolerate unfinished stories easily. Consider the comment in the Oxford Study Bible [RSV]:

> Nothing is certainly known either about how this Gospel originally ended or about the origin of vv. 9–20, which cannot have been part of the original text of Mark. . . . Though it is possible that the compiler(!) of the Gospel intended this abrupt ending, one can find hints that he intended to describe events after the resurrection.[4]

Such speculation is a clear refusal to read the work as it appears in the best-attested readings; it is very much of the same order as the endings tacked on by ancient copyists who could not tolerate a Gospel that ended with frightened women. Interpretation of the ending will necessarily involve scrutiny of our own needs as readers—in this case, suspicion about interpretations that cannot reckon with "for they were afraid" as a conclusion of a Gospel.

Perhaps it should be stated explicitly that the Gospel according to Mark that we are interpreting ends with 16:8. That is not the Gospel read by most generations of Christians. Modern text-critics and editors believe there are good reasons to omit the "spurious" endings that for centuries constituted the conclusion of the church's Gospel. While it would be satisfying to describe our printed text as the original version of Mark's Gospel, greater modesty is advisable. The task of text-critics is to establish the "best" text that can then be printed. Through judicious selections among the alternatives available in the manuscript tradition, scholars can establish a version of the Gospel for which the best arguments can be advanced.[5] The plausibility of text-critical arguments can be tested through a variety of means, both historical and literary. Interpretations that demonstrate coherence in a version of Mark ending with 16:8 add probability to arguments that deal with manuscripts of the Gospel. The reconstruction of an implied audience for whom such a narrative would be appropriate likewise adds plausibility. For example, the abrupt ending makes more sense if the Gospel is addressed to believers than if it were intended as missionary propaganda. Such an implied audience would have to be tested by interpretation of the remainder of the Gospel as well as by historical arguments: Could such an audience have existed in early Christianity as we know it? What setting and function for a narrative might we suggest within such a religious community? The point is that even decisions about what will be printed as the Bible will require arguments that proceed according to agreed-upon ground rules. For our purposes, it is enough to note that the majority of experts in the field of Gospel criticism believe there are good reasons to print as the Gospel according to Mark a version that ends with 16:8. Because that is the case, the format chosen for printing the Gospel ought to make it crystal clear to readers that Mark ends at 16:8. The use of paragraph headings like "longer ending" and "shorter ending," and the use of double brackets in both the Greek New Testament and in the NRSV, is an unfortunate compromise that is more confusing than helpful. One suspects that the use of critical symbols rather than using different size print for alternative versions of the Markan ending represents equivocation on the part of translation committees. The stubborn refusal of commentators to accept sound text-critical arguments in their interpretation of Mark and the continuing creation of hypothetical conclusions say more about commentators than about Mark.

Comments by Brevard Childs in his singular *Introduction to the New Testament as Canon* bear at least some passing comment in this regard.[6] Childs argues that the alternative ending ought to be read as part of the canonical Mark. His concern arises in part from acknowledgment that the Mark known to most generations of Christians included verses after 16:8. Childs seeks a compromise interpretation. He argues that verses 9–20 should be read as the canonical reading of Mark because the verses employ bits and pieces from the remaining three Gospels. The verses, he believes, seek to prevent aberrant readings of Mark that might suggest undue differences from the other Gospels. There is no real problem with reading the verses as part of the canonical Mark because "the same theological point made by the original ending has been retained, but extended," namely the disciples' unbelief in the face of the resurrection.

Such an argument is interesting, but it largely misses the point. Endings are important more for what they do than for the ideas they include. Verse 8 does something radically different as an ending than does verse 20, something that shapes the whole experience of reading the Gospel. It is the whole impact of the canonical Mark that ought to be of interest to readers, not simply the ideas extracted from it. If we agree that the version of the Gospel in the manuscript tradition with the strongest claim to logical priority deserves to be printed in Bibles, it is this version—ending with verse 8—that will function as canon. It is the function of this ending that I wish to explore, with the help of Kermode.

THE EXPERIENCE OF THE ENDING

An ending does things. It can achieve closure, pulling together loose threads from a story, or it can resist closure, refusing to answer burning questions posed in the course of the narrative. Kermode's analysis both in *The Sense of an Ending* and *The Genesis of Secrecy*[7] explores that experience of closure in narrative. His analysis of the wide range of interplay between reader and story necessarily involves attention to the expectations and needs of readers. We write and read stories, he insists, because we must. Stories, and the interpretation of stories, represent a way of dealing with a confusing and "unfollowable" world. His analysis does not seek to replace the reading of stories with something else but to prepare readers to be a more responsive and critical audience. As is the case with other art forms, the Gospel must be experienced; study prepares hearers to listen for themes, for invention, for irony and surprise.

Study is necessary because we are not obviously good readers. In a culture suspicious of words, students need to be coaxed to give them a try. Further, readers must develop a sense of expectancy, learning what to look for and where to find clues. Preparing readers for engaging a narrative with an image or a suggestion makes them susceptible to ideological and institutional biases, of course. Yet without such biases, communication would be impossible. There must be some rules of communication, some sense of what to expect. Kermode has no illusions about objective readings of narratives, but he does seek to prepare critical readers by alerting them to institutional biases. Given the importance of the Bible to the life of the church as well as to the academic community, it is hardly surprising that representatives of such institutions carefully protect their investments by regulating interpretation. We study to see more deeply and to overcome confusion and bewilderment in our reading. Study can, however, protect vested interests and permit personal satisfaction at the expense of what is read.

The ending of Mark's Gospel provides a particular challenge to interpreters. The reason is its failure to resolve the tensions in the story and to provide some sense of closure that seems appropriate to "good news about Jesus Christ." Taken at face value, the concluding verse constitutes a disappointing end: nothing comes of the whole enterprise because the women do not speak. Few interpreters will accept such a reading of the Gospel, of course. For the less sophisticated readers who are familiar with Matthew, Luke, and John, it is difficult even to hear Mark. Endings are automatically supplied, probably much like the familiar "longer ending" printed in the NRSV. Imagination does not even attend to the discord. The same is true of commentators—sensible Bible readers who insist that disappointment in the performance of the women is the result of misunderstanding. One senses a kind of desperation in the otherwise fine study of Schüssler Fiorenza who must at all costs find heroism in the women at the tomb.[8] A similar defensiveness seems to dominate those who argue that the *tromos* and *ekstasis* that take hold of the women at the conclusion of the story, and the fear that drives them to flee, are positive emotions.[9] At least at first reading, the failure of the women to spread the good news is hardly commendable, and the fear with which they are possessed is little different from the fear that plagues the disciples throughout the story. Our need to overcome this experience of disappointment is the primary motor that drives interpretation.

There may well be good reasons to read the ending as hopeful, but that hopeful reading cannot be purchased at the expense of Mark's narrative. I do not wish to belabor the point, but the history of the Markan ending in manuscript and commentary betrays an unwillingness or inability to take the disappointment seriously. It is as if there is an emotional barrier that must be broken through if the Gospel is to be heard.

In the midst of a discussion of Mark 16 in class, in which young interpreters were finding one reason after another for regarding the Gospel's ending as upbeat, one student raised her hand and said, "I read the ending over several times last evening in preparation for class. I thought about it—and I cried." There was something about that experience—an honesty, an ability to read with defenses down, a willingness to acknowledge disappointment—that changed the course of the class discussion.

One of Kermode's great contributions is a willingness to entertain the possibility that there are no satisfying endings—in Mark or in life. Intrigued by the tension between literary form and the formlessness of the world explored by such writers as Kafka, aware of the power of language and story to satisfy and to console, and of the deep human need for satisfaction and consolation, he is well-suited as a critic to examine the experience of reading Mark's Gospel. He is particularly adept at unmasking fraudulent readings that refuse to take Mark's narrative seriously—readings that, more often than not, are proposed by representatives of institutions with considerable investment in interpretation (for example, the church or the learned community); his distaste for Jeremias's approach to the parables is particularly striking, and his critique effective.[10] His critical reflections suggest certain questions are central, and I would like to deal with them. Does the Gospel make sense in light of the ending, or is it nonsense? Are there ways to offer good reasons for one reading or another? And finally, do the troubling verses give reason to look forward to an ending that is inviting and hopeful?

As with many other students of Mark, I wish to focus on the last two verses. In his study, Lincoln characterizes the experience of verses 7 and 8 in terms of promise and failure.[11] Focusing on the response of the reader, I would speak rather of hope and disappointment. Much is invested in a reading of these two verses and their bearing on the argument that the Gospel seeks to make.

"AS HE TOLD YOU": THE ARGUMENT
FOR A SATISFYING ENDING

The astonished women do not find Jesus in the tomb, as they had expected. Instead, they encounter a young man dressed in a white robe. While several interpretations of this figure are possible, we are probably to think of a heavenly messenger. That is surely the way Matthew and Luke heard the term, and both eliminate any possible ambiguity with their embellishments.

The women are appropriately terrified. The herald offers customary assurance that they need not be alarmed. He points to the obvious: Jesus is no longer in the tomb. Hoping to achieve some sort of closure to Jesus' unpredictable career by anointing his body for burial, the women are stunned by one more surprise: Jesus cannot be confined by the tomb any more than by the hopes of his followers or the designs of his enemies. The grave clothes have been shed; Jesus is out of the tomb, on the loose.

Perhaps the most important feature of the herald's announcement is the closing: "Go, tell his disciples and Peter that he is going ahead of you to Galilee; there you will see him, just as he told you" (Mark 16:7). "As he told you." The reminder takes on considerable significance when the verse is read within the context of the whole story. Jesus has, in fact, made such a promise. The little collection of prophecies recounted just prior to Jesus' arrest (14:28–30) include a scriptural reference to Zechariah ("I will strike the shepherd, and the sheep will be scattered;" cf. Zech. 13:7), a detailed forecast of Peter's denial, and the promise that he will precede his disciples to Galilee after his resurrection.

The prophecy of Peter's denial is quite precise. The rhyming couplet (nicely captured in the KJV's "Before the cock crows twice, you will deny me thrice") is repeated by the narrator at the conclusion of Peter's trial: "Then Peter remembered that Jesus had said to him, 'Before the cock crows twice, you will deny me three times.' And he broke down and wept" (14:72). Jesus' prophecy is fulfilled to the letter. Even the detail about the second crowing of the cock is noted carefully (14:72). And while this unlikely scenario of Peter's collapse is being played out in the courtyard of the high priest's house, inside Jesus is being taunted to prophesy by the servants of those who have condemned him to death. Jesus' prophecies, we are reminded, do indeed come to pass, a detail that offers a glimpse into the deeper dimensions of the narrative Mark recounts.

"As he told you." The specific forecast of Jesus' resurrection in 14:28 is only one of many statements Jesus makes about what will happen. Three times Jesus formally predicts his death—and his resurrection (8:31; 9:31; 10:33), predictions that are given the added force of necessity (*dei*, 8:31; 9:11). That "necessity" has to do with the will of God recorded in the Scriptures: "The stone that the builders rejected has become the cornerstone" (12:10, quoting Psalm 118:22); "The Son of Man goes as it has been written of him" (14:21); "But let the scriptures be fulfilled" (14:49).

The collection of parables in chapter four offers figurative predictions of what lies beyond the boundaries of the narrative: planting, despite obstacles, will result in harvests; a tiny seed will produce a full-grown bush. "There is nothing hidden, except to be disclosed," Jesus promises (4:21–24). Jesus speaks to his disciples of the inevitable onset of birth pangs that precede the coming of the Son of Man with the clouds of heaven (13:8). He promises that the Gospel must be preached to all nations (13:10). James and John are told that they will indeed share in his cup and baptism (10:39). His numerous promises have important functions in the narrative. They foreshadow; they give to the story a sense of direction and purpose; they point to what lies beyond the story. Promises that are fulfilled provide a basis for confidence that others will be. His glimpses of what lies ahead create a momentum that drives readers beyond the ending into the period beyond the story. "There you will see him, just as he told you" (16:7). The narrative offers reason to believe that what Jesus promises will take place.

The announcement from the empty tomb that Jesus has been raised—as he said he would be—thus opens a gateway to the future. The disciples will surely see him. Whatever the obstacles, the harvest will come; the tiny seed will grow into a shrub large enough to provide nesting places for the birds; at the end of the birth pangs one can expect new life. There is reason to recount Jesus' story as good news because the reader can believe what Jesus "told you." That, at least, is one argument the narrative offers. There is someone to tell the story, itself an indication that it did not end with fearful women.

"THEY SAID NOTHING TO ANYONE": THE ARGUMENT FOR AN UNSATISFYING ENDING

Were Mark's Gospel to end with 16:7, there would be far less interest in chapter 16, and in Mark's Gospel. It does not. As readers, we have been led to expect something other than verse 8. When Jesus enjoins his bewildered disciples to say nothing about the events on the Mount of Transfiguration, he suggests a limit to their silence: "until after the Son of Man had risen from the dead" (9:9). That Peter, James, and John understand nothing of what Jesus is saying to them only heightens interest in what is to come. Expectations are planted in readers. There will be a time of openness, a time for disclosing and speaking (4:21–22). There is good reason to believe that Jesus' resurrection will mark the transition from one time to another. Yet, in the narrative world at least, that is not to be.

Neither the stirring words of the divine messenger nor the empty tomb succeed in making evangelists of the women who have come to do their duty to a corpse. Like the disciples (14:50) and the young man seized in the garden (14:52), they flee (the word *pheugo* appears also in 5:14 to describe the actions of the swineherds in the land of the Gerasenes, and in Jesus' warnings in 13:14). The reason, we are told, is that "trembling and ecstasy held them fast." They say nothing to anyone—they were afraid, you see (Kermode's paraphrase). The terrible irony is that now is the time to speak. The tomb is empty; the crucified King is alive, vindicated by God, as he said he would be. What is hidden may now come to light (4:21–22); the disciples can tell secret things they were commanded to withhold now that Jesus has risen from the dead (9:9). The faithful women have the opportunity to do what the men could not. And they fail. They flee, just as the men—because they are afraid.

Arguments that the trembling, ecstasy, and fear are positive terms, appropriate to the presence of the divine, seem akin to Matthew's reading of Mark: "So they left the tomb quickly with fear and great joy, and ran to tell his disciples" (Matt. 28:8). Slight changes in wording yield a very different sense; "They left quickly with fear and great joy" is words away from "They fled . . . for they were afraid." Their flight and their inability to do as they were commanded remains.

Insisting that the women told no one "for the present" has little support in the narrative. The story has offered no reason to place confidence in any insiders. While the women at least do their duty, like the disciples of John the Baptist did when they claimed his body and laid it in a tomb (6:29), they do not anticipate a miracle. They come fully expecting to find a corpse. Auerbach's analysis of Peter's performance seems an appropriate reading of the women's performance as well: They come closer to genuine greatness than the other disciples, only to fall further.[12] Even in the face of an empty tomb and testimony to Jesus' resurrection, the women cannot believe in such a way as to perform the most basic task of disciples: testimony. They tell no one the good news. They flee, and we are left to imagine what became of them, and we are left to imagine the fate of Judas, and the naked young man, and Peter, and the Twelve.

If Mark argues that there is a reason to believe the gospel will be preached to the nations, the narrative simultaneously undercuts any confidence in the performance of characters without whom the whole enterprise seems lost.

Mark's Gospel ends with both hope and disappointment. The relationship between the last two verses embodies the critical tension in the story between blindness and insight, concealment and openness, silence and proclamation. The tension is not resolved. Why is this so? To what end does the tension lead? It is to that question we now turn, with the help of Kermode.

DOORS

Kermode's study of endings is driven by a conviction that stories are essential to life as a way of making sense of an unfollowable world. His fascination with Kafka and other existentialist writers arises from the perceived tension between reality and form. Human beings create order and form, so the argument goes, as a necessary response to the formlessness and meaninglessness of the world. To make that argument, to be sure, writers like Kafka must employ traditional forms that purport to represent reality—narrative forms that feature genuine endings— but they do so in such fashion as to create doubts about our ability to make contact with some fundamental order. Kermode senses that there is something hollow, even untruthful, about imitations of a coherent and purposeful reality, however noble the motivations of artists and however necessary their fictions to our sense of well-being. Art imposes order on what is beyond our ordering; it attempts to grasp what is beyond our reach. While one can imagine some ultimate plan or design, it remains out there, unfollowable. Art can achieve meaning, therefore, only at the expense of truth.

Art is most interesting, therefore, for what it tells us about ourselves. It arises from our need for order, a need that seems basic to the species. In analyzing stories, Kermode entertains, with structuralists, the possibility that basic paradigms underlie all narrative:

> Now presumably it is true, in spite of all possible cultural and historical variations, that the paradigm will correspond, the more fully as one approaches a condition of absolute simplicity, to some basic human "set," biological or psychological. Right down at the root, they must correspond to a basic human need, they must make sense, give comfort.[13]

If that is so, the closing verses of the Gospel are all the more intriguing, for the initial experience of the ending suggests that it does not fit the paradigm. The conclusion does little to offer a sense of an ending without which the story makes no sense.

> Mark's book began with a trumpet call: "This is the beginning of the gospel of Jesus Christ, the Son of God" (1:1). It ends with this faint whisper of timid women. There are, as I say, ways of ending narratives that are not manifest and simple devices of closure, not the distribution of rewards, punishments, hands in marriage, of whatever satisfies our simpler intuitions of completeness. But this one seems at first sight wholly counterintuitive, as it must have to the man who added the twelve verses we now have at the end.[14]

Part of the difficulty in conversing with Kermode is that he offers no sustained interpretation of Mark, because that is not his purpose. He offers only hints. He seems willing to entertain the possibility that the ending does "make sense," although such an interpretation is not obvious. He seems most disposed to the imaginative work of people like Austin Farrer, whose creative exploration of literary patterns places him outside the usual guild of Markan scholars.[15] Offering his interpretation of the Markan ending would accomplish little, however, because his major concern is to bring naive readers face to face with the genuinely enigmatic character of Mark: The Gospel generates secrecy, not just secrets. While it holds out the prospect that readers can become insiders, the possibility turns out to be illusory. Placed in this hermeneutical bind, interpreters with institutional allegiances and an investment in coherence and meaning are forced to employ cunning and violence to extract what they need from the text. The experience of disappointment must at all costs be overcome.[16]

Kermode is by no means exempt from such institutional allegiances, of course, and he is capable of employing cunning and violence to achieve his own ends, as he would readily admit. Few would accuse him of violence, but we should not fail to appreciate the single most remarkable act of cunning in his approach to Mark: the selection of Kafka's parable as a controlling image. Here is Kermode's version of the parable:

> A man comes and begs for admittance to the Law, but is kept out by a door-keeper, the first of a long succession of doorkeepers, of aspect even more terrible, who will keep the man out should the first one fail to do so. The man, who had assumed that the Law was open to all, is surprised to discover the existence of this arrangement. But he waits outside the door, sitting year after year on his stool, and conversing with the doorkeeper, whom he bribes, though without success.
>
> Eventually, when he is old and near death, the man observes an immortal radiance streaming from the door. As he dies, he asks the doorkeeper how it is that he alone has come to this entrance to seek admittance to the Law. The answer is, "This door was intended only for you. Now I am going to shut it." The outsider, though someone had "intended" to let him in, or anyway provided a door for him, remained outside.[17]

The parable, introduced in chapter 2, moves in and out of the study and provides Kermode with the dramatic conclusion to his book:

> This is the way we satisfy ourselves with explanations of the unfollowable world—as if it were a structured narrative, of which more might always be said by trained readers of it, by insiders. World and book, it may be, are hopelessly plural, endlessly disappointing; we stand alone before them, aware of their arbitrariness and impenetrability, knowing that they may be narratives only because of our impudent intervention, and susceptible of interpretation only by our hermetic tricks. Hot for secrets, not only conversation may be with guardians who know less and see less than we can; and our sole hope and pleasure is in the perception of a momentary radiance, before the door of disappointment is finally shut on us.[18]

The image gives to Kermode's work a genuine ending; it makes sense of his study and his passion to explore the whole matter of secrecy. Mark, Kermode argues, has no ending in the sense that it can be grasped by any particular reading. The enigmatic conclusion becomes symptomatic of a deeper hermeneutical problem: There can be no ending. Mark will continue to generate new readings. Readings will always be particular—and limited. If ultimate reality is inaccessible to us, as Kafka's parable argues, if the most we can hope for is a glimpse at best, if we are and always will be outsiders, then the lesson for scriptural interpreters seems to be that they would do best to remain satisfied with questions of meaning, never to claim too much for an interpretation, and to bracket out questions of truth from interpretation.

In an important sense, this is quite different from the argument made by Mark's narrative. Consider the differences between Mark's Gospel and Kafka's parable. As in Kafka's work, Mark's narrative generates expectancy. Jesus' parables speak of seed time and harvest, of small seeds and large shrubs. Apparently insignificant beginnings drive toward magnificent conclusions, despite obstacles that stand in the way. Jesus daringly labels the tribulations that lie ahead birth pangs; creation groans in anticipation of what will come. He promises his resurrection and his return with the clouds, when he will gather his elect from the four winds. As in Kafka's parable, there is also disappointment. The world into which the reader is invited is one in which people fail. Longed for resolutions do not occur. Loose ends are not tied up. It is as Jesus says: "the end is still to come" (13:7).

The difference between Mark's story and Kafka's has to do with closure. There is genuine closure in Kafka's parable. The door is shut as the old man dies, and with it the possibility of insight. There is no more waiting. The message is clear: We have been permanently shut out. Meaningfulness, such as it exists, is accessible to us only as we are able to supply it. We remain outside the door, forever.

Mark's Gospel forbids precisely that closure. There is no stone at the mouth of the tomb. Jesus is out, on the loose, on the same side of the door as the women and the readers. The story cannot contain the promises. Its massive investment in the reliability of Jesus' words becomes a down payment on a genuine future. Caught up in the narrative's momentum, the last words of the messenger at the tomb impel the reader beyond the confines of the narrative: "There you will see him, as he told you" (16:7). There will be enlightenment and speaking; the disciples will somehow play the role for which they have been chosen.

The door is a powerful image. It can open to possibilities or it can bar entrance. It is precisely the possibility of opening that makes the conclusion of Kafka's parable—the shutting door—so devastating. Kermode has not attended to such imagery in Mark. The doors in Mark's Gospel are emphatically open: The curtain of the Temple is rent asunder (as is the curtain of the heavens at Jesus' baptism) and the stone is rolled back from the tomb. There is surely disappointment as the women flee, dashing hopes that at least one group of followers will prove faithful. But Jesus is out of the tomb; God is no longer safely behind the curtain. To hear in Mark's elusive ending the strains of Handel's "Halleluia Chorus" would require drowning out the music being performed. But to insist that the discordant ending offers no promise of resolution whatever is to do equal violence to the story. Jesus has promised an end. That end is not yet, but the story gives good reasons to remain hopeful even in the face of disappointment. The possibilities of eventual enlightenment for the reader remain in the hands of the divine actor who will not be shut in—or out.

Kermode's analysis clearly exposes the human need for closure, structure, and control. One can argue theologically from the same premises that interpretation can become a way of defending ourselves against truths that make a claim on us. The argument of Kafka's parables is that whatever truth exists is inaccessible to us—except the truth that we are alone in the face of the impenetrable. Mark's Gospel—and, we might add, the whole Christian tradition—argues that our lack of enlightenment and bondage arise from attempts to box God in or out of experience. All such attempts come to grief in the resurrection of Jesus. He cannot be confined by the tomb or limited by death. In Jesus' ministry, God tears away barriers that afforded protection in the past. God cannot be kept at arm's length. Such a possibility that light dawns even on those who inhabit the realm of darkness is disquieting; it means there is no refuge for the cynical any more than for the naive.

The possibility that the future is open may send interpreters scurrying to the ramparts, fearful for their lives. There is reason for sobriety. The Gospel offers little promise that we have control of our destiny. Interpretation only makes matters worse. The deeper into the narrative we delve, the less control we are promised. If the unresolved ending offers promise, it is surely not because we are encouraged to believe that we can do better than the disciples or the women. We do not "have" Jesus even at the end of the story, and there is no guarantee that we can wrest a promise from him or lock him safely away by hermeneutical tricks. Here Kermode is surely correct. But perhaps that is just where the promise resides. "There you will see him, as he told you." Jesus has promised an encounter with him against which there is no assured defense. God will be put off neither by our failures, or infidelity, nor by our most sophisticated interpretive schemes. And if this "good news about Jesus Christ" is God's work within the intimate realm of human speech, there is reason to hope that our defenses will finally prove insufficient and that we will not have the last word. The history of the Markan ending is perhaps ample testimony that this "gospel" will not be easily dismissed.

One's choice of images by which to open readers to a narrative can be a matter of cunning and violence. A choice is necessary nevertheless, and I believe there are good reasons for choosing an image other than the closed door in Kafka's parable. Given Kermode's fascination with John's Apocalypse, I would suggest this one:

> "These are the words of the holy one, the true one,
>   who has the key of David,
>   who opens and no one will shut,
>   who shuts and no one opens: . . .
> Look, I have set before you an open door, which no one is able
>   to shut."

(Rev. 3:7–8)

Notes

1. David Rhoads's presentation of Mark's Gospel has been prepared on videocassette by the LITE continuing education center at Trinity Lutheran Seminary in Columbus, Ohio. Because Rhoads works from modern editions of Mark, his performance differs from the more famous presentation of Mark by Alec McGowan, who works from the KJV and ends with 16:20 ("Amen"). See D. Rhoads and D. Michie, *Mark as Story* (Philadelphia: Fortress Press, 1982).
2. Andrew Lincoln, "The Promise and the Failure—Mark 16:7, 8," JBL 108 (1989): 283–300.
3. Frank Kermode, *The Sense of an Ending: Studies in the Theory of Fiction* (London: Oxford Univ. Press, 1966).
4. *The New Oxford Annotated Bible* (New York: Oxford Univ. Press, 1977), 1238.

5   For a careful analysis of the logic of text-critical arguments, see Humphrey Palmer, *The Logic of Gospel Criticism* (New York: St. Martin's Press, 1968), 55–111.

6   B. Childs, *Introduction to the New Testament as Canon* (Philadelphia: Fortress Press, 1985), 94–95. It will be of interest later that, according to Childs, the canonical reading of Mark in verses 9–20 clearly rules out a positive interpretation of the terror and amazement of the women at the tomb.

7   Kermode, *Sense of an Ending*, and *Genesis of Secrecy* (Cambridge, Mass.: Harvard Univ. Press, 1979).

8   Elisabeth Schüssler Fiorenza, *In Memory of Her: A Feminist Theological Reconstruction of Christian Origins* (New York: Crossroad, 1983), 316–23.

9   See the brief discussion by Lincoln, "Promise and Failure," 286. More compelling than most are the comments of John Donahue in his *The Gospel in Parable* (Philadelphia: Fortress Press, 1988), 196–97:

> Mark's theology of fear and wonder emerges especially in the resurrection account (16:5, 8) and in the jarring ending of the Gospel, "They were afraid" (16:8). This motif, which throughout the Gospel establishes rapport with the readers and dictates how they should respond to Jesus, now becomes a symbolic reaction to the gospel as a whole. Mark's readers are left not even with the assurance of a resurrection vision but simply with numinous fear in the face of a divine promise.
>
> These reactions of wonder and surprise accompany the revelation of God in Jesus, and they signify the power of this revelation to unsettle and challenge human existence. At the same time, this wonder is fascinating and attracting; it invites people to confront mystery. Such motifs call for a parabolic reading of Mark: for an approach to Mark's Jesus with a sense of wonder, awe, and holy fear.

    Yet even here, "fear" is understood not as incapacitating and blinding but as opening and inviting. This too easily resolves the tension on which the Gospel plays.

10.   Kermode, *Genesis of Secrecy*, chap. 2.

11.   Lincoln, "Promise and Failure," 290–92.

12.   Eric Auerbach, *Mimesis*, trans. W. Trask (Princeton: Princeton Univ. Press, 1953), 24–49. Borrowing a term from Harnack, Auerbach refers to the "pendulation" in such characters.

13.   Kermode, *Sense of an Ending*, 43–44.

14.   Kermode, *Genesis of Secrecy*, 68.

15.   Austin Farrer, *A Study in Mark* (London, 1951).

16.   Kermode, *Genesis of Secrecy*, 71–72 (among many examples).

17.   Ibid., 27–28.

18.   Ibid., 145.

Chapter 2

Is the Joke on Us? Mark's Irony, Mark's God, and Mark's Ending

Brian K. Blount

Life, like Mark, ends badly. In Mark, the protagonist dies. There are two primary variables regarding that death: the human response to it and God's complicity in it.

In Mark's narrative, at least, humans respond poorly. Even though Jesus is the one stirring up controversy and thereby fixing himself squarely in the crosshairs of an unamused Palestinian leadership, his disciples are the ones running for cover. Frightened for their own lives, rattled by Jesus' loss of his, they come so unhinged at the end that Jesus' men are nowhere to be seen and, perhaps even worse, his women are inexplicably seen fleeing the scene of *good* news.

God doesn't come across much better. The cosmic mastermind behind this apocalyptic debacle essentially sets Jesus up in a no-win scenario, overdoses his disciples with fear, and then sends a gaggle of well-meaning but reeling women a cold, divine phantom at the precise moment they desperately need a warm, human embrace.

Mark loves irony. But who exactly is the joke on here? When the high priest mocks Jesus with the question, "Are you the Messiah, the Son of the Blessed One?" (14:61), the reader laughs *with* Mark because she knows that the interrogative jab ironically caresses a truth the lead cleric is too blind and hostile to see. When the crucifying soldiers make a parody of Jesus by dressing him in purple, kneeling down before him, and hailing him as "King of the Jews" (15:16–20), the reader nods knowingly *with* Mark because she understands that what they give Jesus, that is, the dress, genuflection, and salute of royalty, Jesus deserves. When the centurion at the foot of the cross witnesses Jesus' miserable death and guffaws, "Yeah, right, this guy was the Son of God," the reader knows that the joke is on him.

Every time Jesus appears to break the laws of God (e.g., 1:45–3:6), transgresses the purity boundaries set up to keep God's people holy (e.g., 7:1–23), or promulgates an offending vision of God's reign populated with foreigners who are viewed by Mark's Jews as mongrel dogs craving the children's bread (7:24–8:13; 13:10), the reader knows that Jesus' boundary-crossing behavior does not distort God's intention; it clarifies it. The reader knows that Jesus was sent by God to trespass the laws and traditions that separate humans from God and humans from each other.[1] The reader also knows that such actions will inevitably lead to conflict. The people institutionalized to protect those laws and traditions were bound to fight back. Mark's point, though, was clear: In fighting to protect their religious laws and pious traditions, the ritually correct leaders of God's people were actually fighting against God. Even so, when Jesus dies as a direct result of their conspiratorial efforts, *they* win. Jesus' followers certainly believed it; that is why they run.

Then, shockingly, the plot twists. God raises Jesus. That death-defying act validates his ministry and every boundary break it committed. Jesus' way is God's way, the way the narrative characters should have followed, the way the reader must follow. The joke in Mark is on everyone who disappoints or opposes Jesus. And the reader knows it. Clued into the truth at the opening verse, the reader can see what even the characters who follow Jesus cannot: Jesus represents in his person and ministry the in-breaking and the direction of God's future kingdom in the midst of their present lives.

One wonders, though, here at the end, if Mark isn't inflicting his razor sharp sarcasm on the very reader he has for fifteen chapters and seven verses been trying to seduce. Mark wants his reader to believe in the urgency of the moment. Because the kingdom is at hand, he wants her—just as the narrative Jesus wants the characters who hear him—to act, to repent, to believe, and to participate in his boundary-breaking good news. Why is it, then, that instead of good news, we get a story of dim-witted disciples, infuriated leaders, and a Jesus whose proclamations of high standing climax on a criminal's cross? And then, just when it appears that there is some mysterious glimpse of resurrected redemption (16:7) that verifies Mark's irony for the truth that it is, Mark tells us that not only does the moment confuse Jesus' last remaining followers; it frightens them into what appears to be a complete and total stupor. And apparently, if we read Mark right, it is all God's doing. It was necessary that this happen; this is the way the script was written (cf. 14:27).

And so we arrive once more at the mysterious way in which Mark, laughing at somebody, ends his story of "good news." Jesus is dead. Jesus' male disciples have scattered. A remnant, three of Jesus' female disciples, despite having heard him say that his body has already been *anointed* for burial (14:8) and that he would *rise* on the third day after that burial (8:31; 9:31; 10:33–34), come stumbling to his tomb on that very third day with a cache of *oils* to smear across his *corpse*. On top of all that, they don't have a clue how they are going to get past the rock that seals the mouth of the tomb.

Cue God. All of a sudden, the story seems salvageable. An angel is on hand. He explains that Jesus' prophecies about his own resurrection have now come true and, just as he also prophesied (14:28), he is on his way to meet his disciples and Peter in Galilee. All the women have to do is pass the word. But that is when Mark literally snatches defeat right out of the mouth of victory and gives it new life. According to the most ancient manuscripts, he ends at 16:8 with the annotation that the frightened, fleeing women say nothing to anyone because they are afraid. Is that supposed to be it?

Building from the provocative literary observations of Frank Kermode, my good friend and colleague Don Juel offers an assessment. First, though, he does his text-critical homework. He begins by considering the various endings that have been found.[2] The shortest and most difficult reading (16:8) has the distinction of being showcased in the older, more reliable manuscript witnesses. It is also much easier to understand why a scribe would add material to make this stark ending less stark than it is to comprehend why someone would throw out a perfectly reasonable ending where Mary Magdalene not only broadcasts the angel's message about Jesus' resurrection but the resurrected Jesus meets his disciples and commissions them to the universal proclamation of the gospel (16:9–20, the so-called longer ending).

Still, concerns lingered. The grammar of the ending caused as much consternation as its content. No sentence, much less an entire book, could end with a word like *gar* (for, because), the very word that, in the Greek, concludes 16:8. Comparative grammatical research by scholars such as P. W. van der Horst, R. H. Lightfoot, and F. W. Danker countered conclusively that it could.[3]

Others have conjectured that while the most ancient and reliable version of Mark that we now have did end at 16:8, originally there must have been another, more *appropriate* ending that was somehow lost before scribal copying began.[4] Like Professor Juel, I would prefer to engage the text that we have rather than fantasize about the one that might have been.

Still others have argued that the curtness of the ending does not fit the way Mark tends to round off his stories with proper conclusions in the rest of the narrative. Appealing to the abruptness of the Gospel's beginning as well as the manner in which Mark interrupts stories in his narrative in order to insert information (cf. 7:19, 26; 13:14) or indeed posit other entire stories (cf. 5:21–43), responding scholars have demonstrated that Mark's ending is structurally consistent with the rest of his work.[5]

All of this brings us to the appropriate conclusion: When looking for the proper ending to Mark's narrative, look to 16:8. Even that, though, does not solve the problem. As Professor Juel observes, "While we might speak of a scholarly consensus regarding the ending of Mark, there is surely no consensus regarding its interpretation."[6]

Here is where Kermode comes in. He charges that as readers, "We are all fulfillment men [sic], *pleromatists*; we all seek the center that will allow the senses to rest, at any rate for one interpreter, at any rate for one moment."[7] In other words, we all want our narratives to have sensible, meaningful closure. When they do not, we interpret closure into them. Professor Juel maintains that this is precisely what scholarship has done with Mark's ending. Even after rejecting scribal attempts in antiquity to splice on a more satisfying conclusion, scholars have interpreted the ending in a variety of ways that have one thing in common: closure. Fearing that Mark's ending is laughing at them, they mute the sarcasm and level out the irony until what appears on the surface is not really what Mark intended. For a variety of reasons, the ending does not really end here. Instead, Mark has left us with some kind of cipher, whose proper decoding will bring understanding and, most importantly, relief. Such efforts amount to a scholarly attempt to explain Mark's joke to a slow-minded audience whose obtuseness has persisted for over twenty centuries. Professor Juel is right to reject them: 16:8 is where Mark ends. The tragedy of silence does not require decoding; it requires a response.

But not, according to Professor Juel, a response of action. For him, Mark's ending confirms the narrative presupposition that humans are incapable of living up to Jesus' discipleship expectations. The characters in the story do not do so because they are terminally flawed by fear. The reader cannot because she lives in exile outside the narrative's story and time line. No matter how much she desires, she can find no way to revise the literary disaster unfolding before her eyes. What Mark wants, then, is one very simple recognition: There is no justifiable hope for effective human intervention. Humans *have* failed; humans *will* fail to finish Mark's story appropriately. Like the good news itself that clings desperately to the angel because the women will not claim it and set it in motion, the reader realizes that she is totally and irrevocably dependent on God.

I don't think so. Mark's ending lifts the reader to her feet as much as it drives her to her knees. Mark's ending, like the entire Gospel that prefaces it, expects humans to act and believes that they *can*. If it does not, then Mark's ending and the God responsible for its orchestration do not restrict their ridicule to the dull disciples who see but seem never really to perceive and the hostile leaders who view Jesus as a threat; they also mock the reader whom Mark has supposedly let in on the joke. If Professor Juel is right, Mark hasn't been laughing with the reader—he has been laughing at her.

INTERPRETING 16:8: IS THE JOKE ON US?

There is no question that Mark is laughing. His ironic sense of humor seems to play as mischievously with the many interpreters who try to make sense out of the story as it is does with the characters who stumble their way through it. Like any good satirist, he sets up the climactic punch line early and often. He offers Jesus as a prophetic character whose word is utterly reliable. Both the reader and the narrative characters are led to believe that what Jesus promises will be fulfilled. Some of the predictions are almost mundane. Before he enters Jerusalem (11:1–6) and while he is contemplating his final meal with his disciples (14:12–16), he accurately gauges the circumstances that will greet the followers whom he sends ahead to prepare the way. Other predictions are dark and bitter. In the middle of the meal, he forecasts that one of the twelve he has chosen will betray him (14:17–21; 43–45). Still other predictions bite with piercing irony. Jesus tells Peter that he will deny him three times before a cock can crow twice (14:30). There is grit in Peter's response that he will stand by Jesus to the death (14:31). It sounds more like mocking when Mark reveals Jesus standing his ground before the hostile leadership of all Israel while Peter grovels before the accusations of a servant girl and a nondescript passerby (14:66–72). His self-serving lies have just finished leaving his mouth when he hears the male chicken cackle a second time.

The central prophecies are the ones that refer to Jesus' own future. Three times he predicts his death; five times he pledges that he will be raised (8:31; 9:9; 9:31; 10:33; 14:28). Chapter 16 chronicles a very satisfying vindication. Standing before Jesus' empty tomb, the angel declares that, indeed, he has been raised *and* he is already on his way to meet his disciples in Galilee, *just as he had said* (14:28). Right then and there the reader, even though she has no doubt become very skeptical of the disciples, has every reason to believe not only in the successful conclusion to this story but in the disciples' rehabilitated part in it. If Jesus could successfully predict the circumstances surrounding his own death and simultaneously divine the fact and timing of his revival from it, surely something as pedestrian as a promise to parley with his disciples would be just as reliable. But that is precisely where Mark cracks the joke. Just as the people who taunt Jesus at the foot of the cross wonder aloud why the one who promised to save Israel cannot even rescue himself (15:31–32), so now the reader must be wondering how it is that a man who could successfully predict resurrection could possibly be wrong about a mere meeting. No doubt the women must have been wondering it too, even as every step they took made it less and less likely that the meeting would ever take place.

Even in a mocking environment like this one, though, there is no discounting the power of faith. According to R. H. Gundry, "Mark's audience still expect the prediction that the disciples will see Jesus in Galilee to reach fulfillment despite the women's present failure to tell the disciples according to the instructions given them. Too many other predictions of Jesus have reached fulfillment in Mark to leave any doubt that this one will likewise reach fulfillment."[8] But how? That's the question. And that's where the proposals which Professor Juel finds lacking begin to pile up.

First comes the argument that there is more to the story than what first appears. Mark contributes to the misdirection when he pictures the women successfully picking up where the male disciples have woefully left off. Instead of scattering in fear, the women witness Jesus' crucifixion and watch his burial from afar. Staying with him, if just barely, they are determined to tend to him even in death. Even when, stricken with fear, they hastily vacate the scene, hope abounds. Working from Jewish and Pauline parallels, David Catchpole maintains that their fear is not only understandable; it is an appropriate response to the epiphany they have just witnessed.[9] And if that is the case, there must also be an appropriately rehabilitating way around what appears to be their disastrous getaway and subsequent silence. The case of the cleansed leper at 1:44 allegedly provides the way out. The leper's mandate was to maintain silence, but only with the general public. He was ordered to declare himself to the priests. Likewise, proponents of this view argue that while it is true the women did not tell everyone, this does not mean that they did not tell someone, that is, the disciples.[10] Indeed, the existence of a church based on Jesus' resurrection is clear indication that somebody said something. The obvious candidates would be these women.[11]

The problem here is that while Mark does seem from the end of chapter 15 right up to 16:7 to view these women sympathetically,[12] he appears convinced at the end that they fail. Andrew Lincoln is succinct:. "Yet it is at this very point that the reader begins to discover that ultimately women are no different from men—at least in terms of discipleship."[13] Charles Reedy posits structural confirmation for Lincoln's point. By describing the women's flight with the same verb (*pheugein*) used to characterize the behavior of the male disciples and the mysterious young male follower who fled away naked (14:50–52), Mark lowers the women to their same, shameful level.[14] Indeed, as Lincoln points out, Mark likens the women's fear to the same dread that has distastefully marked the behavior of the male disciples throughout the narrative.[15]

Weeden believes he understands the rationale behind Mark's negative portrayal of the women. The evangelist is combating the kind of Christology that emphasizes Jesus' divinity as over against his suffering. Mark attaches this wrongheaded view of Jesus to both the male and female disciples. By narrating their failure, he also implies the failure of their warped Christology.[16] J. D. Crossan has argued that Mark was identifying the women with a different historical problem, namely, the Jerusalem church. The end result, though, was the same. In vilifying the women, Mark vilified the identity connected with them.[17] Telford agrees: "In keeping with his treatment of the disciples throughout the Gospel, Mark [omitted any resurrection stories that chronicled the disciples hearing the good news and thus meeting the risen Christ], I suggest, because these [resurrection] stories served to demonstrate the authority of Jewish Christians as the true bearers or interpreters of Jesus' message, and to legitimate their leadership role over nascent Gentile-Christianity."[18] To protect the Gentile church, Mark vilified the narrative characters who symbolized the Jewish one.

Professor Juel agrees that in ending his story the way that he does, Mark closes on a stirring note of failure: "The story has offered no reason to place confidence in any insider."[19] Still, the breakdown cannot be utterly irreparable. If so, everything Mark has led the reader to believe—that this story is good news (1:1, 14–15), that Jesus really is the Christ, the Son of the Blessed (1:11; 9:7), that Jesus' boundary-breaking ministry into which the disciples and reader are called alike was vindicated by God's act of resurrection (8:31; 9:31; 10:33–34; 14:62), and that this resurrection act would become the key to Jesus' regathering his discipleship corps and refocusing them on his ministry (14:28)—was a lie. Norman Petersen is clear:

> [T]he assumed persona of the narrator becomes a devilish mask in the service of a perversely massive irony. Precisely because for a time—until 16:8—he invited us to believe Jesus and to believe in his and Jesus' imaginative world, a literal interpretation of 16:8 unmasks the narrator and discloses a very nasty ironist who has consistently misdirected our affections and expectations and offered us phony satisfactions from the very beginning.[20]

Or, as Ched Myers puts it, "In this case, the triumph of what I have called the 'betrayal' narrative is indeed complete, such that finally even the reader is betrayed. The story is thus a bitter and even cynical tragedy—hardly 'good news'!"[21] Given the women's fear and flight, the good news ends up being "*no* news." After all, if an angel speaks before what ends up being a *really* empty tomb, does he actually make a sound? When the reader finally gets the joke, she realizes that all along it has been on her.

Several scholars don't believe that Mark is playing a joke on the reader. J. Magness is an illustrative example. He believes that authors like Mark create story gaps, like the huge crevice that follows 16:8, in order to draw the reader into the story. She will be cajoled into participating rather than simply reading. Once she takes the bait, she will see the gap for what it is, a pointer back to structural clues that clarify the gap as meaningful rather than meaningless. In our case, she will find that Mark has established a structural pattern throughout the Gospel that he wants her to find on her own, and then apply to 16:8. The pattern, says Magness, is "speech should succeed silence; and mission should follow flight."[22] In other words, despite how it looks, the women *do* talk.

Petersen tacks in a slightly different direction. Arguing that 16:8 should be read through a full confidence in 14:28 and 16:7, he concludes that Mark intended that his final words be read ironically rather than literally. Though the reader would be drawn into the story this time through irony, she would be snared nonetheless. The end result would be the same. The story would end with success. The reader would not know how it had succeeded, but she would rightfully imagine that it had.[23]

Lincoln brings a challenge that helpfully points the way forward. He argues that the ending cannot be appropriately interpreted unless one places equal literary weight on 16:7 and 16:8, so that they "provide a paradigm for the interplay between divine promise and human failure."[24] Interpreters who argue for the total failure of the women and the collapse of all hope overemphasize verse 8. Those who try to redeem the women and the story put too much stress on verse 7. Those who see the two verses in the more balanced way will recognize "the failure of the women juxtaposed with the promise that is able to overcome it."[25]

I agree. So, I believe, would Professor Juel.[26] The problem is that Lincoln does not tell us *how*. Exactly how, given the bleak scenario at the end, does the promise overcome the failure? Satisfied with his pursuit of the literary matter, he ignores this profoundly practical and ultimately theological one. But he has brought us to the right vantage point. From here we can see that the theological discovery hinges on a very practical recognition. Endings often are not as much conveyers of content as they are motivators to action. Or as Professor Juel puts it, "Endings are important because they do something to readers."[27] Roger Bush claims to know exactly what they do. Working from the perspective of Aristotelian rhetoric, he argues, "The purpose of any speech is to bring the audience to a decision and, to accomplish this, the speaker must bring the audience into a proper frame of mind."[28] Mark's tool is shame. Shaming the reader with this ugly specter of deserting disciples and seceding women, he puts her in the proper frame of mind to pick up the challenge the narrative characters refused and act. "Rather than an abrupt and incomplete closing to the gospel, this pericope is shown to be a well-developed call to action."[29] Myers thinks so too. According to him, Mark wants the reader to make a critical realization. Now that the women have declined this opportunity, it has detoured to her:

> The "dilemma" of the ending is precisely what Mark refuses to resolve for us; he *means* to leave us to wrestle with whether or not the women at the tomb (that is to say, we ourselves) overcame their fear in order to proclaim the new beginning in Galilee (16:8). To provide a "neat closure" to the narrative would allow the reader to finally remain passive; the story would be self-contained, in no need of a readerly response.[30]

But it is precisely this "readerly response" that concerns Professor Juel. He sees the supposition of a reader responding where the women do not as a desperate plea for closure that mutilates the logic of the narrative and overestimates the abilities of the reader: "On what basis are present readers to trust that they can succeed as disciples where Jesus' chosen group failed? If the disciples' problem is that their hearts have been hardened, their eyes unseeing and their ears unhearing, what is to guarantee that we see and hear?"[31] No, Mark's ending is not a call for the reader to end this story properly; it is a demand that the reader finally realize that, if this story is to end rightly, only God will be able to do it. The reader is not forced back upon her own resolve, she is forced to fall down in desperation before God. Ira Brent Driggers focuses the point sharply: "Put simply, Mark's final statement places the reader at the mercy of Mark's God."[32]

There are two reasons why I disagree. The first involves Professor Juel's point about closure. He is right to record that the problem with most attempts to finish Mark's story positively is that they are really exercises in reducing the tension caused by the women's final flight and silence. But here's the irony: The one solution to the problem that brings a more stable closure than any other is his own, the one that puts the onus on God. After all, God, whether implied as a character in the story (so Driggers) or understood as the orchestrating mastermind behind it, is the one entity who is utterly dependable, even at the point of Jesus' demise. Even then, even as Jesus cries out, "My God, my God, why have you forsaken me?" the reader knows that God has not. The reader knows her psalms as well as Mark does, and she recognizes that Jesus is quoting Psalm 22 and that by the end of it God delivers the petitioner and champions God's cause. So the reader, depending on God, is not surprised that the tomb is empty, and surely is not anxious if the final reckoning rests with God.

God is the ultimate relief pitcher. When God gets on the mound, the reader can in all good conscience head on home. Despite how things look, this game is already won. I would argue that the only ending that both involves the reader *and* keeps her on edge is the one that draws *her* into the relieving role. To be sure, God will ultimately close history out, but the middle relief belongs to her. And that is exactly where Mark's irony digs in. The reader is sure about God.[33] But Mark, through his revelations about the weaknesses of those who consider themselves to be strong Jesus followers, has taught her that she can never be sure about herself. It is, after all, Professor Juel himself who recognizes quite appropriately that if this story were placed in the hands of the reader, it would have just as precarious a future as it had in the hands of the frightened women at the tomb: "If the disciples' problem is that their hearts have been hardened, their eyes unseeing and their ears unhearing, what is to guarantee that we see and hear?"[34] Absolutely nothing. And that is precisely why, far from being a comforting closure, the prospect of a readerly response is riddled through and through with anxiety.

The second reason is that Mark's narrative is written with the expectation that the reader will be motivated by the story to pick up her cross and follow, that is, to act. Right from the start of the narrative at 1:1, when he makes the reader privy to critical information that even Jesus' narrative disciples lack, it is clear that while Mark is writing about Jesus and the cast of characters who either follow, intersect with, or oppose him, he is writing to and for the reader. Just in case a tiring reader might forget that, he throws in winking asides (7:19; 13:14) meant only for the reader to hear. The reason the drama surrounding Peter's "confession" in chapter 8 works is that the reader knows not only that Peter is right but that he is simultaneously wrong. By the time she gets to 8:29, she already knows Jesus' fate; it is part of her documented past even as it remains the disciples' uncertain future. So when Jesus instructs them in the matter of picking up a cross and following behind him (8:34), what befuddles them is crystal clear to her. *She* is the one being asked to pick up the boundary-breaking ministry that led to Jesus' cross; *she* is the one being asked to follow.

Mary Ann Tolbert agrees: "Each individual who hears the word sown by the Gospel of Mark . . . is given the opportunity—as have all the characters in the story—to respond in faith or fear."[35] What does that mean for Mark's ending? "It is intended to move its hearers to respond, to excite their emotions on behalf of Jesus and the gospel message."[36] Here even Professor Juel seems to agree: "Caught up in the narrative's momentum, the last words of the messenger at the tomb impel the reader beyond the confines of the narrative: 'There you will see him, as he told you.' "[37]

Tolbert theorizes that Mark's foundational call to the reader comes in the Gospel-orienting parable of the Sower (4:3–9): "Mark's Gospel purposely leaves each reader or hearer with the urgent and disturbing question: What type of earth am I? Will I go and tell? Indeed, one's response to the seed sown by the Gospel of Mark reveals in each listeners' heart, as did Jesus' earlier preaching, the presence of God's ground or Satan's."[38] The problem is that with this statement Tolbert strips the reader of the very responsiveness she had earlier championed. She agrees that Mark is writing to the reader and demanding from her a discipleship response. Yet, in the end, she declares that readers actually cannot choose whether to respond or not. Earth is soil; it does not get to decide whether it is good or bad. A good soil reader will respond not because she decides to do so, but because that is her nature. The bad soil reader, whose pool outnumbers the good soil reader's pool three to one, will behave badly whether she wants to respond appropriately or not. Clearly, in this case, Mark's laughter would have to be as piercingly focused on the reader as it was on his narrative characters. Through fifteen chapters and seven verses he was about the business of preparing her to make a critical and dangerous decision about responding positively to the demands of his gospel story. Only at the crucial end moment does he drop the news that her particular make-up has already decided for or against her. Depending on which type of soil she finally discovers herself to be, her gospel learning process might well have been a cruel ruse. Should she catch on that she is bad dirt, her predicament would prove to be wickedly laughable. She would know what to do, but the nature God had given her would prevent her from actually doing it. Even for the good soil reader, there is not much of a victory. In the end, her preordained, preprogrammed response was not really a response at all.

Of course, Professor Juel would reject such mockery because he never thought the reader was being asked to respond by making up for the male and female disciples in the first place. Indeed, he never had any confidence that she would have been able to comply properly even if she had been asked. Yet, if he is right, Mark's laughter must ring against the reader here as well. Having trained the reader to see the difference between appropriate and inappropriate Jesus following, and having called the reader to take up her cross and respond, suddenly, here at the end, Mark tells her that he was really kind of just thinking and then writing out loud. He really wasn't talking to *her* after all. And even had he been, he wouldn't have expected that she would have been up to the task. Why did Mark tell the reader this kind of story if this was how he intended to end it? Why write for a reader at all if you ultimately have no use for her? Was he taunting her, or was he placing a true opportunity in her hands?

A BOUNDARY-BREAKING ENDING

Mark's Gospel is a textbook on boundary trespass. I am deeply indebted to Professor Juel's characterization of this narrative and the Jesus it portrays as boundary-breakers for the cause of God's reign.[39] My own work takes its cue from this recognition and attempts to build from it.[40] Indeed, and perhaps ironically so, I want to build from it here. Professor Juel helps us see Mark's portrayal of a God who shreds the fabric of the sky and breaks loose in human reality. In Jesus' ministry, the God who had been stashed behind the veil of the heavens at the opening of the Gospel and cloistered behind the curtain of the temple at its end slashes into free and open access with the characters in the story and the reader to whom the story is written. Jesus' boundary-breaking ministry is a recapitulation in real time of what God has already accomplished for the end of time. Mark's Jesus breaks through the traditional boundaries, the purity codes and ritual expectations, that have designated too many as too impure, too broken, too diseased, too destitute, too sinful, and too ethnically distasteful to be acceptable before God and therefore acceptable within proper human community. Most importantly for our study of the story's ending, though, Mark himself shatters what most reasonable people would consider an appropriate definition of *good* news.

Professor Juel starts me on my way: "The ending of Mark's Gospel provides a particular challenge to interpreters. The reason is its failure to resolve the tensions in the story and to provide some sense of closure that seems appropriate to 'good news about Jesus Christ.'"[41] But the ending makes sense *if* one crosses over into Mark's world where *good* news is ironically redefined. I would argue that in the structure of Mark's narrative world the reader is misled if she goes searching for the good news with a narrow focus on Jesus. From the moment immediately following his baptism, when he is driven into a barren wilderness filled with wild beasts, until his agonized plea from the cross, what happens to him is mostly bad. The *good* news is not what happens to Jesus as a result of his boundary-breaking behavior; the *good* news is what Jesus' boundary-breaking behavior causes to happen for others. Jesus' person and ministry is the good news that God unleashes in the world *for others.*

Mark's use of the term ("good news") enforces my point. At 1:1, he declares his work to be the good news *about* Jesus Christ.[42] The good news was about Jesus, not for him. It was good news *for* all those in spiritual, physical, and sociopolitical bondage whom Jesus encountered. According to 1:14–15, it is about Jesus' central preaching message: the reign of God. The good news is that, in his person and ministry, Jesus represents this reign. Mark then narrates Jesus' actual representation of that reign through all varieties of boundary-breaking, institution-threatening kinds of behavior. As early as 3:6, the leaders of the people have so tired of his act that they seek a way to destroy him. Professor Juel seems convinced: "The reasons for Jesus' death arise from his conflict with those in charge of human affairs, the religious and political authorities. It is their need to live within the bounds of the law that requires Jesus' execution."[43] Realizing this, by 8:35 and 10:29, in his next two explicit references to the good news, Jesus finds it necessary to inform his disciples that should they follow his lead and represent the boundary-breaking reign of God in their lives and ministries, they too will suffer. When they become good news for others it will be bad news for them! Yet Jesus seems convinced that, despite the resistance, the boundary breaking will prevail; the good news will win out. In his final two uses of the term, 13:10 (still in a context of suffering!) and 14:9, he implies that, because of their kingdom representation of God's reign, the greatest boundary of all—the ethnic one that separates Jew and Gentile—will be broken down. Yet in a world where Jews and Gentiles were often engaged in hostile and bitter conflicts, the messenger and appointed orchestrator of such *good* news was not necessarily going to be well received.

Therein lies the problem that helps us make sense of 16:8. The angel spills a critical clue when he mentions Jesus' destination. Tolbert senses something: "Literal geography is not the point, for Galilee represents the time of sowing, and the message of the empty tomb is that the time of sowing still continues."[44] Morna Hooker picks up on this idea when she recognizes that following Jesus into Galilee is the equivalent of following him on his path of discipleship.[45] Is that a problem? It is if that discipleship entails as much boundary breaking as Jesus' did! After all, the characters in the narrative now know as well as the reader does exactly where that kind of good news discipleship ends up.

That brings me to what I think is the most pertinent question:. Why, exactly, are the women afraid? The reverent-awe-in-the-face-of-epiphany answer having been rightfully dismissed, we are pushed in search of more fertile ground. We find it in Galilee. As Lincoln points out, the fear Mark has described here in 16:8 has been characterized as a negative trait.[46] That is, Mark has described it negatively in the context of the Jesus ministry that spans most of its time and energy in Galilee. In fact, of the eleven other uses of the verb ("to fear") that he finds, seven of them occur in the Galilee portion of the ministry (4:41; 5:15, 33, 36; 6:20, 50; 9:32), one of them occurs in Judea as Jesus and his disciples are on the way from Galilee to Jerusalem (10:32), and the ones that occur in Jerusalem or its environs do not target the disciples at all. They refer to the fear the leaders have either of Jesus or the crowd that sympathizes with him (11:18, 32; 12:12; 16:8). The disciples' fear is structurally connected with Jesus' representation of the reign of God in Galilee. Of course, the reader knows (and by the seventh indication of that fear, 10:32, so do the disciples) that because of his ministry there, Galilee leads inevitably (cf. 8:31) to Jerusalem.

Throughout that Galilee ministry and on up into Jerusalem, the male disciples, and particularly the Twelve, have been the ones, on the surface of the story narrative, who have been invited to follow in Jesus' boundary-breaking wake. They are the ones explicitly called in chapters 1 and 2. They are the ones who are taught by Jesus to perform the same acts of exorcism, miracle, and authoritative teaching that characterize his own preaching ministry (cf. 3:13–19; 6:7–13, 30). Though the women have been numbered implicitly among the disciples, we have not yet seen them singled out as boundary-breakers on the narrative surface. Here, at 16:8, they too are drawn directly in. They are invited through this call back into Galilee to reignite a fire that the cross in Jerusalem was supposed to have extinguished. They are to be accomplices no more; the angel solicits them to take their place front and center as perpetrators of the good news. *Their* actions will restart the dangerous boundary-breaking preaching ministry in the place where it began: Galilee. They will therefore become as identifiable with that ministry as their male counterparts already were. That is why they are afraid, and that is why, like their male counterparts, they take off.

In the midst of all this, while most readers are scrambling around to determine the location of the good news in a Gospel where so many bad things are happening, the women are on the run because, even though they have been a part of it all along, it is only now that they finally understand it. *They are afraid of the good news.* Going to the disciples and then going on to Galilee would start them inevitably on this good news kind of way. Like Jesus, they would initiate and then become the very boundary breaking they declared. They would become boundary breakers for others in the way that Jesus had been for them. There is a cost for that. That is what Galilee means. It is not the angel that they fear; they fear his message and what it means for their lives.

READING THE READER BACK INTO THE STORY

> For those who imagine that a successful ending is available to interpreters as some kind of achievement, the ending will be disappointing, even crushing. The women finally fail, as do the disciples and everyone else. All that is left is a promise—a promise made by the one whom God raised from the dead.[47]

My disagreement with Professor Juel is only on the small but critical point signalled by the two words "everyone else." There is no doubt that this is a disastrous ending. Every narrative character Mark introduces blows up in failure. All we have left is the promise from the utterly dependable, incredibly powerful God that this story will work. In fact, according to the angel, Jesus is so certain that, even before the narrative reveals the women's response, he has already started his trip back north to Galilee in anticipation of the infamous meeting (16:7).

Here is why Jesus is right to hope: It is all God's fault. God is the one who sets this up. In the same way that God inexplicably connects death to life, God networks suffering with the boundary-breaking proclamation and enactment of the good news. Either God is making a joke or God is making plans. The joke is on the opponents who think that the suffering they inflict will forever stifle the good news. The plan involves the development of disciples outside the story in the same way that Jesus tried desperately to develop the character trait of discipleship inside the story. Where even Jesus failed, the God who has the power to raise from the dead will succeed.

God will handle this. Only God can. God will step into the breach cracked open at the end of 16:8 and take up the cause the women refuse. The key is not *that* God will do it; the key is *how* God will do it. After all, God is already in the story; the angel is demonstrative proof of that. And while in the story, God does not take it over. God's modus operandi throughout has been the enlistment of human agents to enact the divine cause. God breaks in at the baptism, but then solicits Jesus to act. God breaks through at the transfiguration, speaks to the disciples, but steps away and waits for them to respond. God comes through at the empty tomb, but instead of lighting up the morning sky with a demonstrative, faith-inspiring indication of the glorious handiwork, whispers a dangerous word of instruction to three women whom the omniscient angel must already know are too frightened to deliver. At the end, and beyond the end, when Jesus goes off searching for human representation in Galilee, God establishes yet again the desire to make and use human disciples. If God is so determined to use them in and beyond the story, why does it make sense to suggest that God has neither the desire nor the power to use them to finish the story? Let God stay in character. Keep God looking for human disciples willing and able to overcome their fear of this good news and thereby finish the story Mark's Jesus started. That is why Mark writes this Jesus story in the first place: to let would-be disciples know that God is searching for them, to finish it.

The emphasis then is on the reader. Mark does not expect her to succeed, to achieve; Mark only wants her to follow. In fact, because of the connection between suffering and following, it is quite likely that her acts of discipleship, like Jesus' own ministry, will end up in defeat rather than victory. It is not her success that will finish the aborted story; it is her following.

Appealing to Kermode, Driggers, following Professor Juel, says no: "So also with Mark's ending, we are given no way out of the dilemma. Or, as Kermode would have it, we are given no way *in*. We are regulated to the status of outsider."[48] But that is precisely the point. The reader does not want to be *inside* the story because she already knows that everybody *in* the story gets stopped by either servant girls and nondescript passersby, crosses, or good news. The reader's vantage point is an advantage she will want to maintain. She reads from the future. Like the reign of God itself, the reader is never inside; she is always outside. The reign of God is the future boundary-breaking reality invading the boundary-driven world of the present. So is the reader—the flesh-and-blood reader, that is.

It is the implied reader who, like the male and female disciples in the story, will likely fail to follow. The implied reader is a narrative construct, an idealized audience who learns as the story unfolds and, while let in on some of the secrets of the narrator (like the fact of Jesus' divinity at 1:1), cannot escape the time line of the story. The existence of this reader is implicit within and therefore beholden to the structure and reality of the story itself. Driggers, then, is correct when he declares that "Mark strips the reader, leaving him naked and exposed. Mark takes away everything the reader thought he had."[49] But he is only correct in the case of the constructed, implied reader. The implied reader is a fool. And surely if

Mark knew anything about such a construction, he would agree. The joke is on the implied reader because he is caught up in the story time line, in its present. He is therefore trapped at its ending. It is the implied reader who cannot, just as Professor Juel declares, do a thing about what is going on. Having been led to believe all along that he was more privileged than the characters in the story, that he was being brought along by the narrator to know the story's inner mysteries, here at the end, all he has is a dead Jesus, an empty tomb, women running from it, and not a clue what to do next. You don't hear laughter from that?

What, though, has Mark taken from the flesh-and-blood reader in the Markan community of the first century? She first reads this story some four decades after the narrated events themselves took place. What has Mark taken from every flesh-and-blood reader since then? They forever read from their vantage point in the future. The flesh-and-blood reader exists with Mark. Both Mark and the flesh-and-blood reader are always future to the narrative time and thus future to the implied reader. They can see what the implied reader cannot. In this case, they see from the faith context of a community that has survived. So, right from the start, the ending does not do the same thing to the flesh-and-blood reader as it does to the implied reader. Just as what was unclear for the disciples throughout most of the narrative was clear for the implied reader, what is shocking for the implied reader is completely expected by the flesh-and-blood reader.

The implied reader knew Jesus was the Son of God, even when he was dying on the cross. He may not have understood it, but he knew it. The characters did not even know it, not for sure. When the centurion jibes, "Yeah, right, this guy was the Son of God," the characters are dismayed *and* taunted. The implied reader, though dismayed, is not taunted; he knows the soldier speaks the ironic truth. The flesh-and-blood reader is neither dismayed nor taunted. She knows for certain that Jesus was (past tense!) raised (the implied reader will only ever have the ambiguity of an empty tomb), *and* she knows that his resurrection became the foundation of a new movement.

I could write a story today about the sinking of the *Titanic* and end it at the moment the hull disappears beneath the icy waters of the North Atlantic as life boats drift solemnly at a distance. The implied reader of my story, stopped forever there with the ending of my plot line, has little reason to hope that there will be any good news from this point on. As far as he is concerned, tied as he is to the time line of the story itself, the life boat occupants are as dead as the souls trapped on the sunken ship. The flesh-and-blood reader, reading *with* me, will already know the ending and the promise it will bring those survivors. She will know about the ship that finds them in the night and rescues them. The implied reader cannot tell, because except for what the narrator shows him, he cannot see. He is blind. But the flesh-and-blood reader does not need to see. She already knows the future, and she brings that future with her to the narrative's present ending. The tragedy is still overwhelmingly sad. She knows, though, that there will be a remnant. So does Mark's flesh-and-blood reader.

Indeed, the flesh-and-blood reader is the only one the angel can count on anyway. The story cannot do anything to the implied reader. He is enslaved to Mark's narrative. The implied reader is a statue moved only when the narrator moves it. He has no life of his own; he cannot do anything of his own. Not so with the flesh-and-blood reader. With her, we move out of the passive realm into the world of active, knowledgeable possibility. For her, the call to Galilee-like discipleship, while still just as frightening, is possible.

NO JOKE—FINISH THIS STORY

Death is the natural result of life. That is the way God has constructed things. A person can say he believes in life after death all he wants; it is still natural to fear death. Professor Juel is right; only God can make death come out right. That, after all, is what Jesus' resurrection here at the end of Mark is all about. But that does not mean that we simply sit around and wait, even faithfully so, for death; we do something with our lives in spite of the fact that no matter what we do, our lives will always end in death. We still follow. In fact, the more faithfully we follow the boundary-breaking Jesus story as chronicled in Mark's Gospel, the more likely it will be that suffering and death may come sooner rather than later. God is a part of that too. Yet that is the life of discipleship to which God calls us. It is at that difficult moment when we confront such a discipleship decision, when, like the women, we know what we are supposed to do, but fear the consequences of doing it, that Mark's ending speaks to us—not in jest but in hope—that we will finish this story.

Notes

1. For a fuller discussion of Jesus as a boundary breaker, see Donald H. Juel, *A Master of Surprise: Mark Interpreted* (Minneapolis: Fortress Press, 1994); Brian K. Blount, *Go Preach! Mark's Kingdom Message and the Black Church Today* (Maryknoll, NY: Orbis Books, 1998).
2. See Donald H. Juel, *The Gospel of Mark* (Nashville: Abingdon Press, 1999), 167. Juel lists the five alternative endings as (a) 16:8; (b) 16:8 plus the longer ending that includes verses 9–20 in some later manuscripts; (c) 16:1–8 plus a shorter ending that consists of a celebratory and summary verse; (d) 16:1–8 plus the longer and shorter endings; (e) 16:1–8 plus the longer ending with additional comment about the disciples' unbelief, which is found in a single manuscript. For other succinct accountings, see W. R. Telford, *The Theology of the Gospel of Mark* (Cambridge: Cambridge University Press, 1999), 144–45.
3. For listing of citations see Andrew T. Lincoln, "The Promise and the Failure: Mark 16:7, 8," *Journal of Biblical Literature* 108, no. 2 (1989): 284 n. 4; see also Morna Hooker, *The Gospel according to Saint Mark* (Peabody, MA: Hendrickson Publishers, 1991), 387; I. Brent Driggers, "At the Mercy of Mark's God: Reader Exclusion in Mark 16:8," conference presentation, Mid-Atlantic Region of Society of Biblical Literature (Baltimore, 2002), 3.
4. See Craig A. Evans, *Mark 8:27–16:20*, Word Biblical Commentary (Nashville: Thomas Nelson, 2001), 538, for a listing of scholars proposing this solu-

tion: H. B. Swete, C. H.Turner, C. E. B. Cranfield, V. Taylor, R. H. Gundry, C. A. Evans.

5. Cf. Thomas E. Boomershine and Gilbert L. Bartholomew, "The Narrative Technique of Mark 16:8," *Journal of Biblical Literature* 100 (1981): 214; Richard W. Swanson, "'They Said Nothing,'" *Currents in Theology and Mission* 20 (1993): 39.

6. Juel, *Master of Surprise*, 108 (see above, p. 2).

7. Frank Kermode, *The Genesis of Secrecy: On the Interpretation of Narrative* (Cambridge, MA: Harvard University Press, 1979), 72.

8. Robert H. Gundry, *Mark: A Commentary on His Apology for the Cross* (Grand Rapids: Wm. B. Eerdmans Publishing Co., 1993), 1009.

9. David R. Catchpole, "The Fearful Silence of the Women at the Tomb: A Study in Markan Theology," *Journal of Theology for Southern Africa* 18 (1977): 8–9; Marie Sabin, "Women Transformed: The Ending of Mark Is the Beginning of Wisdom," *Cross Currents* 48, no. 2 (1998): 160–64.

10. Cf. Catchpole, "Fearful Silence of the Women"; Elisabeth Schüssler Fiorenza, *In Memory of Her: A Feminist Theological Reconstruction of Christian Origins* (New York: Crossroads, 1983), 322; Elizabeth Struthers Malbon, *In the Company of Jesus: Characters in Mark's Gospel* (Louisville, KY: Westminster John Knox Press, 2000), 64–65.

11. Cf. Swanson, "'They Said Nothing,'" 147. For a complete accounting of those holding this position, see Driggers, "At the Mercy of Mark's God," 3.

12. Thomas E. Boomershine, "Mark 16:8 and the Apostolic Commission," *Journal of Biblical Literature* 100 (1981): 229–32.

13. Lincoln, "Promise and the Failure," 288–89. See also Mary Ann Tolbert, "Defining the Problem: The Bible and Feminist Hermeneutics," *Semeia* 28 (1983): 294–95; Hooker, *Gospel according to Saint Mark*, 387.

14. Charles J. Reedy, "Mk. 8:31–11:10 and the Gospel Ending: A Redaction Study," *Catholic Biblical Quarterly* 34 (1972): 229.

15. Lincoln, "Promise and the Failure," 286–87. After tracking Mark's use of the verb for "fear" in 16:8 (*phobeisthai*), Lincoln draws the following conclusion: "So, of the other twelve references to fear in the narrative, only one can be judged to be part of a positive response (5:33) and then it belongs to the set phrase 'fear and trembling'; one is ambiguous (6:20); and ten, including all the references to the disciples, have negative connotations" (287). Driggers, finding negativity implicit even in 5:33, is even more forceful: "Instead, we are left with a fear that Mark consistently contrasts with faith, a fear hardly worthy of emulation, a fear that—by virtue of the causal—renders the women silent," ("At the Mercy of Mark's God," 9).

16. Cf. Driggers, "At the Mercy of Mark's God," 4–5; Theodore J. Weeden, *Traditions in Conflict* (Philadelphia: Fortress Press, 1971).

17. As cited in Boomershine, "Mark 16:8," 230–32.

18. Telford, *Theology of Mark*, 159.

19. Juel, *Master of Surprise*, 116 (see above, p. 8).

20. Norman R. Petersen, "When Is the End Not the End? Literary Reflections on the Ending of Mark's Narrative," *Interpretation* 34 (1980): 162.

21. Ched Myers, *Binding the Strong Man: A Political Reading of Mark's Story of Jesus* (Maryknoll, NY: Orbis Books, 1988), 400.

22. J. Lee Magness, *Sense and Absence: Structure and Suspension in the Ending of Mark's Gospel* (Atlanta: Scholar's Press, 1986), 90.

23. Petersen, "When Is the End Not the End?" 163: "But because the apparent interruption in 16:8 proves to be only an artfully penultimate closure, we must also recognize that the ultimate closure to Mark's story comes in the reader's imaginative positing of the meeting in Galilee."

24. Lincoln, "Promise and the Failure," 293.
25. Ibid., 296.
26. Cf. Juel, *Master of Surprise*, 112. Juel prefers the nomenclature of hope and disappointment rather than promise and failure.
27. Juel, *Gospel of Mark*, 171. See also Juel, *Master of Surprise*, 110–11 (and see above, pp. 8–9).
28. Roger Anthony Bush, "Mark's Call to Action: A Rhetorical Analysis of Mark 16:8," in *Church Divinity 1986*, ed. John H. Morgan (Bristol, IN: Wyndham Hall Press, 1986), 26.
29. Ibid., 28.
30. Myers, *Binding the Strong Man*, 401–2.
31. Juel, *Gospel of Mark*, 174.
32. Driggers, "At the Mercy of Mark's God," 2.
33. So Juel: "But to insist that the discordant ending offers no promise of resolution whatever is to do equal violence to the story. Jesus has promised an end. That end is not yet, but the story gives good reasons to remain hopeful even in the face of disappointment." Juel, *Master of Surprise*, 120. So Driggers: "God will bring to light what has been hidden in darkness. God will bring forth a bountiful harvest out of barren circumstance. Fallibility will be turned—in some mysterious way— into proclamation and genuine following in the way of the Lord." Driggers, "At the Mercy of Mark's God," 22.
34. Juel, *Gospel of Mark*, 174.
35. Mary Ann Tolbert, *Sowing the Gospel: Mark's World in Literary-Historical Perspective* (Minneapolis: Fortress Press, 1989), 298.
36. Ibid., 295–96.
37. Juel, *Master of Surprise*, 120.
38. Tolbert, *Sowing the Gospel*, 299.
39. Cf. Juel, *Master of Surprise*.
40. Cf. Blount, *Go Preach!*
41. Juel, *Master of Surprise*, 111 (and see above, p. 4).
42. Cf. Blount, *Go Preach!* particularly pp. 84–85, for my discussion of the construction, which positions Jesus Christ as an objective genitive.
43. Juel, *Gospel of Mark*, 163.
44. Tolbert, "Defining the Problem," 298.
45. Hooker, *Gospel according to Saint Mark*, 392.
46. Lincoln, "Promise and the Failure," 287.
47. Juel, *Gospel of Mark*, 176.
48. Driggers, "At the Mercy of Mark's God," 12.
49. Ibid., 14.

Chapter 3

The Face Is Familiar—I Just Can't Place It

C. Clifton Black

I

Mark's Gospel ends with both hope and disappointment. The relationship between the last two verses [16:7 and 16:8] embodies the critical tension in the story between blindness and insight, concealment and openness, silence and proclamation. The tension is not resolved. Why is this so?
    Donald H. Juel, *A Master of Surprise: Mark Interpreted*

Donald Juel did not suffer gladly any attempt to dilute Christian theology's bittersweetness and so betray the gospel. For that reason, he resisted all efforts of those whom Frank Kermode calls "the pleromatists": those so unnerved by unresolved tension that they are determined to cobble up filler (*plērōma*) for narrative gaps.[1] Chief among Markan pleromatists are the scribal houses that have provided us endings beyond Mark 16:8—particularly the contributors to the Textus Receptus that gave us Mark 16:9–20, immortalized in the King James

Version—probably on the assumption that the women's terrified silence while fleeing the empty tomb was no way to conclude a Gospel (cf. Matt. 28:8b–20; Luke 24:8–53; John 20:3–21:25). A shrewd exegete, Juel was adept at unmasking modern commentators' subtler ways of giving Mark a satisfying conclusion.[2] Pressing himself for an answer to his own question about Mark's refusal to resolve his Gospel's tension, Juel suggested a literary-critical reply immediately transposed into a theological key, so eloquent that it justifies extended quotation here:

> Kermode's analysis clearly exposes the human need for closure, structure, and control. One can argue theologically from the same premises that interpretation can become a way of defending ourselves against truths that make a claim on us. . . . Mark's Gospel—and, we might add, the whole Christian tradition—argues that our lack of enlightenment and bondage arise from attempts to box God in or out of experience. All such attempts come to grief in the resurrection of Jesus. He cannot be confined by the tomb or limited by death. In Jesus' ministry, God tears away barriers that afforded protection in the past. God cannot be kept at arm's length. . . . Jesus has promised an encounter with him against which there is no assured defense. God will be put off neither by our failures, or infidelity, nor by our most sophisticated interpretive schemes. And if this "good news about Jesus Christ" is God's work within the intimate realm of human speech, there is reason to hope that our defenses will prove insufficient and that we will not have the last word.[3]

Plucked from the context of Juel's comprehensive exegesis, this formulation seems emphatically anthropological. Taking his cue from Kermode—whose Norton lectures (1977–78) descry the foibles and fate of his fellow literary critics—Juel speaks here about *human* need and its disappointment, *human* speech and its undoing, *our* ultimately unavailing stratagems to defend *ourselves*, *our* lack of enlightenment and bondage, *our* failures and infidelity and schemes. To be sure, Mark's Gospel offers abundant testimony to all these things. It does so, however, in sustained, dialectical tension with an element that fascinated Juel as far back as his doctoral dissertation at Yale:[4] the character of the God who has opted to meet Israel and Mark's readers in Jesus Christ. It is not only the case in the Second Gospel that *homo religiosis* is the constant bungler who plays faith false. Neither is it only the case in Mark that "Jesus is out, on the loose" from the tomb, that "God is no longer safely behind the [temple] curtain" rent in twain, that "[all] doors in Mark's Gospel are emphatically open."[5] True as these things are, in Mark's Gospel it is also—and, to my thinking, more pointedly— the case that God is *Deus absconditus atque praesens*: as Samuel Terrien translates, "God [who] is near, but [whose] presence remains elusive."[6] With this and other cues taken from Terrien's seminal contribution to biblical theology, it is my aim in what follows to trace in Mark's Gospel some outskirts of the fundamentally elusive God.

II

That St Mark's thought runs cyclically is a thesis which needs no advocate.
Austin Farrer, *St Matthew and St Mark,* 2nd ed.

It may have been Norman Perrin who most sensitively attuned Markan exegetes to the subtle yet unmistakable threefold pattern of predictions concerning the persecuted and vindicated Son of Man, arranged and elaborated in that Gospel's central section (8:31; 9:31; 10:33–34).[7] There is, however, another tripartite structure within Mark that, though not neglected, has received less attention: the triptych composed of Jesus' baptism (1:9–11), transfiguration (9:2–8), and death (15:33–41). These episodes have not always been correlated with the interpretive care that they invite. Their verbal and conceptual similarities may not be quite so obvious as those of the passion predictions in Mark 8:22–10:52. In addition, these tableaux are more widely separated from one another than the Son of Man sayings concentrated in three contiguous chapters. It may also be that these episodes have triggered the action of an almost unconscious, form-critical default mode that tends to separate rather than conjoin them: Mark 15:33–41 as the climax of the Gospel's passion narrative; 1:9–11, a mythic account of a virtually undisputed event in the life of Jesus; 9:2–8, an outright epiphany myth.[8] In any event, it seems to me that Jesus' baptism, transfiguration, and death in Mark beg joint consideration as mutually interpretive. Consider:

1. Their location is critical. The transfiguration story lies in almost the dead center of the Second Gospel, whose bookends are the baptism and death of Jesus.
2. All three anecdotes are drenched in imagery that is apocalyptic or revelatory.
3. As I hope to demonstrate, Mark's intervening narrative provides important commentary on how these episodes are interconnected and should be interpreted.
4. The punch line of all three affirms Jesus as God's Son—a comparatively rare claim in this Gospel (see also 1:1[9]; 3:11; cf. 5:7; 12:6; 13:32; 14:61).
5. Although the tenor of Mark 15:39 is debatable, the validity of Jesus' divine sonship remains incontestable. In 1:11 and 9:7—and *only* here, in Mark—God is the speaker. Jesus' affiliation with God, by divine decree, could not be more intimate. While these verses have understandably occupied a central place in scholarly constructions of Markan Christology (Jesus as *Son*),[10] they are no less significant for construing Mark's presentation of *God*.[11] While it would be absurd to reduce every

aspect of Mark's portrait of Jesus and of God's kingdom to no more than a few verses, by these assertions the evangelist could not send his readers a clearer signal that theology and Christology are complementary and inseparable. If we want to learn something about God in Mark's Gospel, attention must be paid to him who is identified as God's Son.

In this light, let us stipulate at the outset that Mark 1:9–11, 9:2–8, and 15:33–41 are of an interwoven, interpretive piece. Each merits examination in its own right, but to isolate any one of these pericopae from its narrative counterparts risks exegetical misapprehension.

III

Behold: I send my messenger before your face,
Who will prepare your way.

Mark 1:2a[12]

Perhaps by the evangelist's design, it is unclear to whose face and whose way Mark's epigraph refers. Having read the Gospel's title (1:1), which seems aimed at the book's readers, at first one might interpret the conflated quotation from Exodus 23:20/Malachi 3:1 as continued address to that audience: Thus, God, whose voice authorizes the prophet, sends his messenger before the reader's face, to prepare the reader's way. While that messenger could refer to Jesus Christ (1:1), 1:3 and especially 1:4 seem instead to identify God's *angelos* as John the Baptizer. Reasoning backward: If the one crying in the wilderness (1:3a) is identical to the one who prepares "your way" (1:2c), then "the way of the Lord" (1:3b) appears to be the way of Jesus Christ, before whose face God's messenger is sent (1:2b). Notice how intricate is the web of associations that Mark already is spinning. First, the way of the reader merges into the way of Jesus Christ, a theme the evangelist will expressly develop in terms of discipleship in 8:27–9:1 (N.B. *hē hodos,* v. 27; *akoloutheitō moi,* v. 34). "Your" (*sou*) way (1:2c), Mark's apparent adjustment to Malachi 3:1 LXX, stresses by repetition both Christ and Christ's follower, before whose face the herald is dispatched. Second, "the way of the Lord" (Mark 1:3b), which in Isaiah 40:3 originally referred to the Lord God of Israel, retains that sense in Mark (thus, 11:9; 12:9, 11; 12:29–30; 13:20, 35) while at the same time associating "the Lord" with Jesus (thus, 2:28; 5:19–20; 7:28; 11:3; 12:36–37). A similar identification is suggested by the phrase poetically parallel with "your way," *pro prosōpou sou,* "before your face." In this Gospel, the way that Jesus "faces" suggests God's own self-revelation in the Old Testament (Mal. 3:1: *ûpinnâ-derek lĕpānāy* [MT]; *kai epiblepsetai hodon pro prosōpou mou* [LXX]). Third, the very fact that the reader must reason backward to peel away these layers of meaning provides an important key to Mark's theology: The significance of Jesus in this Gospel depends on faith's hindsight, not only upon the resurrection and death and life of Jesus[13] but also upon Scripture, which is now regarded as speaking prophetically of him and his gospel (1:2–3). In this light, Scripture also discloses a different aspect on John the Baptizer, who now appears as *Elias redivivus* (1:4–8; cf. 2 Kgs. 1:8), the prophet who would precede the day of the Lord, turning minds around (*metanoia*, Mark 1:4; cf. Mal. 3:5–6).

Thus, Mark readies us for Jesus' baptism, a denouement no less crucial in this Gospel for its early placement. The straightforward description of Jesus' coming from Nazareth to be baptized in the Jordan by John (Mark 1:9)—with its implied subordination of Jesus to the Baptizer, which other Gospels strive mightily to undo or at least mitigate[14]—is contrasted with the astonishing phenomena that attend his emergence from the waters: Jesus' vision (*eiden*) of the heavens' rending (*schizomenous tous ouranous*) and the descent of the Spirit upon him (1:10). The imagery is conspicuously prophetic and apocalyptic (see 1 Sam. 10:6; Ezek. 1:4–21; Rev. 1:10; 4:2); unlike John's Gospel (1:32–34) but entirely in accord with the association forged in Mark 1:2–3, only Jesus and the reader are privy to this disclosure by God. The revelation is completed by a rumbling reverberation (*bat-qôl*, "the voice's daughter") from heaven (1:11), which, unlike Matthew's presentation (3:17), is directed solely to Jesus with the reader as eavesdropper:

A "You are my Son,
B the beloved,
C in whom I am well pleased."

As in 1:2–3, Mark has adopted a familiar Old Testament formula (there, Isa. 40:3; here, Ps. 2:7) but has modified that basis in theologically significant ways. First, in poetic stich A, Mark lets stand the climactic announcement of divine adoption for Israel's king in Psalm 2, a coronation hymn. This, tied to the imagery of water and spiritual unction, recalls Jesus' identification as *Christos*, "anointed one," in Mark 1:1.[15] Second, rather than continuing to quote Psalm 2:7c as it appears in the Septuagint (*egō sēmeron gegennēka se*, "Today I have begotten you"), in stich B Mark shifts to the appositive *ho agapētos*, "the beloved," whose closest Septuagintal counterpart is in Genesis 22: Isaac, "the beloved son" (*ton huion sou ton agapēton*) of Abraham, who is offered up in sacrifice by divine command.[16] Instead of returning to Psalm 2, with its saber rattling before the nations of the earth (vv. 8–12), in stich C Mark rounds out the heavenly acclamation with a muffled echo of Isaiah 42:1ab, the introduction to the first of Deutero-Isaiah's Servant Songs: "This is My servant, whom I uphold/My chosen one, in whom I delight" (NJPS; see also Matt. 12:18; 2 Pet. 1:17). The same servant, of course, is the one upon whom God's Spirit has been placed (Isa. 42:1c), the one "smitten and afflicted by God; . . . wounded because of our sins, crushed because of our iniquities" (Isa. 53:4d–5ab NJPS).

So familiar is Mark's account of "Elijah's" preparatory address and Jesus' baptism that we might easily overlook a cluster of important and occasionally subversive claims in this presentation. Jesus is God's anointed, beloved Son, the unique beneficiary of God's own Spirit, on whom divine favor rests; by his conduct, Jesus aligns himself with Scripture's promise of Israel's realignment with the Lord's way. And like all Judea (1:5), Jesus implicitly "turns" (*metanoeō*), allowing himself to be baptized among sinners. This becomes the occasion *not* for a public proclamation of his own authority but rather for a passive acceptance of God's dramatically revelatory acclamation, made known only to him (and to us). Precisely in connection with coronation hymns such as Psalms 2 and 110, Samuel Terrien reminds us of the theological and political perils they courted: "As the adopted son of the Godhead, the [Davidic] king could do no wrong, and autocratic caprice easily trespassed the limits of Yahwistic ethics. Presence as royal adoption represented a deterioration of the Hebraic theology of presence."[17] When such trespass occurred, it was an easy yet catastrophic step to confuse Israel's "rock," the Lord who was the real instrument of the nation's deliverance (Ps. 18:1–3, 31–32, 46), with a vigorous, militarily triumphant king (vv. 28–29, 33–34; cf. Pss. 2:8–9; 110:1). Repeatedly, Mark's Gospel will undermine such braggadocio by depicting Jesus as humble servant (9:35; 10:43–45; 11:7–10), ironically echoing the sovereign's own hymnic acknowledgment of God's self-abasement and appearance of weakness (Ps. 18:35).[18] The undercutting of presumptions about Davidic lordship is probably suggested by Jesus' "putting of David in his place" in Mark 12:35–37; it is surely at work in Jesus' self-presentation as another, very different rock: the "beloved son" rejected by the builders yet laid by the Lord as cornerstone (Mark 12:6, 10–11, quoting Ps. 118:22–23). As the Second Gospel unfolds, Jesus will demonstrate the habits acquired by living in the divine presence—"the will of God," as Mark 3:35 sums it—but such conduct will consistently baffle those entrenched in conventional religious and social mores (1:27; 2:1–3:6, 21b–34; 6:1–6a). That stage is set in Mark 1:1–11: God will be God, binding himself, intractably anointing and eventually sacrificing his own beloved Son, in the face of unrepentant humanity's repeated efforts to fabricate a god in human image.

IV

. . . and he was transformed in front of them.

Mark 9:2c

The transfiguration of Jesus in Mark 9:2–8 has long seemed to me among this puzzling Gospel's most enigmatic passages—not so much on its own terms but as regards its function within the evangelist's comprehensive scope. Bultmann assumed that this legend was originally a post-resurrection appearance story that had been later relocated into the narrative of Jesus' ministry "to serve as a heavenly ratification of Peter's confession [in 8:29] and as a prophecy of the Resurrection in pictorial form [see 8:31]."[19] Whatever one makes of the tradition-critical assessment,[20] this explanation leaves much unanswered. If Mark did not consider heavenly ratification of a Christian confession and a pictorial dramatization of Jesus' resurrection needful in chapter 16, following discovery of the empty tomb and the herald's announcement of Jesus' resurrection, why on earth would Mark think it appropriate in chapter 9? In fact, Mark 9:2–8 directly refers neither to Peter's confession, as such, of Jesus as Messiah, nor to the promise of Jesus' resurrection (8:31).

The most obvious narrative clue to this episode's placement just here in the Gospel seems to be Jesus' warning, in Mark 8:38, that "the Son of Man [would] come in the glory [*en tē doxē*] of his Father with his holy angels [or messengers: *meta tōn angelōn tōn hagiōn*]." This, I think, sets us on a proper footing for interpreting 9:2–8, for the latter passage immediately fulfills two aspects of that promise: On a mountain or in hill country (*eis oros*), the biblical topography of divine revelation (Exod. 19:3–25; 24:12–18; 1 Kgs. 19:8), Jesus is brilliantly transformed (Mark 9:2–3) in a manner evocative both of the *kabhod* or *shekinah*, God's essential splendor (Exod. 16:10; Num. 14:10; Ps. 56:5, 11), as well as of apocalypticism's supernatural imagery (Dan. 7:19; 12:3; 2 Esd. 7:97; Matt. 13:43; Rom. 12:2; 2 Cor. 3:18; Phil. 3:21; Rev. 3:5; 4:4; 7:9, 13). Attending the metamorphosed Jesus are figures that intertestamental Judaism surely considered "holy messengers," namely, Elijah and Moses (Mark 9:4; cf. Mal. 4:5–6; Sir. 45:1–22; 48:1–16; Philo, *Mos.* 2.2.3.187). In a real sense, then, the glimpse of glory given to Jesus' intimates (Peter, James, John, and us as readers) in 9:2–8 immediately satisfies Jesus' promise in 9:1: "Truly I tell you, there are some standing here who will by no means taste death until they have seen that God's sovereign rule has come with power." Should one counter that 9:1 probably refers to the Son of Man's cataclysmic advent, portrayed by Jesus in Mark 13:24–31, then one must explain (1) why Mark uses an intensive double negative in 9:1 (*ou mē*, "by no means"), which, if referring to the final *parousia*, would unnecessarily invite instantaneous disproof; (2) why Mark would later insist that the timing of historical catastrophe is unknown to all—including the Son—but only to the Father (13:32), thus placing Jesus in needless contradiction with himself at 9:1; (3) why, in view of the evangelist's repeated references to God's inbreaking kingdom (1:15; 3:34; 4:11, 26, 30; 9:47; 10:14–15, 23–25; 12:34) and the Son of Man's present activity (2:10, 28; 8:31; 9:9, 12, 31; 10:33, 45; 14:21, 41), Mark must be referring in 9:1 to the final apocalypse. More likely, I think, Mark 9:2–8 invites interpretation within the proximate context of 8:27–9:1/9:9–13, as well as with the remote yet kindred declaration in 1:1–11.

Christologically considered, the primary burdens of Mark 9:2–8 are to coordinate and to counterbalance at least three kinds of claims made by the material that frames the passage: the relationship between Jesus and his Israelite precursors, the distinctive identity of Jesus with respect to God, and the point at which such things may be properly declared. Very much as we witnessed in this Gospel's opening verses, Mark 9:2–8 seems at pains both to demonstrate the continuity of Jesus' messiahship with scriptural precedent and to show where Jesus surpasses all precedent. Thus, whereas popular opinion mistakenly equates Jesus with Elijah or one of the prophets (8:27–28), Peter identifies Jesus (correctly, from Mark's viewpoint: 1:1) as the Christ (8:29) but is hushed (8:30) and instructed about the Son of Man's God-given destiny (8:31; N.B. the divine agency implied in *dei*, "it is necessary"). A comparable pattern unfolds in 9:9–13: The disciples are again sworn to secrecy until after the Son of Man's vindication (v. 9), of whose unjust suffering "it has been written" (*pōs gegraptai,* v. 12); in the meanwhile, the disciples' confusion over Elijah's mission must be dispelled, then accurately reassessed (vv. 10–13). Wedged between these disputes (N.B. *epetimēsen,* "rebuked," 8:30, 32–33; *suzētountes,* "arguing," 9:10) is the hilltop revelation, which, at God's direct instigation, obscures even as it clarifies.

The narrative of Jesus' transfiguration reprises, with subtle variations, the same motifs announced in Mark 1:1–11: an apocalyptic vision, a divine declaration, and their scriptural foreshadowing. "After six days" (9:2; an allusion, perhaps, to Moses' ascent of Sinai in Exod. 24:16), Jesus leads a trio up (*anapherei*) a high mountain (cf. Mark 1:10, "going up [*anabainōn*] from the water"). Instead of Jesus' beholding the Spirit's descent from the riven heavens (1:10), this time the disciples have thrust before them (*emprosthen autōn*) a vision of Jesus' radiance and his conversation with Elijah and Moses (9:2–4). Notice that the key verbs in Mark's narration—*metemorphōthē,* "was metamorphosed," (v. 2) and *ōphthē,* "there appeared" (v. 4)—are conjugated as so-called divine passives, indicating God's agency as in the comment that no human fuller could have bleached garments so luminous (v. 3; recall the passive participle, *schizomenous,* "were split," in 1:10). Moses too had reflected the divine effulgence when proximate to God's glory over the tabernacle (Exod. 34:29–35); like Moses, Elijah had experienced a theophany upon Sinai/Horeb (1 Kgs. 19:8–18). Beyond these obvious correspondences, this pair in Mark 9:4–5 is significant in other ways. By the first century CE, a parallelism between the lives and ministries of Moses and Elijah had become so well established in Jewish tradition that Elijah appears as *Mosi redivivus.*[21] Moses and Elijah are explicitly linked in Malachi 4:4–5 as tandem heralds of the Lord's day.

A cloud descended over Sinai (Exod. 24:16); a voice spoke to the prophet on Horeb (1 Kgs. 19:12–13). So also here: A cloud overshadows the participants (cf. Luke 1:35); from the cloud comes a *bat-qôl,* largely reiterating what was uttered at Jesus' baptism—this time, however, addressed to his disciples (Mark 9:7):

A   "This is my Son,
B   the beloved:
C   Listen to him."

The critical difference between the two heavenly announcements in Mark lies in stich C. This surely is no accident. It is a direct order to pay attention *to Jesus,* quoting from Deuteronomy, in which Moses enjoins Israel's obedience to a forthcoming prophet, like him, whom the Lord God would raise up (18:15).[22] By distinguishing Jesus from Elijah and Moses—only Jesus is transfigured; only he is singled out by the heavenly voice—it now should be clear what the *bat-qôl* at the baptism suggested: The Son *agapētos* is the Son *yāḥîd,* "only" or "unique." A father's love for such a son is fathomless, precisely because there is no other.[23] The substance of what Jesus' disciples should obey is left nonspecific, therefore all-encompassing. In the Gospel's immediate context, what they must heed is God's design that the Son of Man suffer and be vindicated (8:31), their adoption of his way as theirs (8:34–35), an injunction against reporting what they have seen until after the resurrection (9:9), and an assurance that all proceeds according to divine plan (9:12–13). For those able to see, Elijah has already returned in the person of John the Baptizer (1:2–8; cf. 9:12a); this time, however, he has not escaped the murderous clutches of Ahab and Jezebel *redivivi* (9:13; cf. 6:14–29; 1 Kgs. 19:1–3; 21:1–16).

An odd but critical point remains unaccounted for: Peter's confused, frightened suggestion to Jesus transfigured that three tents (*treis skēnas*) be built for him and his heavenly interlocutors (Mark 9:5–6). On its face, the referent appears to be the Feast of Booths, or Tabernacles (Lev. 23:39–43), a popular harvest festival whose significance here is less than conspicuous. While Josephus and doubtless other Jews remembered such thanksgiving celebrations as occasions for political turmoil (*A.J.* 13.372–73; *B.J.* 6.300–309), three disciples on a hill do not a riot make, not even potentially. Probably underlying Peter's addled proposal is Israel's religious memory of the wilderness tabernacle as the Lord's "mobile home" (Exod. 25:1–31:18; Lev. 26:11–12; Rev. 21:3) and, by imaginative extension, eternal dwellings for the righteous (Luke 16:9; 2 Cor. 5:1). A forerunner and constituent of the Solomonic and Herodian temples, the tabernacle was both liturgical shrine and oracular venue ("the tent of meeting"; Exod. 27:21; 29:43–44).[24] If Peter intended to house divine disclosure by creating sacred dwelling places, that hope is dashed. The evangelist dismisses his proposal (Mark 9:6); the supernatural colloquy evaporates (9:8); the four descend the mount (9:9). Like Elijah from Horeb (1 Kgs. 19:15) and Jesus from the Jordan (Mark 1:12–13), the disciples are redirected into the world (9:9–29), having gotten from God something considerably more than Elijah's "thick silence" (1 Kgs. 19:12–13) yet altogether different from that prophet's political marching orders (19:15–18). They must pay attention to Jesus, the moving nexus and veiled disclosure of divine mystery that asserts, without clear resolution, a supremacy more radiant than any fuller can bleach and a suffering that overshadows like a cloud.[25] The beloved Son encountered on this mountain is *beyond* glory (*doxa*); he is, in the most literal sense, *para*dox.

V

. . . facing him, he beheld that thus he had expired.

Mark 15:39

In this, the Second Gospel's climax, Mark operates at the peak of his rhetorical and theological powers, but with a profound reserve, an exquisite narrative braiding that disowns blatancy in favor of a completely subliminal statement. In Mark, Jesus' death is a near perfect, albeit macabre, inversion of his transfiguration: Every gleam of radiance is now suffocated by darkness, all splendor dissolved into lifeless shame. For Mark's reader, ancient or contemporary, there is nothing heroic about how Jesus dies.[26] Yet the resonance of 15:33–41 extends far beyond 9:2–8, reaching deeply into this Gospel's first verses. In its manner of expression, it is as though the evangelist were proclaiming, "More than merely the brute fact of what has been repeatedly forecast [in 8:31; 9:31; 10:33–34] is now laid before you. Listen. Look [4:3]. Behold how completely this one's nadir corresponds to his zenith."

As he is wont, the evangelist begins simply by setting the clock: "When it came to be the sixth hour . . . until the ninth hour" (Mark 15:33; cf. 1:9: "And it came to be in those days"; 9:2: "And after six days"). In crucifixion (15:24), Jesus has been elevated (cf. 15:30, 32: "Come down from the cross"), even as at transfiguration he ascended a high hill (9:2) and at baptism came up from the water (1:10). At three in the afternoon, the whole land falls under eclipse (15:33)—a weird, contrapuntal composite of Jesus' unearthly radiance on the mount (9:3) with "all of the Judean countryside and the Jerusalemites" that once went out to the Jordan (1:10). In 9:2a, Jesus and his disciples were at first "alone by themselves," before the appearance of Elijah with Moses (9:4). Similarly, Jesus was at first numbered among a plethora (1:5), then paired with John (1:9), before Mark concentrated our attention on a transaction between Jesus alone with the Spirit (1:10). In chapter 15, there are unnumbered passersby (vv. 29, 31, 35), narrowed down to a runner (v. 36) and a centurion on watch (v. 39), and a pair of fellow victims on either side of Jesus (v. 27) who occupy exactly the positions of "honor" that another pair have requested of Jesus before being corrected about "[his] baptism" (10:35–40). In 1:11 there was a heavenly voice (*phōnē*); in 9:7, a voice (*phōnē*) from a cloud; in 15:34 and 37, the loud voice (*phōnē megalē*) of Jesus himself, who cries out with need (*boaō*). Into all three tableaux, Mark carefully reintroduces Elijah: first, as John the Baptizer (1:6–7); later, in the hilltop colloquies (9:4, 11); finally, in the response of hard-of-hearing bystanders (15:35–36), whose foolish hope that Elijah may miraculously rescue Jesus is ignorant that Elijah has already come—and was decapitated for his trouble (6:14–29; 9:12–13). They no more know what they are saying than did Peter in his building proposal (9:6). In his baptism and transfiguration, Jesus stood out from the rest; so too in his crucifixion—though never in his life has Jesus appeared so alone (15:34, 40). Given the many changes that the evangelist is obviously ringing, one wonders if he has selected with precision the very word for Jesus' death—"expired," *exepneusen* (15:37 and 39)—which of course is cognate with "the Spirit" (*to pneuma*) that, at his baptism, literally "came down into him" (*katabainon eis auton,* 1:10).[27]

Mark's dense network of repetitions—some minor, others refracted—comes into sharp focus at three critical moments in 15:33–41: the centurion's statement in 15:39, the revelatory sign in 15:38, and Jesus' anguished question in 15:34. To begin with the last, let us not only filter out Jesus' words from the cross in other Gospels but also renounce any exegetical legerdemain that would dull the knife edge of the psalmist's lament (22:1).[28] While the evangelist has manifestly determined to end the story of Jesus as he began it, with scriptural context (cf. Mark 1:2–3), the proffered wine in 15:36 would have sufficed to satisfy mere strategy (Ps. 69:21).[29] As Samuel Terrien has noted, of all the laments in the Psalter, Psalm 22 most passionately disclaims any sense of the petitioner's sin, from which, as in Psalm 51:9, the Lord was typically urged to hide his face.[30] In that psalm, the penitent prays not to be expelled from the divine presence (*milĕpānêkā* / *to prosōpon sou,* "your face," 51:11 [Heb. v. 13]). By contrast, in Mark 15:34, Jesus stares with the psalmist (22:1) into God's unveiled face— which now resembles an abyss—and asks why the Almighty has left him in the lurch. By adopting the Hebrew text and opting to translate it with an additional personal pronoun, in 15:34 the evangelist has intensified the heart-searing question: *ho theos _mou_ ho theos mou,* "*my* God, my God" (cf. Ps. 21:2 LXX: *ho theos ho theos mou,* "God, my God"). Not only that: Jesus hurls back to the absent God the comparably intense, personal address that the voice from heaven has twice used for the beloved Jesus: *ho huios mou* (Mark 1:11; 9:7). It is as none other than the beloved Son, going faithfully as it is written of him (14:21), that the crucified Jesus prays to the God who is absent in his hidden presence.

Whatever else may be signified, surely it is the presence of the elusive God that Mark 15:38 asserts, "And the curtain of the temple [*to katapetasma tou naou*] was split in two, from top to bottom." Again note Mark's use of the verb in passive voice, suggesting divine agency of the destruction. Notice too that Mark does not say what Matthew does (27:54), which is often smuggled back into Mark: that the centurion witnessed the curtain's rending and, on the basis of this and other extraordinary phenomena, deduced Jesus' sonship. Such a maneuver sometimes constitutes an exegetical basis to differentiate exactly which cultic appointment Mark intends: the outer curtain, covering the Jerusalem temple's entrance from its forecourt (which would have been visible to spectators outside), or the inner curtain, separating the temple's interior from its most sacred precinct, the Holy of Holies. Complicating interpretation is the fact that the Septuagint and Josephus employ *to katapetasma* for both (outer curtain: Exod. 26:37; 38:18; Num. 3:10, 26 LXX, among others; *A.J.* 8.75; *B.J.* 5.212; inner curtain: Exod. 26:31–35; Lev. 21:23; 24:3 LXX, among others; *A.J.* 8.75). Even if we put aside what was visible from Golgotha—a red herring, as Mark says nothing of this—it is questionable that the evangelist would have rigorously discriminated between *to katapetasma* and *to kalymma,* the proper name for the entryway's drapery. In any case, the inner curtain is probably the referent in Mark 15:38. So far as we know, the outer curtain had no special religious significance, which probably explains the New Testament's exclusive use of *to katapetasma* (here in Mark, plus Matt. 27:51; Luke 23:45; Heb. 6:19; 9:3; 10:20).[31]

All that said, what does Mark 15:38 *mean?* Characteristically, the evangelist offers no interpretation of the veil's breach; to do so would attempt exposure of the God who remains hidden from us, even from Jesus. Still, for perhaps the only time in this Gospel, Mark allows the reader a vision of something unseen by any figure in the story. Does Mark offer us adequate resources to infer its meaning? The traditional exegesis is that "God's judgment has fallen on the temple."[32] In that there may be truth. Yet it says too little, merely restating Mark 13:1–2 (perhaps also 11:15–19) and leaving the *purpose* of such judgment unspecified. In my view, the simplest answer that squares with evidence available elsewhere in this Gospel is that, by God's deliberate intervention, there is no longer any shield between the holy presence and the world around it. (Here we might recall that *naiō,* the verbal cognate of *ho naos,* "temple," fundamentally means "to dwell" or "to inhabit.") Even prior to the resurrection, Jesus' death spells the defeat of any human attempt to localize divinity—whether in a religious structure, such as a temple or tabernacle (thus also 9:5–6), or in the religious imagination that would fix God in the heavens—which, like the curtain in 15:38, have been decisively ripped asunder (*schizō*), spiritually penetrated, and cut down by God (1:10). The expiration of the beloved Son coincides with and is ratified by the apocalyptic release of God's living yet covert, holy presence.

That which remains is the centurion's declaration and the circumstances prompting its utterance (Mark 15:39): "And when the centurion, the bystander facing him, saw that thus he had died, he said,

A   'Truly,
B   this man [*houtos ho anthrōpos*],
C   was God's son [*huios theou ēn*].' "

Although the syntactic elements are shuffled, the pattern is the same as in 1:9 and 9:7. The material difference lies in the speaker. In previous verses, the voice has issued from the heavens or from a cloud. Here, for the first and only time in the Gospel, the voice acknowledging Jesus as God's son belongs to a human character.[33] Readers familiar with the commentary tradition will immediately spot the exegetical difficulties. Is this statement to be taken at face value, with all its attendant ironies: A Gentile recognizes this Jewish victim as faithful ("God's son"), perhaps even the Messiah ("God's Son")?[34] A Roman legionnaire who ludicrously betrays his imperial oath and acclaims a dead Jew as *divi filius,* like unto the divine Augustus?[35] Or is the irony even deeper: Far from offering a Christian confession, does the centurion sarcastically utter the last in a long series of taunts, true (from Mark's point of view) though not for one moment believed by their speakers (see also 14:61, 65; 15:2, 9, 12, 17–18, 26, 32)?[36]

Many commentators are determined to slice the Gordian knot, offering reasons for one alternative or another. If, however, we remain true to the spirit of "the mystery of the kingdom of God" (Mark 4:11), I consider it imperative that the circumstances of this climactic utterance be held firmly in mind while leaving unresolved, to eyes open or shut to faith, its precise significance. The believing reader has been given access, at Jesus' baptism and transfiguration, to faith's evidence that what the centurion says is indeed true—whether *he* knows and believes it or not.[37] The evangelist does not lead us down any path of the soldier's psychology, so there we ought not go.[38] The unbelieving or undecided reader, however, is put on notice: This side of the kingdom's coming, the only empirical evidence that can truthfully support the claim that Jesus is God's Son is nothing other or beyond that which the centurion regards, that is, a dead Jew ("facing him" or "opposite him," *ex enantias autou*) who thus has died (*houtōs exepneusen*). "The critical tension" that Juel discerned in Mark "between blindness and insight, concealment and openness, silence and proclamation" is, indeed, "not resolved" with the report of Jesus' resurrection at the empty tomb (16:7–8). And neither does Mark unravel it with the centurion's announcement at the cross (15:39).

VI

How long till I come and see the face of God?

Ps. 42:2b Goodspeed

As Christopher Burdon perceptively comments, "Mark's is literally a gospel of 'following,' not of Jesus' 'abiding' as in John's or of his being 'in the midst' as in Matthew's."[39] Through Jesus, God outruns everyone in Mark. Occasionally, to the consternation of later Trinitarian thought, God outstrips even Jesus, his beloved Son (Mark 7:24–30; 13:32; 15:34). Ultimately, if not expressly, that is the point underlying the venerable question of Mark's "theological geography" or, in its late reformulation, "boundary-crossings."[40] Arguably, God's self-concealing revelation is the primary element in Mark's presentation of suffering discipleship and its christological corollary, which, somewhat misleadingly, has too often been epitomized as "the Messianic secret." For when we speak of Mark's Jesus—his baptism, transfiguration, death and resurrection; his gospel of the kingdom and way of discipleship; all of the religious and cultural definitions exploded by the Messiah's apocalypse—are we not probing, at bottom, a particular theology of divine presence and its "mysterious revelation"?[41] Are we not invited by this evangelist to reconsider where God is truly found and, in the process of that search, to discover what the true God looks like—the One whose power is revealed in power's renunciation, whose glory is cloaked in suffering self-abnegation?[42] "Truly, thou art a God who hidest thyself, O God of Israel, the Savior" (Isa. 45:15 RSV). Thus did Second Isaiah marvel. The record is clear that the evangelist Mark agreed.

So did Don Juel. He learned it from Luther[43] and thrived in its reinforcement by his *Doktorvater* Nils Dahl.[44] Juel understood that theology is not an inquiry that pursues the divine as an object but, rather, a clarification and communication of the inherently mysterious operation by which God pursues and transforms humanity into the *imago Dei*. Writ large across Scripture, exemplified by the Second Gospel, that divine pursuit is utterly free, uncontrollably gracious, ever present yet forever elusive. Aping the Almighty, we seek God in comfortable zones, precincts of power, among the pious; constantly we are startled that God's kingdom already is among us, its Messiah enthroned where we least expect. At our best, we want him enshrined; at our worst, we want him dead. Though elusive, Jesus will not collude with our delusions. He refuses to keep still on a holy hill. He won't stay buried. Roving, relentless, Jesus persists in calling disciples into a Sabbath of which he is Lord, along a way he makes sacred though never safe. They follow where glimpses of God's presence are traceable yet intractable, where the Face, made familiar among us, can never be placed.

Notes

1. Frank Kermode, *The Genesis of Secrecy: On the Interpretation of Narrative* (Cambridge, MA: Harvard University Press, 1979), 72–73; see also idem, *The Sense of an Ending: Studies in the Theory of Fiction* (London: Oxford University Press, 1966).
2. Donald H. Juel, *Mark,* Augsburg Commentaries on the New Testament (Minneapolis: Augsburg, 1990), 230–31; idem, *The Gospel of Mark,* Interpreting Biblical Texts (Nashville: Abingdon Press, 1999), 167–76.
3. Juel, *Master of Surprise: Mark Interpreted* (Minneapolis: Fortress Press, 1994), 120–21 (and see above, pp. 11–12).
4. Donald H. Juel, *Messiah and Temple: The Trial of Jesus in the Gospel of Mark,* SBL Dissertation Series 31 (Missoula, MT: Scholars Press, 1977).
5. Juel, *Master of Surprise,* 120 (and see above, p. 11).
6. Samuel Terrien, *The Elusive Presence: The Heart of Biblical Theology,* Religious Perspectives 26 (San Francisco: Harper & Row, 1978), 170.
7. See Norman Perrin, "Towards an Interpretation of the Gospel of Mark," in *Christology and a Modern Pilgrimage: A Discussion with Norman Perrin,* ed. H. D. Betz (Claremont, CA: New Testament Colloquium, 1971), 1–78.
8. See, for example, Martin Dibelius, *From Tradition to Gospel* (New York: Charles Scribner's Sons, 1934), 275–79.
9. The textual evidence for and against the original occurrence of *huiou theou,* "son of God," in Mark 1:1 is so evenly balanced as to be irresolvable with confidence. Consult Adela Yarbro Collins, "Establishing the Text: Mark 1:1," in *Texts and Contexts: Biblical Texts in Their Textual and Situational Contexts: Essays in Honor of Lars Hartman,* ed. T. Fornberg and D. Hellholm, assisted by C. D. Hellholm (Oslo and Copenhagen: Scandinavia University Press, 1995), 111–27.
10. See especially Jack Dean Kingsbury, *The Christology of Mark's Gospel* (Philadelphia: Fortress Press, 1983), 47–155.

11. In this connection, see David Fredrickson, "What Difference Does Jesus Make for God?" *Dialog* 37 (1998): 104–10.

12. Here and elsewhere all translations are my own unless otherwise noted.

13. Hence, Willi Marxsen's celebrated insight that "Mark composes backward": *Mark the Evangelist: Studies on the Redaction History of the Gospel* (Nashville: Abingdon Press, 1969), 32. It is important to note that Donald Juel was among the translators of this seminal German volume (1956) into English.

14. Matthew (3:13–17) articulates the theological problem and his own resolution of it on the lips of John and Jesus; Luke (3:21) shifts the baptism itself into an adverbial clause; in the *Gospel according to the Hebrews* (per Jerome, *Against Pelagius* 3.2), Jesus flatly resists his family's invitation that he be baptized with them, on the grounds of his sinlessness.

15. As Donald Juel notes in *Messianic Exegesis: Christological Interpretation of the Old Testament in Early Christianity* (Philadelphia: Fortress Press, 1988), 59–88, both Psalm 2 and 2 Samuel 7 (Nathan's oracle to David) may have been interpreted messianically by some Jews even before the Christian era.

16. While many commentators correctly note that the christological issue of adoptionism is not in view in 1:11, Mark's decision to depart from Psalm 2 LXX at precisely the point of verse 7c (*egō sēmeron gegennēka se,* "I have begotten you today") might suggest, to the contrary, a deliberate decision to avoid that intimation.

17. Terrien, *Elusive Presence*, 294. Likewise, a serious danger attached to the priesthood lay in "the corruptibility of the mediating agent" (p. 400).

18. So also Juel: "The more one knows about the background of the [royal] imagery in Mark, the more striking is the account. . . . Jesus should be among the mighty, in the great city that served David as his citadel, not among sinners who have come to repent for their sins" ("The Origin of Mark's Christology," in *The Messiah: Developments in Early Judaism and Christianity,* ed. J. H. Charlesworth [Minneapolis: Fortress Press, 1992], 457).

19. Rudolf Bultmann, *History of the Synoptic Tradition,* rev. ed. (New York: Harper & Row, 1963), 260.

20. Rendering a firmly negative verdict to his article's titular question is Robert H. Stein, "Is the Transfiguration (Mark 9:2–8) a Misplaced Resurrection-Account?" *Journal of Biblical Literature* 95 (1976): 79–96.

21. For documentation, consult Jerome T. Walsh, "Elijah," *Anchor Bible Dictionary* (New York: Doubleday, 1992): 2:463–66.

22. See, among others, Joel Marcus, *The Way of the Lord: Christological Exegesis of the Old Testament in the Gospel of Mark* (Louisville, KY: Westminster John Knox Press, 1992), 80–93.

23. Though the nuance may have been lost on audiences lacking Hebrew, *agapētos* ("beloved") is employed throughout Genesis 22 LXX to translate *yāḥîd,* "only" or "unique" (vv. 2, 12, 16). Margaret E. Thrall, "Elijah and Moses in Mark's Account of the Transfiguration," *New Testament Studies* 16 (1970): 305–17, points up Mark's emphasis on Jesus' superiority.

24. See Richard Elliott Friedman, "Tabernacle," *Anchor Bible Dictionary* (New York: Doubleday, 1992): 2:292–300.

25. As Morna D. Hooker observes, "[O]n the rare occasions when [Mark] uses the word *doxa* [8:38; 10:37; 13:26], he links it every time with the suffering and death of Jesus and his followers." Hooker, "'What Doest Thou Here, Elijah?' A Look at St Mark's Account of the Transfiguration," in *The Glory of Christ in the New Testament: Studies in Christology in Memory of George Bradford Caird,* ed. L. D. Hurst and N. T. Wright (Oxford: Clarendon Press, 1987), 70.

26. *Pace* John J. Pilch, "Death with Honor: The Mediterranean Style Death of Jesus in Mark," *Biblical Theology Bulletin* 2 (1995): 65–70, which argues that "Jesus' [stoic] death proves that he was reared well."

27. Bas M. F. van Iersel suggests that such resonance with 1:10 would explain why, in 15:37 and 39, Mark avoids the far more common verb *apethanen*, "he died" (15:44; 1 Cor. 15:3–5). Van Iersel, *Mark: A Reader-Response Commentary,* Journal for the Study of the New Testament: Supplement Series 164 (Sheffield: Sheffield Academic Press, 1998), 477. Though ingenious, S. Motyer's proposal that the *velum scissum* amounts to a Markan Pentecost overreaches the textual evidence ("The Rending of the Veil: A Markan Pentecost?" *New Testament Studies* 33 [1987]: 155–57).

28. On this point, observe the cautions of Raymond E. Brown, *The Death of the Messiah: From Gethsemane to the Grave,* Anchor Bible Reference Library (New York: Doubleday, 1994), 2:1049–51.

29. In addition, Kenneth E. Bailey highlights the fabric of associations between Mark's crucifixion narrative and the book of Lamentations. See "The Fall of Jerusalem and Mark's Account of the Cross," *Expository Times* 102 (1991): 102–5.

30. Terrien, *Elusive Presence*, 323.

31. Cf. David Ulansey, "The Heavenly Veil Torn: Mark's Cosmic *Inclusio,*" *Journal of Biblical Literature* 110 (2001): 123–25, suggesting a correspondence between the heavens in Mark 1:10 and the starry sky depicted on the outer curtain, as Josephus describes it (*B.J.* 5.5.4).

32. O. Michel, "*naos,*" in *Theological Dictionary of the New Testament,* ed. G. Kittel and G. Friedrich (Grand Rapids: Wm. B. Eerdmans Publishing Co., 1967): 4:885.

33. In 3:11, the wording is exact but the voice belongs to the unclean spirits. In 12:6 and 13:32, the speaker is Jesus but the wording is only approximate (*huion agapēton, ho huios*).

34. Compounding the interpretive problem here is the lack of a definite article for *huios* ("son") in the Greek text. In idiomatic Koine, however, no article is necessary when a predicate precedes the verb "to be." See the discussions in T. Francis Glasson, "Mark xv. 39: The Son of God," *Expository Times* 80 (1969): 286; and Philip B. Harner, "Qualitative Anarthrous Predicate Nouns: Mark 15:39 and John 1:1," *Journal of Biblical Literature* 92 (1973): 75–87.

35. Philip H. Bligh, "A Note on Huios Theou in Mark 15:39," *Expository Times* 80 (1968): 51–53; Tae Hun Kim, "The Anarthrous *Huios Theou* in Mark 15,39 and the Roman Imperial Cult," *Biblica* 79 (1998): 221–41.

36. Whitney T. Shiner, "The Ambiguous Pronouncement of the Centurion and the Shrouding of Meaning in Mark," *Journal for the Study of the New Testament* 78 (2000): 3–22. Juel's later interpretation is also attracted toward a similar conclusion: Donald H. Juel, "The Strange Silence of the Bible," *Interpretation* 51 (1997): 5–19.

37. A rehearsal for this enigmatic confession occurs in Mark 14:3–8, where Jesus—not the woman with the alabaster flask—interprets the suggestion of royal anointing (1 Sam. 10:1; 2 Kgs. 9:6) as a proleptic funeral preparation.

38. See Earl S. Johnson, Jr., "Mark 15,39 and the So-Called Confession of the Roman Centurion," *Biblica* 81 (2000): 406–13. For an opposing—to my mind, unconvincing—exegesis, see Howard M. Jackson, "The Death of Jesus in Mark and the Miracle from the Cross," *New Testament Studies* 33 (1987): 16–37.

39. Christopher Burdon, " 'Such a Fast God'—True and False Disciples in Mark's Gospel," *Theology* 90 (1987): 94; see also idem, *Stumbling on God: Faith and Vision in Mark's Gospel* (Grand Rapids: Wm. B. Eerdmans Publishing Co., 1990), esp. 42–52.

40. The literature is vast. Representative are Elizabeth Struthers Malbon, "Galilee and Jerusalem: History and Literature in Marcan Interpretation," *Catholic Biblical Quarterly* 44 (1982): 242–55; Gerd Theissen, "Lokalkoloritforschung in den Evangelien," *Evangelische Theologie* 45 (1985): 481–99; Sean Freyne, "The Geography of Restoration: Galilee-Jerusalem Relations in Early Jewish and Christian Experience," in *Restoration: Old Testament, Jewish, and Christian Perspectives,* ed. J. M. Scott, Journal for the Study of Judaism: Supplement Series 72 (Leiden: E. J. Brill, 2001), 405–33; William Loader, "Challenged at the Boundaries: A Conservative Jesus in Mark's Tradition," *Journal for the Study of the New Testament* 63 (1996): 45–61; Brian K. Blount, *Go Preach! Mark's Kingdom Message and the Black Church Today* (Maryknoll, NY: Orbis Books, 1998).

41. In this connection, T. A. Burkill, *Mysterious Revelation: An Examination of the Philosophy of St. Mark's Gospel* (Ithaca, NY: Cornell University Press, 1963), remains a worthwhile study.

42. See Dorothy A. Lee-Pollard, "Powerlessness as Power: A Key Emphasis in the Gospel of Mark," *Scottish Journal of Theology* 40 (1987): 173–88; Claude Wiéner, "Voyant Qu'il Avait Ainsi Expiré (Marc 15,39)," in *Pense la Foi,* ed. J. Doné and C. Theobald (Paris: Assas Éditions, 1993), 51–58; William C. Placher, "Narratives of a Vulnerable God," *Princeton Seminary Bulletin* 14 (1993): 134–51.

43. "But one is worth calling a theologian who understands the visible and hinder parts of God to mean the passion and the cross" (*The Heidelberg Disputation* [1518]) in *Luther: Early Theological Works,* ed. J. Atkinson [Philadelphia: Westminster Press, 1962], 290–91).

44. Nils A. Dahl, "A Neglected Factor in New Testament Theology," *Reflection* 75 (1975): 5–8; repr. in *Jesus the Christ: The Historical Origins of Christological Doctrine,* ed. D. H. Juel (Minneapolis: Fortress Press, 1991), 153–63. John R. Donahue, "A Neglected Factor in the Theology of Mark," *Journal of Biblical Literature* 101 (1982): 563–94, remains the most acute appropriation of Dahl's insight for the exegesis of Mark that I know.

Chapter 4

Unsettling Generosity: Fearful Disciples on This Side of the Text

D. Cameron Murchison

In *A Master of Surprise,* Donald Juel probes the complex ending of Mark's Gospel and kneads the themes of disappointment and promise as the former is expressed in the women's failure to say anything to anyone and the latter is expressed in the heavenly messenger's reiteration that the disciples would see Jesus in Galilee, just as he had told them.[1] In doing so, Juel offers a hermeneutical approach that can fruitfully be applied to reading a number of texts in the Gospel, perhaps the Gospel as a whole. The approach may be stated thus: When we encounter disciples and followers astonished or disbelieving in Mark's narrative, we are facing the same dialectic of disappointment and promise that operates so intensely at the end of Mark's Gospel. In these settings we see the tension between the fundamental theological claim of trustworthiness for all that Mark represents as manifestations of God's present reign in the world and the fearful response of disciples more ready to make peace with the death of the gospel than to enter into its promise.

Moreover, in identifying the hermeneutical approach, Juel not only offers us a way to read the story in the text but also a way to attend to "the world in front of the text."[2] That is, this tension between disappointment and promise, between fearfulness and gladness, between making peace with the constraints of the world as we think we know them and being open to the freedom of God who does more than we ask or think—this very tension is something into which Mark's narrative invites us as we reckon with some of the important moments of our world and of our lives in it.

The plan of this essay is to focus on certain texts in Mark's Gospel that probe those of us standing on this side of the text with the tension of disappointment and promise. In doing so, we will see that the dilemma of Easter is constantly at work in Mark's narrative, constantly confronting disciples and near disciples— then and now—with a surprising promise of life in virtue of the reality of God's reign even as we bend toward the disappointing readiness to make peace with the death of the gospel.

Writing not as a biblical scholar but as a practical theologian, I will focus on several texts that have in common a concern with the material conditions of human well-being. As we will see, the texts share with the unsettling ending of Mark a certain recalcitrance of disciples and near disciples at the promise of the gospel—ranging from hesitancy, to objection, to disbelief. Whatever the form of their reservation, they pose a particular case of the women fleeing in fear from the empty tomb, succumbing to definitions of reality that make the gospel unbelievable. The stories portray occasions in which the disciples' assumptions about the material conditions of human well-being are challenged and confronted by a gospel that proposes a very different way of understanding the material world. Reading the stories in this way will not be an innocuous matter but will confront those of us standing on this side of the text (especially, perhaps, those of us who may be standing in the midst of North American affluence) with a gospel that proposes surprising understandings of the material conditions of *our* well-being.

MARK'S STORIES OF FEEDING MULTITUDES AND OUR CONSUMING PASSION

Donald Juel's own comment upon the appearance of two feeding stories in Mark[3]—five thousand in 6:35–44 and four thousand in 8:1–9—argues with others for the intentionality of the repetition of two stories so strikingly similar. What is of narrative (hence dramatic) importance is not that Jesus did the same miracle twice but that the disciples were stuck in the same unbelieving response to the unanticipated power of God's reign in their midst. Both stories echo the provision of manna in the story of Israel's exodus from Egypt. Both stories acknowledge the material basis of human well-being in having food for nourishment. While the earlier story tells of the disciples' awareness of the crowd's need, the second story recounts Jesus' compassion for the people in his bringing attention to their need for sustenance. But no matter who first calls attention to this inescapable need for food as a material condition of human well-being, both the stories share the portrayal of disciples as uncomprehending when it comes to Jesus' claim about how the need will be satisfied.

In essence, Jesus challenges the disciples to trust that the needed material resources do not have to be generated by some extrinsic economic activity, but rather that the material reality needed will appear in the midst of communal activity that is gratefully focused on God's generosity. In the first story, the assumption that the needed resources can only be derived from economic activity is explicit. Not only do the disciples suggest to Jesus that the people can be sent away "so that they may . . . buy something for themselves to eat" (6:36), but when challenged by Jesus to give the crowd something to eat themselves the disciples immediately assume that the burden of economic activity has been transferred from the people to the disciples: "Are we to go and buy two hundred denarii worth of bread, and give it to them to eat?" (6:37). If the second story is less explicit about the disciples' assumption that material resources are only available through well-defined economic activity, it no less powerfully displays the disciples wonderment about alternatives: "How can one feed these people with bread here in the desert?" (8:4).

Jesus' response in both stories deals with the question of material resources not by recourse to economic activity but by communal activity that arranges itself receptively and gratefully around God's promise of generous blessing and shares what is given with all. And the report of the stories is that they all ate and were satisfied (6:42; 8:8). Moreover, the satisfaction is not represented as minimalist but abundant—as baskets full are left over (6:43; 8:8).

Thus, the feeding stories challenge the assumption that the material conditions of human life are best met by economic behaviors by which we provide for our own security. Instead, these stories unsettle such pre-Easter convictions by proposing that God satisfies the material conditions of human life by providing enough, when what is given is received in thanksgiving (as a blessing from a generous God) and mediated through neighborliness (by a readiness to share).

As disciples on our (North American, affluent, Christian) side of the text, we join in the recalcitrance of Mark's disciples from a special vantage point. For like it or not, we have been shaped in our convictions about the material conditions of human well-being by the success of production-oriented capitalism that has led inexorably to consumer-oriented capitalism. As Rodney Clapp explains the progression, the Industrial Revolution displaced home production with the factory system. "Suddenly this economic system could produce many, many more goods than the existing population, with its set habits and means, could afford and consume."[4]

The result has been a turn to advertising that early on succeeded in introducing an array of products and services that eventually replaced traditional home production with store-bought commodities. But more importantly, a new ethos was shaped "in which the good life is attained through the constant acquisition and consumption of new products and new experiences." Moreover, advertising took as part of its necessary task not only serving the needs that people already had but also creating new ones.[5] The oft-noted experience of being part of a culture where the pace at which wants are converted into needs accelerates with increasing rapidity is not an accident.[6] The material conditions of human well-being in the context of consumer capitalism require it.

Oddly, though, the material condition of human well-being turns out in this system fundamentally not to be about materialism or physical goods. "As Colin Campbell puts it, individuals consume for the 'pleasure which they derive from the self-illusory experiences that they construct out of the images or associations attached to products.'"[7] As a consequence, modern consumers are continually and perpetually and deliberately dissatisfied. "Fulfillment and lasting satisfaction are forever just out of reach. . . . Unique to modern capitalism and consumerism are the idealization and constant encouragement of insatiability—the deification of dissatisfaction."[8]

As a consequence, North American Christians on this side of Mark's text that tells of the feeding of the multitudes are likely to behave with a disappointment akin to that of the women fleeing in silence from the empty tomb, rather than to embrace the promise that empty space offers. Inevitably we are encouraged to understand that "persons consist basically of unmet needs that can be requited by commodified goods and experiences. Accordingly, the consumer should think first and foremost of himself or herself and meeting his or her felt needs. The consumer is taught to value above all else freedom, defined as a vast array of choices."[9]

Rare is the person who does not treasure some significant aspect of such multiplication of choices. But this univocal definition of freedom as choice easily seduces us into a failure to wonder whether many of our choices add anything significant to the quality of our lives. Moreover, it also blinds us to some of the values that are lost when consumer choice becomes the driving mechanism. Rodney Clapp cites the work of Alan Ehrenhalt, who has detailed the way in which concentration on choice and marketing has weakened communities.[10] The outcome is most notable in the disappearance of small, locally owned commercial establishments beneath the rising tide of large discount stores.

There is no doubt that the latter serve the alleged freedom of virtually unlimited choice in the average shopper's experience. But the virtually unnoticed cost of this freedom is the loss of a communal sense deriving from carrying out commerce in a network of ongoing, long-term relationships between customers and merchants, where the relationships are more important than the price of a particular item. What we have gained in the bargain is more, less expensive choices. What we have lost is the fabric of community itself.

Our particular form of economic activity is as second-nature to us as was that of the disciples. They could not imagine satisfaction of the material needs of the multitude apart from sending the crowd away to purchase what was needed. We cannot imagine satisfaction of our material needs apart from the freedom to choose—except that we live with the irony that as modern consumers we are perpetually unsatisfied, because, as we have seen, we have embraced the illusion that the images and associations we have attached to the products we choose will accompany our acquisition of the things themselves. Disciples then and now find it difficult to trust Jesus' claim that the material basis of our well-being resides elsewhere than in our commonplace economic practice.

But then and now Jesus poses a different vision that echoes the promise in the midst of disappointment. He prioritizes communal bonds over conventional economic practice. Instead of sending the multitude off to buy, he asks the disciples to bring the resources at hand forward, and then he takes, blesses, and shares them. Overflowing satisfaction of the need is the result. The language of both stories makes plain that Mark ties them closely to the early church's eucharistic practice. Both the stories and the Eucharist provide a foretaste of the eschatological fulfillment where all are fed and satisfied by God's hand.

Thus, the insatiable assumptions of our consumerist economy are unsettled by the gospel. Its promise is found in what God provides when the disciples, led by Jesus, generously and gratefully offer their resources to the community and discover how what appears to be very little can satisfy beyond all expectations. Thus, it invites those of us on the consumerist side of the text to find ways to practice resistance against economic habits that form us as insatiable choosers, even at the expense of community. We are no less likely than the women at the tomb to disappoint in our response, no less likely than they to make peace with the death of the gospel rather than enter into its promise. But the God who has fed Israel with manna in the wilderness, the crowds with loaves and fish in Mark's stories, and the church in the Eucharist continues to hold forth the promise. Indeed, the church's continual immersion in the promise by its practice of the Eucharist is perhaps one of its primal acts of resistance against the presumption of the material conditions of human well-being that our economic milieu sponsors.

MARK'S ACCOUNT OF THE MAN WITH MANY POSSESSIONS AND OVERSPENT AMERICANS

If the feeding stories in Mark manifest disciples hesitant to understand the material conditions of human well-being as Jesus does, the story of the person of wealth who comes to Jesus shows one who could not quite believe and thus who did not follow (10:17–31). The encounter does not start out as one that involves a focus on life's material conditions. Indeed, it begins with an explicit naming of what might be considered spiritual conditions as the subject of the encounter.

A man approaches Jesus in a quest to know what he must do to inherit eternal life. The first response he receives from Jesus maintains the same framework for the conversation, as Jesus lists the commandments that define the existence of people before God. To the confident, though not obviously arrogant, response by the man that he has lived this pattern of life for a long time, Jesus answers by (apparently) suddenly changing the terms of the conversation. No longer operating solely in a spiritual realm, he turns directly to the material: "You lack one thing; go, sell what you own, and give the money to the poor, and you will have treasure in heaven; then come, follow me" (10:21). Here the man confronts the outer limits of his readiness for discipleship, going away grieving, "for he had many possessions" (10:22).

The man seems to have presumed that the cost of discipleship would not extend to his material circumstances. But Jesus seems to assume that the material conditions of his existence represent not a resource for discipleship but precisely an alternative to it. Indeed, the emphasis of Jesus' summons to the man falls not on helping the poor by divesting himself of his possessions (however helpful such a transfer of wealth might be to the poor) but upon following Jesus with an abandon that holding many possessions precludes.

Mark's account of this encounter suggests that predictable, perhaps excessive, concerns about the material conditions of human existence are fundamentally incompatible with following Jesus with abandon. The man with many possessions is cut off from discipleship in this sense because he is too embedded in his material reality. His quest for "eternal life" is not so earnest as to countenance a redefinition of his relationship to what he has. He goes away grieving, but go away he does.

What is at stake in the story becomes increasingly clear as Jesus turns his attention to the disciples, stating plainly, "How hard it will be for those who have wealth to enter the kingdom of God!" (10:23). Whatever one makes of interpretive approaches that have seen in the "eye of a needle" a name for a small city gate alongside the main gate or that read "camel" as "cable,"[11] a very strong hyperbole remains in Jesus' striking image of the difficulty that someone who is rich has in entering the kingdom of God. And it is one that deeply disturbs the disciples.

They quickly draw the (inescapable?) conclusion that none with many possessions can find their way into God's kingdom, only to have Jesus counter with the same gospel logic that unsettled the women at the empty tomb: "For mortals it is impossible but not for God; for God all things are possible" (10:27). And then in counterpoint to the negative instance of the young man who had already departed, Peter speaks for the disciples in recognition that God had already made possible for them the abandonment of the ordinary assumptions about the material conditions of their existence: "Look, we have left everything and followed you" (10:28). This counterpoint with the man of wealth is precise. He could not leave much of anything, and so could not follow. The disciples had (only by God's power) left everything and did follow. Disappointment not unlike the women fleeing in silence is seen in the one case, joyous embrace of the promise in the other. The cost of their discipleship had extended to their material world— house, brothers, sisters, mothers, children, fields (10:29)—all the appurtenances of livelihood and community. They had thus followed with the requisite abandon and were living into the promise that these would be given, again, overflowing in the community of those following Jesus.

Thus, both in negative (the man of wealth) and in positive illustration (the disciples), the unsettling work of God manifests itself in this story as well. The material conditions of life are closely tied to the life of discipleship. No stewardly management of the material domain is called for by Jesus, but straightforward abandonment of it in readiness to follow him. What perplexes (the man of wealth decisively and the disciples initially) is the apparent impossibility of the demand. Sadly, that is all the young man ever grasps in the story, leaving him in his unsettled disappointment. Fortunately, the disciples are made aware of the power of God at work in ways different from worldly possibility, planting them in the midst of unsettling promise.

Reading on our side of the text introduces some very important variables. Middle-class Americans, however sure they may be that they do not represent wealth or riches, are especially likely to be as confounded as the young man in the story by this encounter with Jesus. This is because of what Juliet Schor calls "the new consumerism."[12] We are likely to go away grieving not merely because we have so much but because we want so much more, sucked as in a vortex into a culture of upscale spending.

Noting that competitive acquisition has long been an American institution, Schor points out that a monumental shift has occurred in the way it is practiced. Whereas the average American in the early post–World War II decades practiced this competitive acquisition with reference to those in his or her own earnings category, or perhaps with reference to those a rung higher on the economic ladder, in recent decades things have changed dramatically. "Today a person is more likely to be making comparisons with, or choose as a 'reference group,' people whose incomes are three, four, or five times his or her own."[13]

At the heart of this shift is the fact that our lifestyle aspirations are formed by different points of reference. Family and neighborhood have been replaced by the people alongside whom we work, together with colleagues in our own and related professions. Moreover, real-life friends have been augmented by media "friends." Consequently, says Schor, "we watch the way television families live, we read about the lifestyles of celebrities and other public figures we admire, and we consciously and unconsciously assimilate this information."[14] The obvious rub in this newer reference group is that it has been extended not merely horizontally but vertically as well: "When a person who earns $75,000 a year compares herself to someone earning $90,000, the comparison is sustainable. . . . But when a reference group includes people who pull down six or even seven-figure incomes, that's trouble."[15]

Schor reckons that there are both dramatic and pedestrian examples of how this vertical stretching of reference group operates. She describes a dramatic instance of an urban literary reference group that includes poet-waiters earning $18,000 a year, teachers who make $30,000, and editors or publishers who may earn six-figure incomes. Their common aspiration to be part of this one urban literary reference group can have serious effects. It "exerts pressure to drink the same brand of bottled water and wine, wear similar urban literary clothes, and appoint apartments with urban literary furniture."[16] Obviously the pattern is untenable for those at the lower economic end of the reference group. What may

appear to be a simple matter of chronic dissatisfaction for the low-end participants in such a vertically extended reference group as this can turn into something more socially devastating: "When the children of affluent suburban and
impoverished inner-city households both want the same Tommy Hilfiger logo
emblazoned on their chests and the top-of-the-line Swoosh on their feet, it's a
potential disaster."[17]

But the most important point of Schor's analysis for many of us living on this
side of Mark's text about the man of wealth and the disciples before Jesus lies in
the more pedestrian illustrations of these vertically stretched reference groups:
"People in one-earner families find themselves trying to live the lifestyle of their
two-paycheck friends. Parents of modest means struggle to pay for the private
schooling that others in their reference group have established as the right thing
to do for their children."[18] And these extended reference groups are also in the
midst of product innovation and lifestyle marketing that has the effect of constantly raising the standards for the whole group.

The result of this process as reflected in research into social and economic
aspirations among Americans is that "85 percent aspired to be in the top 18 percent of American households. Only 15 percent would be satisfied by 'living a
comfortable life' or something less. Only 15 percent would be satisfied ending
up as middle-class."[19] Yet the pattern of economic growth in the United States
has been moving in exactly the opposite direction, with the top 20 percent earning an increasing share of income, with the income share for every group beneath
them falling. "So four-fifths of Americans were relegated to earning *even less* than
the people they looked up to, who were now earning and spending more."[20]

The dynamic process that Schor narrates is full of irony. While many Americans have experienced substantial improvement in their material comforts, they
report a diminished sense of material well-being: "The story of the eighties and
nineties is that millions of Americans ended the period having more but feeling
poorer."[21] And while many had much more, they also found their quality of life
squeezed at the level of family finance (1) by debt service that had risen to 18 percent of disposable income, (2) by pressure to work longer hours or to send a second earner into the workplace, and (3) by overspending, which has undermined
savings even among the financially better-off households.[22]

Moreover, family finances are not all that is at stake. As pressure on private
spending has escalated, support for public needs has slackened. "Education,
social services, public safety, recreation, and culture are squeezed. . . . People
respond to inadequate public services by enrolling their children in private
schools, buying security systems, and spending time at Discovery Zone rather
than the local playground."[23] Thus, people who have the resources "try to spend
their way around these problems,"[24] but that does nothing to restore the lost
experience of social support—of community—over time.

Schor's analysis of the overspent American offers an important prompt for
self-awareness for many of us who approach Mark 10:17–31. It suggests that we
have our own version of "many possessions" that make abandoned response to

Jesus' call to discipleship deeply problematic. Of course, it is not necessarily that we have many possessions in relation to our immediate points of reference, however many we may have by historical and global standards. For in relation to our immediate points of reference, Schor has shown how they have been extended vertically and how they inexorably enmesh us in aspirations for more in the way of material satisfactions. So whether we *have* many possessions, or merely *aspire to* many more possessions, we may easily find ourselves in solidarity with the shock and grief of the one who went away from rather than went after Jesus.

The unsettling dynamic of Mark's surprising ending operates in our particular encounter with this story as well. It is perhaps more obvious in our own case than that of the man in the story that our relationship to possessions represents not a resource for faithful following of Jesus but an impediment to it. For what we are challenged to divest ourselves of by the story is not necessarily an accumulation of possessions, but of our willing (if unacknowledged) embrace of vertically extended reference groups that threaten both personal/familial and public goods. It may not be our actual acquisitions so much as our relentless aspirations that keep us from the abandoned following of Jesus that he invites. Schor's account of the "new consumerism" makes plain that this is a formidable impediment. We have neither time nor energy both to follow Jesus and to live under the relentless pressure of the reference group our economic culture offers.

Thus, we stand poised between the man who is disappointed by the "unrealistic" claim the gospel makes on his life, and the disciples who have been seized by the generous promise of the gospel and enabled to "leave everything" in their following of Jesus. What is especially interesting is that what they left has special resonance for those of us who may be asked to leave a pattern of reference groups that focuses everything on market exchanges (that is, how we can get what our reference group convinces us we need). We can hear the disciples' abandonment of houses, families, and fields as a call to leave behind the economic comparisons that undermine both the quality of our lives and the public goods they inevitably ignore. And we can hear Jesus' promise of a hundredfold blessing of houses, family, and fields as a promise of new community, defined as a reference group that is extended horizontally rather than vertically, with Jesus at its center. In this new community, concern for the social goods that we share in common matters more than the personal goods we competitively acquire.

The story of the man with many possessions poses for us another Markan surprise, a challenge not to succumb to definitions of reality that make the gospel unbelievable. In particular, it invites us to understand the material conditions of our well-being in ways alternative to that of "overspent Americans." It invites us into community not with reference groups that drive us relentlessly toward upscale spending, but into community formed and defined by Jesus, where we find people and means of livelihood that honor what a generous God gives us together more than what any of us acquires alone. In showing us what abandonment is required for faithful discipleship, it threatens to disappoint us as we have been formed by our economic culture. But, more importantly, it gives us a fresh promise that God's generous provision for even our material well-being is richer than we have heretofore imagined.

MARK'S ACCOUNT OF THE ANOINTING
AT BETHANY AND LUXURY FEVER

Mark's version of the anointing of Jesus at Bethany by a woman with a jar of "very costly ointment" (14:3–9) is another point at which Mark surprises us with his vision of the material conditions of human well-being. It offers a somewhat odd twist on the question. In the previous accounts we have considered, stress has fallen on basic, self-referential needs—either to provide for oneself through consumptive behavior (the feeding of the multitudes), or to secure one's sense of well-being by accumulation of possessions. In this story, however, the dramatic conflict revolves around two, conflicting, other-regarding courses of action.

Those who viewed with anger the woman's act of anointing voice one of these other-regarding courses of action. They might easily be seen as having thought they had learned Jesus' lesson in the encounter with the man who had many possessions. They wanted such a costly possession sold and the proceeds given to the poor (cf. 10:21). They apparently believe that renunciation of such a luxurious item is consistent with Jesus' understanding of the material conditions of human well-being—renunciation that converts the luxury item to a more generous and sustaining use.

But given what we have already seen in relation to Jesus' encounter with the man of wealth, we should not be surprised when he disputes this first, other-regarding course of action. It is not that material possessions have value only in their capacity to be converted into useful resources for the poor. It is rather that material possessions lack value to the extent that they become impediments to following Jesus with abandon.

Therefore, Jesus surprises these onlookers with an interpretation of the woman's act as consistent with genuine discipleship. He sees in her act a second, other-regarding gesture that represents authentic, abandoned discipleship. By rejecting the onlookers' account of her action, Jesus challenges the assumption that every faithful economic act is renunciatory in style. Instead, he affirms an act that uses something luxurious, economically considered, since Mark is careful to say that the ointment was "very costly." But what is being affirmed is not wanton, profligate, unctuous, or self-aggrandizing use of the luxurious ointment. What is being affirmed is an abandonment of the luxury commodity (it is not being retained to secure the woman's self-image by accumulation) and the utilization of it as a sign of and commitment to God's strange reign in the world ("she has anointed my body beforehand for its burial" [14:8]).

What distinguishes the act of the woman is precisely that it is other regarding. Her act takes something luxurious as not to be hoarded for self. Instead, this something luxurious is abandoned to the presence and purpose of God as it unfolds before her. Thus, the story brings into sharp focus how faithfully to account for luxurious materialism in the life of discipleship. While it is not difficult to imagine then or now different settings where the faithful abandonment of luxury materials might move in a different direction, in her particular setting the woman "has done what she could" (14:8). And her action brings us full circle to what the women at the end of the story (16:1–8) are not able to do, that is, to anoint Jesus' body for burial.

Once again it is pertinent for us as readers of Mark to take stock of the geography on our side of the text, specifically in the midst of what Robert Frank has aptly called "luxury fever." Noting the availability of an incredible range of luxury consumer items for the superrich—ranging from propane grills costing more than $5,000, to Patek Philippe wristwatches for $17,500, to pleasure craft that cost $1.5 million to run and maintain annually, to vacation homes priced in the high $700,000s, to cases of wine auctioned for $112,500—Frank argues that such expenditures ought not be ignored on the grounds that they constitute just a small fraction of total spending. Such purchases, he believes, "are far more significant than might appear, for they have been the leading edge of pervasive changes in the spending patterns of middle- and even low-income families. The runaway spending at the top has been a virus, one that's spawned a luxury fever that, to one degree or another, has all of us in its grip."[25] To make the point concrete, he reminds us that as $5,000 grills become prominent on the market, buying a $1,000 grill begins to appear frugal. "More troubling still is the possibility that, with ready opportunities to spend five times that amount and more, I might fail to notice anything strange about spending $1,000 to replace my $90 gas grill."[26] Similarly, Frank observes that "except for the growing presence of Patek Philippe and other similar products in the marketplace, many fewer upper-middle-class buyers would have purchased wristwatches costing $1,000."[27]

The reality of "luxury fever" leads to two large results that echo those discovered by Schor in her investigation of the "overspent American." Both personal/family life and communities suffer. The former happens because, whereas the uppermost incomes have been growing, the incomes of middle and lower-income families have not. "The median earner in the United States has essentially the same income now, in real terms, as in 1979, and earnings of those in the bottom 20 percent of the income distribution have actually declined by more than 10 percent during the same time span."[28] The consequence is that such increased spending has to be financed by reduced savings and increased indebtedness. For individuals and families the consequence has been burgeoning consumer debt and a bankruptcy boom.[29] Moreover, at the personal and family level, there are other costs as well, especially decreasing time away from work, which has led to diminished quality for both personal and work life.[30]

Beyond the personal sphere, the public sphere has paid a price as well: "Apart from high rates of increase in public spending on medical care and income transfers for the elderly, the past two decades have been a time of across-the-board retrenchment in public goods and services of all sorts."[31] Frank goes on to detail the ways in which money freed up by a slackened rate of increase in expenditures on luxury goods could be used for such social goods as clean drinking water, improved air quality, food inspection, improved pay for public school teachers, bridge and highway maintenance, and drug treatment and prevention programs.[32]

All of this describes our side of the text and conditions how we are most likely to hear Mark's story of Jesus' anointing with costly ointment. Our first instinct is unlikely to be one that expresses anger at the use of such a luxury commodity. Perhaps we might have preferred a slightly less costly ointment ourselves, but we are likely to have been influenced sufficiently by the purveyors of the most costly ointment to ensure that the ointment we would use is more costly than it would have been otherwise. More importantly, we would probably not understand the onlookers who questioned, "Why was the ointment wasted in this way?" (14:4). The understanding of the material conditions of human well-being sponsored by the luxury fever of our economic culture does not worry about waste, else it would have already taken stock of the personal and social costs it leaves in its wake.

Yet the truly curious point to ponder is that Jesus did not worry about waste in the case of the costly ointment either. It is certainly not the case that he failed to understand the material conditions of the poor, much less failed to recognize their fundamental economic need. Indeed, he recognized both the continuing and inescapable presence of the poor in the human community, along with the fundamental obligation of kindness toward them (14:7). But there is a sharp difference between our disregard of waste and his. We disregard waste because it interferes with our cultural value of locating ourselves socially by means of upscale spending. Jesus disregarded waste because in this particular case it manifested an act of devotion to the peculiar reign of God as it was about to transpire in his own death. Just as we ought not make more of his bracketing of the needs of the poor in this story than the text warrants, so we ought not make more of his bracketing of restraint on waste in this particular case than the text supports. Unlike our economic culture, Jesus is not unmindful of the personal and communal damage that can be done by "luxury fever."

What enables Jesus to transcend the common-sense economic needs of the poor as he receives the act of devotion from the woman with costly ointment is his sure knowledge that the materially destitute will have no hope apart from God's power to reign even in the midst of death. The "wasteful" act of anointing is testimony precisely to this power of God and is thus the hope for the world—especially for the poor. The surprise for us in this story of Mark is that the curious comfort we might take from it at first glance is taken away upon deeper reflection. For the story calls us not to wanton acts of wastefulness that are so much a part of our luxury-fever culture. Instead, it calls us to abandoned embrace of God's redemptive power that is most intensely at work where death pretends to reign. Here is the ultimate condition for the well-being of the human community.

At one level this surprising story that Mark narrates is a disappointment to figures standing in and in front of the text. Within the text, it disappoints onlookers and the poor alike in bracketing for the moment the obvious material requirements of human well-being. On our side of the text, it disappoints those of us who mistakenly believe we have an ally for the wastefulness of luxury fever in Jesus. But at the deepest level, this story of the anointing holds promise for all of us. It holds the promise that all forms of wastefulness and disintegration—which reach their nadir in the event of Jesus' death—are answered by this one anointed for burial, who yet promises to make himself known in Galilee.

FEARFUL DISCIPLES ON THIS SIDE OF THE TEXT

So these texts that share a common concern with the material conditions of human well-being—the feeding of the multitudes, the man with many possessions, and the woman anointing Jesus with costly ointment—manifest recalcitrant disciples and near disciples hesitating, objecting, and disbelieving. As the gospel is narrated in these stories relative to various material conditions of human well-being, it encounters on our North American side of the text disciples and near disciples similarly hesitating, objecting, and disbelieving. Our hesitancy, objection, and disbelief are framed in terms of the consuming passion for new products and new experiences, of the vertically extended reference groups of overspent Americans, and of the luxury fever that engulfs our economic culture.

As a result, we recapitulate in our encounter with these stories the interwoven themes of disappointment and promise that Donald Juel has tellingly described in his analysis of Mark's unsettling ending to the Gospel. We constantly stand ready to enact the theme of disappointment in our reading of the stories by letting our culture's understanding of the material conditions of human well-being rule out of court the view of reality the stories propose. But by standing before the stories with all the accoutrements of our economic self-understanding, we stand in a place where the gospel's promise of God's present reign can open us to truly abundant life.

Notes

1. Donald H. Juel, *A Master of Surprise: Mark Interpreted* (Minneapolis: Fortress Press, 1994), 113–16 (and see above, pp. 6–8).
2. Donald H. Juel, *The Gospel of Mark* (Nashville: Abingdon Press, 1999), 29–30.
3. Ibid., 41.
4. Rodney Clapp, "The Theology of Consumption and the Consumption of Theology," in *The Consuming Passion: Christianity and the Consumer Culture,* ed. Rodney Clapp (Downers Grove, IL: InterVarsity Press, 1998), 183.
5. Ibid., 185.
6. Juliet B. Schor, *The Overspent American: Upscaling, Downshifting, and the New Consumer,* (New York: Basic Books, 1998) 6.
7. Clapp, "Theology of Consumption," 186.
8. Ibid., 188.

9. Ibid., 191.
10. Ibid.
11. C. S. Mann, *Mark: A New Translation with Introduction and Commentary*, Anchor Bible (Garden City, NY: Doubleday, 1986), 402.
12. Schor, *Overspent American*, 4.
13. Ibid.
14. Ibid.
15. Ibid.
16. Ibid.
17. Ibid., 5.
18. Ibid.
19. Ibid., 13.
20. Ibid., 14.
21. Ibid., 18.
22. Ibid., 19–20.
23. Ibid., 21.
24. Ibid.
25. Robert H. Frank, *Luxury Fever: Why Money Fails to Satisfy in an Era of Excess* (New York: Free Press, 1999), 3.
26. Ibid., 11.
27. Ibid., 17.
28. Ibid., 45.
29. Ibid., 45–48.
30. Ibid., 48–52.
31. Ibid., 53.
32. Ibid., 54–63.

Chapter 5

When the Ending Is Not the End

Marianne Meye Thompson

Virtually all introductions to or discussions of the Gospel of John make note of its dualism, also referred to as its "binary oppositions" or "bipolarity."[1] In John's symbolic universe, everything seems to be depicted in pairs of stark opposites: light and darkness, Spirit and flesh, truth and error, belief and unbelief, knowledge and ignorance, salvation and judgment, life and death, freedom and slavery, love and hate. People belong to one realm or the other and are characterized by one reality or the other. Hence, those who believe have been born of the Spirit, walk in the light, know the truth, and have salvation and eternal life. But those who do not believe are of the flesh, walk in the darkness, are ignorant of the truth, are already condemned, and destined for death. The Gospel, painting in broad strokes of black and white, seems to have no room for anything in shades of gray.

In John's "realized eschatology," the dualistic categories of the Gospel describe both the current status and the ultimate destiny of human beings. Those who believe in Jesus *have* "eternal life" since they have "passed from death to life" (3:16; 5:24). But those who do not believe "come under judgment," and are indeed "condemned already" (3:18; 5:24). The realities typically promised for the end time, such as salvation and eternal life, are actually available in the present time and enjoyed by those who believe. Because of the emphasis on believing, John's dualism has been called a "dualism of decision."[2] That is to say, John's dualism is neither ontological nor eternal. Rather, one becomes part of one realm or the other through one's decision about Jesus. Such a worldview could readily lend itself to triumphalism, for dualism can easily become a tool to divide everyone into two camps and to assume that one can know, in the present, who is "in" and who is "out" for all eternity, and that such a determination rests upon the individual's attainment of faith.

In this essay, I would like to suggest that John's dualism cannot be used as a template to assess the current or future status of individuals, because their ultimate destiny is actually not known until "the last day." Put differently, the promise of salvation, given in the present time to those who believe, is just that: a *promise,* which will be fulfilled on the last day when God shall raise them up to eternal life. In order to argue this point, I will look at explicit theological statements in the Gospels that seem both to manifest and support John's virtually absolute dualism, consigning all people either to life or death. I will also suggest how certain narratives of John fit his dualistic worldview. But once we have surveyed that evidence, I will raise some questions which suggest that ultimately John's eschatology, while it does unquestionably emphasize the present realities of salvation and life, nevertheless clearly maintains the expectation of future resurrection. Since resurrection is God's act, the destiny of individuals is determined not by their belief in Jesus but by God's act of giving them life, both in the present and in the future.

DUALISM IN NARRATIVE AND THEOLOGY

The most explicit statement of purpose found in the Gospel of John occurs at 20:30–31: "Now Jesus did many other signs in the presence of his disciples, which are not written in this book. But these are written so that you may come to believe that Jesus is the Messiah, the Son of God, and that through believing you may have life in his name." This statement neatly pulls together key ideas in the Gospel. It reminds the reader that Jesus had done "signs," a term for the miracles of Jesus that is unique to John, and that his disciples were witnesses of them (2:11). It highlights the designations "Messiah" and "Son of God," which arguably are central to John's Christology. Moreover, it underscores the point that the purpose of the ministry of Jesus was to bring people to life through faith. Hence, this statement points to the desired response to Jesus—both during his own ministry and also among the readers of the Gospel. Bringing together the emphases on signs, faith, and life, given through the Messiah, the Son of God, this statement expresses simply and forthrightly the purpose for which the Gospel was written. It brings a sense of closure to the Gospel, in part because it summarizes what has regularly been portrayed in it: People have come to faith in Jesus as the Messiah and Son of God.

Furthermore, this statement of purpose also recalls the prologue of the Gospel, where the ministry of Jesus and the narrative of the Gospel are summarized as follows:

> He was in the world, and the world came into being through him; yet the world did not know him. He came to what was his own, and his own people did not accept him. But to all who received him, who believed in his name, he gave power to become children of God, who were born, not of blood or of the will of the flesh or of the will of man, but of God. (1:10–13)

Here is the Gospel of John in a nutshell: The very one through whom the world was created was not recognized by the world. Even "his own" did not accept him. But there were those who did welcome him, who believed in him, and they were given the power to become God's children. Again, the possibilities are portrayed in dualistic terms. The prologue uses one set of terms to express what the purpose statement of 20:30–31 phrases another way: The purpose of Jesus' ministry was to bring people to faith so that they might have life from God. In keeping with the emphases of these passages, Alan Culpepper has summarized the "plot" of the Gospel in this fashion:

> Plot development in John, then, is a matter of how Jesus' identity comes to be recognized and how it fails to be recognized. Not only is Jesus' identity progressively revealed by the repetitive signs and discourses and the progressive enhancement of metaphorical and symbolic images, but each episode has essentially the same plot as the story as a whole. Will Nicodemus, the Samaritan woman, or the lame man recognize Jesus and thereby receive eternal life? The story is repeated over and over. No one can miss it. Individual episodes can almost convey the message of the whole; at least they suggest or recall it for those who know the story.[3]

In other words, the statement of purpose of the Gospel of John lays out what is at stake in the Gospel as a whole and in each individual episode: Jesus did signs in the presence of his disciples; the disciples professed faith; they are given life. Or, they accepted him; believed in his name; and became children of God. No matter how it is phrased, the dualism of John comes to expression in or is implied throughout the Gospel.

Let us turn then to examine a few representative narratives of the Gospel and the ways in which they embody the apparently unambiguous dualism of the Gospel of John. The account of the first sign at Cana, the changing of water to wine, ends with the summary statement, "Jesus did this, the first of his signs, in Cana of Galilee, and revealed his glory; and his disciples believed in him" (2:11). Given the fact that we have noted John's penchant for a description of reality in clear-cut and opposing terms, it is not particularly surprising that the conclusion simplifies a somewhat enigmatic story. We read: Jesus manifested his glory; his disciples believed. But the story that leads up to this point is enigmatic on a number of counts: It is not clear what Mary expects Jesus to do when she informs him that the wine has run out; Jesus' reply to her appears rude; and his explanation that "[his] hour has not yet come" scarcely provides an adequate reason why she should not be bothering him. Yet it is clear that Jesus' promise, that those who follow Jesus will see "heaven opened," the revelation of God in and through him (1:51), has begun to be fulfilled. "[H]e revealed his glory; and his disciples believed in him."[4] These disciples have begun to recognize who Jesus is and have believed in him; the implication to be drawn from John 20:30–31 and other passages is that they will receive eternal life.

As has often been noted, the narrative structure of the second miracle at Cana manifests a pattern similar to the first: Someone makes a request of Jesus; he offers a rejoinder that apparently distances him from the petitioner; the petitioner then renews the request in some fashion; and Jesus essentially fulfills the desired request. In John 4, a royal official from Capernaum asks Jesus to come heal his son, and although Jesus seems initially to rebuff the man, he does carry out the healing, albeit from a distance. The narrative picks up at this point and runs as follows:

> Jesus said to him, "Go; your son will live." The man believed the word that Jesus spoke to him and started on his way. As he was going down, his slaves met him and told him that his child was alive. So he asked them the hour when he began to recover, and they said to him, "Yesterday at one in the afternoon the fever left him." The father realized that this was the hour when Jesus had said to him, "Your son will live." So he himself believed, along with his whole household.

This account links faith to the word of Jesus. Jesus says, "Your son will live." The man's slaves confirm to him that his child is indeed alive. Later, the father realizes that his son's healing occurred because Jesus had said "Your son will live." Because of the authority and power of Jesus' word, the man believes: "So he himself believed, along with his whole household." Again, as in John 2, Jesus' action—here, healing through his word—is the occasion for faith in him. In this narrative we hear echoes of the condensed gospel found in the prologue, as well as adumbrations of the summary statement of John 20:30–31. Jesus came to his own; while not all believed, those who did were given power to become God's children. The purpose of the Gospel is to allow its readers likewise to come to faith in Jesus and so to receive the life that his word promises and conveys.

In both these accounts, the narratives reflect neatly one of the key theological ideas of the Gospel—namely, that response to the revelation of God in Jesus signals the movement from ignorance to knowledge, from error to truth, from darkness to light, from death to life. As Culpepper notes, each episode summarizes the whole "plot" of the Gospel in miniature. It would be easy to add to these two episodes. John 9, for example, plays most explicitly on the themes of darkness and light, as it shows the "enlightening" of a man who had been blind, and the blinding of those who see. The story ends with the enlightened man confessing his faith, "Lord, I believe." Again, the episode ends with a note of the man's faith in his Lord; his response demonstrates the truth of the assertions in the prologue and anticipates the ending, which promises readers who make the same confession that they will have life in the name of Jesus.

As has already been noted, the purpose statement of John implies, although it does not state explicitly, John's dualism, inasmuch as it refers to those who believe and have life in Jesus' name (20:30–31). The opposites—unbelief and death—are assumed. In John 3:18 we read, "Those who believe in him are not condemned; but those who do not believe are condemned already, because they have not believed in the name of the only Son of God," a point echoed at the end of the same chapter in the statement, "Whoever believes in the Son has eternal life; whoever disobeys the Son will not see life, but must endure God's wrath" (3:36). In Jesus' discourse about his authority (chap. 5), the same point is asserted: "Very truly, I tell you, anyone who hears my word and believes him who sent me has eternal life, and does not come under judgment, but has passed from death to life" (5:24).

All these statements—and many more in John could be adduced—link together belief in Jesus with eternal life. Some verses state their opposites explicitly: Unbelief leads to death. Elsewhere it is simply assumed. Those who believe have life, and one either believes or does not. These are the only two options John presents. Responses—including wonder, marvel, praise, awe, fear, and doubt, which are typical responses to Jesus' deeds in the other Gospels—are missing from John. Even "doubting Thomas" is given only two options: Do not be unbelieving (*apistos*), but believing (*pistos;* 20:27). He is not told to move from doubt to faith but from unbelief to belief; then he will have eternal life.

In sum, from whatever angle one examines John—whether from individual narratives or the overt theological statements—the dualism of John comes to expression, either explicitly or implicitly. There are two realities, the realms of death and of life, and one moves from the one to the other through faith in Jesus. Not only are these two circles of reality nonintersecting, but people are clearly and unambiguously identified with one or the other. The badge of their identity is faith.

AMBIGUOUS NARRATIVES AND ENDINGS IN THE GOSPEL OF JOHN

We have noted a typical paradigm of the Johannine narratives, and I have suggested that this paradigm embodies the dualistic theology of John. But the situation is not nearly so simple. In fact, quite a number of the narratives of John break the neat, clear-cut pattern, and are far more complex and less tidy than the above analysis suggests. There are, first of all, narratives that do not end with a statement that someone believed in Jesus. To be sure, the prologue foreshadows a mixed response, asserting that while "his own" did not receive him, nevertheless, many did. John 6 gives us an instance of a narrative with a mixed ending or, perhaps better, a series of mixed endings. Although there are numerous responses to Jesus—the acclamation of him as prophet (6:14), the desire to make him king (6:15), various questions directed to him (6:28, 30), and finally the request that Jesus give to them the bread of which he has spoken (6:34)—there is no explicit statement that any of those making such responses and requests have put their faith in Jesus. In fact, the first explicit comment on any sort of response to Jesus shows that the response is negative: Jesus' hearers are skeptical of his claims, and he warns them against "murmuring" (6:43). And the situation gets worse before it gets better, leading to disputes (6:52), offense (6:61), and abandonment (6:66). Apparently only the Twelve remain with Jesus, and Simon Peter confesses to Jesus their faithfulness and their understanding of his identity: "Lord, to whom can we go? You have the words of eternal life. We have come to believe and know that you are the Holy One of God" (6:68–69). Knowing who Jesus is has led them to faith; they have put their trust in his life-giving words.

In some ways, the mixed response does not come as a shock in a Gospel that has already warned its readers that when the Word became flesh and "came to his own, his own received him not." The narrative of John 6 is but another example of the "Gospel in a nutshell," for both negative and positive response are portrayed here, in keeping with the assertions of the prologue. But the matter is more complex, for the narrator comments that it was because of Jesus' words that "many of his disciples turned back and no longer went about with him" (6:66). In other words, we do not read that many in Jesus' audience refused to believe, but that many of those who apparently had believed no longer walked with him. It is his *disciples* who abandon him. Earlier Jesus' words had brought the official and his whole household to faith; now his words lead his disciples to desert him. This is no light matter, as indicated by the fact that the narrator takes pains to note that Jesus was not caught unaware by this turn of events: " 'Among you there are some who do not believe.' For Jesus knew from the first who were the ones that did not believe, and who was the one that would betray him" (6:64). And then, only a few verses later, Jesus reveals that he knows his betrayer is in their midst. This time the author notes, "He was speaking of Judas son of Simon Iscariot, for he, though one of the twelve, was going to betray him" (6:71). Not only do some of his disciples abandon him, but one of the Twelve will betray him.

Such statements make us rethink the earlier narratives, with their straightforward presentations of Jesus' action and the human response of faith. These narratives present the way it was supposed to be: Jesus revealed his glory; his disciples believed. The narrative comes to its proper ending; the case is closed. But what if those who abandoned Jesus, as recounted in John 6, were among those who had been at the wedding feast in Cana? Was Judas among those who had earlier "beheld his glory" and "believed in him"? While these early narratives of the Gospel seem to fit well with John's dualistic worldview, it becomes clear before too much time has passed that the neat, happy ending may well be far less assured than suggested by the terse summaries and explicit statements about the faith of Jesus' disciples and others.

As we look more closely at several other narratives in John, it becomes clear that many of them are pervaded by similar tensions that are not resolved by the endings of the narratives. The narrative about Nicodemus in John 3 is a classic example of a narrative from the Fourth Gospel with an ambiguous ending. Indeed, the whole character of Nicodemus is subject to numerous interpretations.[5] Initially he comes to Jesus at "night," which has been taken as evidence of his affinity with darkness. He struggles to understand what Jesus labels "earthly matters," clearly indicating that he will be unable to comprehend the "heavenly matters" that Jesus will proclaim, again putting him on the wrong side of the dividing line between life and death. Later Nicodemus appears to defend Jesus (7:50–52), but ironically when Jesus is given the hearing that Nicodemus urges, he is eventually crucified. Nicomedus's final act, with Joseph of Arimathea, is to ensure Jesus' royal burial. This act could be taken as at last manifesting his full understanding that Jesus is the "King of the Jews." But perhaps it is ironic that Nicodemus's last act is to seek to put Jesus into a tomb. While at other times the narrator inserts an interpretative or guiding remark, nothing helps the reader to know how to appreciate the significance of Nicodemus's actions. Has he moved from unbelief to belief, from darkness to light, from death to life? Has he believed in Jesus? Has he received life in his name? Oddly enough, in a Gospel that paints the alternatives in the strongest opposing terms and cares a good deal about bringing people to faith, there is no clear answer to the question of Nicodemus's destiny.

Another example of ambiguous characterization in John is the man who is healed at the pool of Beth-zatha. He is typically contrasted with the blind man who is healed in John 9. Whereas the blind man squares off with the Pharisees as he defends Jesus, ultimately confessing him as Lord, the man at the pool reports to the Pharisees what Jesus had done. Both men acknowledge what Jesus had done, but for the one it becomes the point of departure for faith, and for the other it apparently becomes the point of departure for betrayal of Jesus. Curiously, though, the man at the pool has shown some preliminary response to Jesus. He takes up his mat and walks, thus violating the Sabbath—the very thing Jesus has come under criticism for in this chapter. He is thus portrayed as obedient to Jesus' word and as imitating his deeds. Just as Jesus receives his command from the Father and does only what the Father does, arguably this man has only done what Jesus has told him to do. That appears to be the right response to Jesus. But no final account of the man is given. Does he become, like Judas, one who betrays Jesus? Or does he follow the course of the blind man, eventually professing faith?

In sum, not only are there ambiguous endings to several of the stories, but the sense of assurance that at first appears captured by the assertion "they believed" crumbles upon discovery that it was exactly those who believed who later abandoned and betrayed him. In short, "they believed" guarantees nothing. The road from "they believed in him" should lead to "and had life in his name," as the theological assertions and purpose statement of John make so clear. But sometimes "they believed" leads to "many of his disciples turned back and no longer went about with him" (6:66), or to "Judas . . . was going to betray him" (6:71). Thus, even the positive endings to the narratives of the Gospel of John are not true "endings." Rather, these "endings" point beyond themselves; they anticipate some other ending, yet to come.

THE END

The assertion that the endings of the narratives in John seek an ending yet in the future might seem to ring false to John's "realized eschatology." Final decisions about judgment and salvation, life and death, have already been made. Indeed, so strong is John's emphasis on the present reality of salvation and life that not a few commentators, following the lead of Rudolf Bultmann, have argued that the traces of futuristic eschatology still discernible in the Gospel are essentially foreign to it.[6] Jesus does not speak of a judgment to come; he speaks of a judgment already past. So, for instance, he says, "Very truly, I tell you, anyone who hears my word and believes him who sent me has eternal life, and does not come under judgment, but has passed from death to life" (5:24). This would in fact fit very well with some of the narratives and their endings, particularly those that show someone coming to or expressing faith. Presumably the royal official is one of those who has heard the word of Jesus, believed in him, and so has received eternal life; he has passed from death to life. What need is there then of any further ending to his story? The need, as suggested earlier, is that the general truth of Jesus' statement does not tell us how it works out in the particular. If it is true that those who have faith have "passed from death to life," it is also true that some of those who had once been Jesus' disciples abandoned, deserted, and betrayed him. It is apparently not the initial moment of faith that determines whether one has "passed from death to life"; it is the ending of the story that counts.

But often the argument that John contains a realized eschatology includes the assertion that John has reinterpreted the future resurrection as a present experience of faith, either eliminating or muting the future hope and promise of resurrection. For a number of reasons, I deem this reading of John to be mistaken.[7] John contains the affirmation that the Father gives life through the Son to those who believe in him, but it also contains the promise that they will be raised up "at the last day." The language of being "raised up" remains consistently linked with "the last day." One can see the difference, for example, in John 5, where two statements are made about the life-giving work of the Son.

> "Very truly, I tell you, the hour is coming, and is now here, when the dead will hear the voice of the Son of God, and those who hear will live." (5:25)

> "Do not be astonished at this; for the hour is coming when all who are in their graves will hear his voice and will come out—those who have done good, to the resurrection of life, and those who have done evil, to the resurrection of condemnation." (5:28)

According to these passages, the *dead* hear the voice of the Son of God and *live,* but those who are *in the graves* come out to *resurrection.* The statement in 5:25 describes a present reality—the hour is "now here"—while the statement in 5:28 portrays a resurrection yet in the future. John nowhere says that the resurrection has already happened or is experienced in the present. Jesus' words to Martha, "I am the resurrection and the life," maintains the same distinction between "life" and "resurrection." In 11:25–26, Jesus explains the meaning of "resurrection" when he says, "Those who believe in me, even though they die, will live." The one who experiences physical death will live again. In the Farewell Discourses, when Jesus anticipates his own resurrection, he promises his disciples, "Because I live, you also will live" (14:19). Although Jesus returns, through his resurrection, to the life he has always had with God, it is through resurrection that such a return occurs. Death cannot rob him of life; he returns to the life he had with God. Because he has been raised to life, he now lives with God. And this clarifies the meaning of the second part of Jesus' revelatory statement, "I am the life." In light of the Gospel's description of eternal life as fellowship with God, as a participation in the life of the Father through the Son, the verse seems to mean that not even physical death can sever that fellowship. Those who are presently alive in God, those who "know God" (17:3), will not experience death as a threat to that fellowship and participation in eternal life. Death did not destroy Jesus' relationship to God; it will not destroy the relationship of the believer to God. Nevertheless, death is a reality, and the life-giving God overcomes it—through resurrection. The hope of believers is that God will do for them what God has done for Jesus Christ. But this means that the ending which the narrative endings anticipate is the day of resurrection.

This observation brings us to a second point. Not only does the final ending anticipated in the Gospel of John lie in the future, but it lies in God's hands alone. If human faith guarantees nothing, it is because it is God who guarantees everything. This is repeatedly emphasized in the Gospel. For example, in the narrative of Jesus' encounter with Nicodemus, Jesus states, "Very truly, I tell you, no one can see the kingdom of God without being born from above" (3:3), a statement that is then paraphrased in verse 5 by glossing "born from above" with "born of water and Spirit." The birth of which Jesus speaks is not achieved through human agency—"not of blood or of the will of the flesh or of the will of man" (1:13), but "from above," "of the Spirit," that is, "of God" (1:13). At minimum this must mean that it is God's action, not human agency, that brings about this birth. What the reader waits to discover in the narrative is not so much whether Nicodemus comes to faith and so receives life, but whether God's Spirit has "blown where it wills" and given new life to Nicodemus. This is a more frightening proposition, because it wrests control from the human agent in order to emphasize the initiative of the divine agent. What gives life is not faith but the Spirit of God. As we read elsewhere in John, "It is the spirit that gives life; the flesh is useless" (John 6:63). Insofar as flesh represents human agency and effort, it "profits nothing."

Or, take the narrative of those who abandon Jesus in John 6. As noted earlier, those who do so are called Jesus' disciples; they could have been among those who had earlier seen the glory of Jesus and believed in him. But now, taking offense at his hard words, they desert him. In this same chapter, however, Jesus explains faith not primarily with reference to the believer but with reference to God. Thus he says, "No one can come to me unless drawn by the Father who sent me; and I will raise that person up on the last day. It is written in the prophets, 'And they shall all be taught by God.' Everyone who has heard and learned from the Father comes to me" (6:44–45). While there are many interpretations of the meaning of such phrases as "drawn by the Father" and "taught by God," it is difficult to find a way to read these statements without making it clear that for people to have faith in Jesus, *God* must do something: *God* must draw, and *God* must teach. The wind must blow, and the wind blows where it wills.

How then does one explain those who abandon Jesus? The Gospel offers no ultimate theological solution to this problem, but it does offer a promise. Jesus, the Good Shepherd, speaks of his knowledge of and care for the sheep: "My sheep hear my voice. I know them, and they follow me. I give them eternal life, and they will never perish. No one will snatch them out of my hand. What my Father has given me is greater than all else, and no one can snatch it out of the Father's hand" (10:27–29). Throughout John 10 and the various discourses about the sheep, they do little but hear and follow; they make no decisions and choose no paths. Their choosing, their deciding, their faith, plays no role in what happens to them. They simply follow the one who leads them. And they are given a promise: "No one will snatch them out of my hand." But of course the other narratives of John have alerted us that some of those who appeared to have been Jesus' sheep went astray and wandered from him. Such scenes might make one a bit uneasy about the promises of the Good Shepherd. Yet the Good Shepherd has promised to hold the sheep; the one who was raised from the dead has promised that his own will also be raised to life. In the end, everything depends upon the One who makes such promises, and whether that One can be trusted with the lives of the sheep.

Notes

1. Mark Stibbe, *John's Gospel,* New Testament Readings (London: Routledge, 1994), 124; D. Moody Smith, *John,* Abingdon New Testament Commentaries (Nashville: Abingdon Press, 1999), 43. But John Ashton argues that the "vertical opposition" of the Gospel is not properly dualistic, since the contrast between heaven and earth simply reflects beliefs about the relative location of heaven and earth. The horizontal opposition, moral or ethical in its character and played out on earth, is genuinely dualistic (*Understanding the Fourth Gospel* [Oxford: Clarendon Press, 1991], 207).
2. This phrase comes from Rudolf Bultmann; see, for example, *Theology of the New Testament* (New York: Charles Scribner's Sons, 1951, 1955), 2:21. For recent discussion, see Ashton, *Understanding the Fourth Gospel,* 207.
3. R. Alan Culpepper, *Anatomy of the Fourth Gospel: A Study in Literary Design* (Philadelphia: Fortress Press, 1983), 88–89.

4. On the ongoing disagreement over the role of signs and sight in John, see the discussion in Marianne Meye Thompson, *The God of the Gospel of John* (Grand Rapids: Wm. B. Eerdmans Publishing Co., 2001), 106–26.

5. See Jouette Bassler, "Mixed Signals: Nicodemus in the Fourth Gospel," *Journal of Biblical Literature* 28 (1989): 635–46.

6 Bultmann in fact attributes them to the so-called ecclesiastical redactor who attempted to tame the Gospel's "dangerous statements" and bring its eschatology in line with traditional eschatology; see, e.g., *The Gospel of John* (Philadelphia: Westminster Press, 1971), 261.

7. I have argued this view at some length in Thompson, *God of the Gospel of John*, 80–87.

Chapter 6

The God Who Will Not Be Taken for Granted: Reflections on Paul's Letter to the Romans

Beverly Roberts Gaventa

Among the striking observations in Donald Juel's treatment of Mark 16 is that "Jesus is out, on the loose, on the same side of the door as the women and the readers."[1] This unsettling way of putting things builds on Juel's earlier observation that the tearing of the heavens at Jesus' baptism declares that the protective barrier between humanity and God is gone and that God, "unwilling to be confined to sacred spaces, is on the loose in our own realm."[2] The inescapability of God not only unsettles Mark's narrative; in Juel's view, it unsettles interpreters, scholarly and otherwise, who desire to wrest control over the text from "the divine actor who will not be shut in—or out."[3]

That God is "on the loose" serves not only as a challenging reading of Mark's Gospel but as a provocative way of epitomizing Paul's Letter to the Romans. Admittedly, this leap from Mark to Romans is disconcerting—and for good reason. Any movement from interpreting a narrative to interpreting a letter brings with it certain challenges. And the movement from Mark's particular Gospel, with its narrative gaps and awkward syntax, to the careful argumentation of Romans only heightens the difficulties.[4] Yet in its own distinctive way, Romans no less than Mark reflects the understanding that God is "on the loose," that God cannot be contained either in the argumentation of Paul or by the craftiness of Paul's interpreters.

GOD AS TAKEN FOR GRANTED

Paul's letter to believers at Rome, a city he had not yet visited and a group of believers most of whom he had not met (although see the greetings in chap. 16), has generated a nearly endless procession of questions and proposals. Research in recent years has addressed a number of important questions about the purpose and occasion of Romans, its rhetorical genre, and its audience.[5] Yet it remains the case, as Juel's own esteemed teacher Nils Dahl observed about New Testament theology in general, that students of this letter pay too little attention to God.[6]

One recent major study of Pauline theology that does begin with God is J. D. G. Dunn's *The Theology of Paul the Apostle*, a work that identifies Romans as offering interpreters their best access to Paul's theology.[7] Dunn opens his exploration of Pauline theology with a chapter on God, yet early on he depicts God as belonging among Paul's "taken-for-granteds," by which he means that " 'speech about God' was part of the shared speech of the first Christian congregations." Because these common beliefs were also thoroughly Jewish, "Paul did not have to explain or defend his belief in God," since it was a "fundamental" part of his own tradition. Dunn goes on to say that Paul's "conversion had not changed his belief in and about God," so that "his most fundamental taken-for-granted remained intact."[8] Elsewhere Dunn insists that those things that are taken for granted are not things to which Paul is indifferent.[9] Nevertheless, the expression "taken-for-granted" appears to imply that God belongs among the presuppositions of Paul's thought, that the precise issue of God's identity has no real impact on Paul's theology. Indeed, Dunn speaks of several "levels" in Paul's theology, so that Paul's inherited view of God and Israel occupy one level, while the events of Jesus' death and resurrection occupy another level.[10] The chapter on Jesus Christ stands at considerable remove from the initial discussion of God, and here it becomes clear that what changes in Paul's theology following his conversion changes because of his encounter with and understanding of Jesus Christ, while his understanding of God remains stable. It is Christ who endows Paul's work as "theologian, missionary, and pastor" with its coherence. When Dunn sums up Paul's theology, he identifies its "focal and pivotal point" as Christ. Christ is a mediator figure for Dunn, not simply in the sense of being God's agent but in the sense that Christ becomes the occasion by which human beings experience God.[11]

The distance Dunn appears to place between God and Christ raises numerous questions. Francis Watson has unpacked the sheer impossibility of speaking of God in Paul's thought apart from reference to Christ and the Spirit and vice versa.[12] Even the opening words of Romans reflect the difficulty involved. To affirm that Paul is *both* "a slave of Jesus Christ" *and* "set apart for the gospel of

God" (author's translation) surely means that those two designations belong to one another, which makes it difficult to distinguish the "taken-for-granted" understanding of God from the new event of Jesus Christ. How can God and Christ occupy two levels when God's gospel and Jesus Christ stand here connected to one another?

What concerns me at present is the unfortunate expression "taken-for-granted," with its apparent implication that the gospel involves no real challenge to Paul's previous understanding of God. Dunn correctly claims Paul always knew that God was one, creator, sovereign, judge, and faithful to Israel.[13] Yet surely these descriptors are strained when Paul speaks of the Gentiles of Thessalonica as God's beloved (1 Thess. 1:4), or when he concludes that "neither circumcision nor uncircumcision is anything" (Gal. 6:15), or when he identifies God as the one "who raised Jesus our Lord from the dead" (Rom. 4:24). How can a "taken-for-granted" God possibly justify the *ungodly* (Rom. 4:5)? Dunn's "taken-for-granted" God provides us with scant means of understanding the repeated "now" of Paul's Letter to the Romans (e.g., 3:21; 5:9, 11; 6:22; 8:1; 13:11). The impossibility of restricting the identity of God to predefined categories emerges into plain sight in Romans. Indeed, it is not too much to say that the God of Romans is very much "on the loose." The God of the promises of Scripture (1:2) is faithful, but faithfulness does not imply predictability. God is also free, not to be confined to human expectations about God's judgments and responses.

Perhaps the first hint of God's freedom comes already in the salutation of the letter. Here Paul describes the gospel as "promised beforehand through his prophets in the holy scripture" (1:2 NRSV), language that reflects God's commitment to Israel, the people from whom the prophets come and for whom God sends them. In other words, this line invokes the ancestral expectations of God's faithfulness. Yet when Paul describes his apostleship, he anticipates "the obedience of faith among all the Gentiles" (1:5 NRSV). Already the scope of God's actions extends in new directions—God is faithful to the promise but not restricted in fulfilling it.[14]

Indeed, the letter contains a string of arguments that might be summarized as "God will not be restricted. God is on the loose." The first major section of the letter insists that God is not restricted even by the implacable forces of Sin and Death (1:18–8:39). If that is the case, then clearly God's freedom will not be restricted by some narrow, fixed definition of election (chaps. 9–11). And, finally, God cannot be limited to a sliver of human life that is designated "ethics" (12:1–15:13).

GOD'S FREEDOM IN RESPONSE TO SIN AND DEATH

As E. P. Sanders famously observed, in Paul's thinking, the solution precedes the problem, but in the structure of Paul's argument in Romans, the problem precedes the solution.[15] Although the apocalypse Paul refers to in Galatians 1 and Philippians 3 invaded his life and destroyed that life and its understandings (Paul's preexisting "solutions"), in Romans an initial declaration of the gospel in 1:17 yields to an extensive statement of the problem of the human condition as the gospel reveals that problem. And Paul expounds the situation in unrelenting terms. From 1:18 through 3:20, he depicts the extent of Sin among both those under the law and those outside it. As one, humanity falls short of God's glory (3:20), whether by the refusal to acknowledge God or by an acknowledgment twisted into self-congratulation. With the declaration of God's intervention of grace in 3:21–31, readers may imagine that this exploration of the human condition has come to an end, but in chapter 5 it returns, as the recollection of Adam serves to show how the powers of Sin and Death captured all of humanity. Again, the end of chapter 5 declares the "free gift of grace" (5:15), and chapter 6 finds humanity transferred to the dominion of righteousness, but once more 7:7–25 introduces the problem of Sin's grasp of the law, so that even the impulse of humanity to do good is maimed by Sin.

Leander Keck has perceptively observed that these three passages move in the manner of a spiral, with Paul "each time going deeper into the human condition, and each time finding the gospel the appropriate antidote."[16] This spiral, then, involves not only Sin, in that Sin captures humanity in its grasp, but also God's own intervention. Here it is that Paul's understanding that God is "on the loose" comes into play, for God's intervention also "spirals," in the sense that God's action encompasses more as the spiral continues.

The first stage in the spiral comes to its climax in 3:19–20, followed by a statement of the good news in 3:21–26, a text that is often regarded as a restatement of 1:16–17. Exegetical problems abound here, but the general logic of the passage is sufficiently clear: All human beings fall short of God's glory, and all are rectified freely through the grace of redemption in Christ Jesus, grace that results from God's own action in putting Christ forward. The act Paul describes is unilateral in the sense that it is God alone who accomplishes this event.

Yet there is also a qualification having to do with faith, since verse 22 stipulates that "the righteousness of God" is "through the faithfulness of Jesus Christ for all who believe" (NRSV).[17] I am inclined to think that the phrase "all who believe" does not limit the range of God's righteousness; instead, "all who believe" acknowledges that only those to whom faith has come have received the gift of seeing God's action for what it is. The phrase works in a fashion similar to 1 Corinthians 1:18, which frankly acknowledges two irreconcilable views of the cross; to some it appears foolish, and to others it is God's power.[18] Yet most recent commentators understand this statement as somehow limiting the scope for God's action, so that God's saving righteousness applies only to believers.[19] For example, Brendan Byrne describes faith as the "vehicle" of the operation of redemption, since through faith "God is able to draw sinful human beings into the scope of the divine righteousness."[20] Regarding Paul's comments on faith in Romans 3–4, Dunn goes so far as to say that God "would not justify, could not [*sic!*] sustain in relationship, those who did not rely wholly on him."[21] Granting that conventional (and certainly majority) view for the present, we would conclude that the first cycle reflects the conviction that the gospel reveals that now God deals with Sin differently. The implacability of human rejection meets with God's own offering up of his Son, an offering that has its effect on all those who believe.

This is not, however, Paul's final statement in Romans about the scope of God's redemptive action. In the second stage of the spiral, Paul introduces not only the extent of human rebellion against God but also humanity's capture by the powers of Sin and Death. Sin "entered" the world through the transgression of Adam, bringing with it Death and its unavoidable, unyielding grasp. But Paul finds that the universal consequence of Adam's action has an equally universal consequence in Christ's gracious death: "Therefore, just as one man's trespass led to condemnation for all, so one man's act of righteousness leads to justification and life for all" (5:18).

Numerous attempts to limit this statement fail, since the comparison Paul makes will only work if the scope of God's gospel includes "all."[22] To contrast Adam's death-giving act, an act that invades the entire human sphere, with Christ's life-giving act, and then insist that Christ's action pertains only to some, or only to those who respond, would make no sense at all. As Charles B. Cousar puts it directly: "Nothing is said about Christ's having made life 'potentially' available to all and that faith is necessary to turn the potentiality into reality. (Certainly death is not pictured as a potential destiny.)"[23] Even if the first stage of the spiral imagines that God's redemptive action concerns only those who believe, the second does not.[24]

In its third stage, the spiral cannot become more inclusive, but it does become more invasive. As Paul W. Meyer has demonstrated in his landmark study of Romans 7, students of Paul have too long been distracted by questing for the identity of the "I" of the passage, and in the process of looking for the speaker, interpreters have failed to see that Paul's attention here returns to the power of Sin.[25] The power of Sin is such that it has even the law in its grasp. The law is not to be equated with Sin (7:7); on the contrary, the law itself is "holy and just and good" (7:12). Nevertheless, Sin seized an opportunity presented by the commandment (7:8); Sin "revived," Sin worked through the law to deceive and kill (v. 11). Sin's power is such that it can make use *even* of God's good and holy instrument, the law, and can corrupt even the laudable desire to do what is right.

Again in this final stage of the spiral, Paul writes about the response of God. In this instance, however, the response is not the putting forward of Christ as God's righteousness for those who believe. Neither is it the death of Jesus that defeats Death for all. Now the response of God is to condemn Sin itself (8:3) and to liberate not only humanity (7:25) but all of the cosmos. The final section of Romans 8 brings the spiral of God's action to its completion: God "did not withhold his own Son" recalls the language of 3:21–31 as well as 5:6–21, with its claim that Jesus' death reveals that God's grace suffices even for human rebellion.

The God who defeated Sin in Jesus' death will finally defeat all those other powers arrayed against the power of God (see also 1 Cor. 15:24–28).

The downward spiral of the human condition is more than matched by what we might regard as an "upward" spiral of God's intervention. God cannot be restricted by Sin and Death, for God will finally defeat both those enemies and all others. God is "on the loose."

GOD'S FREEDOM AND THE ELECTION OF ISRAEL

Despite intense scholarly disagreements about the contours, even the coherence, of Romans 9–11, there is widespread agreement that this portion of the letter fundamentally concerns the faithfulness of God.[26] Important features of Romans 1–8 make the question of God's faithfulness an urgent one. If there is "no distinction" between Jew and Greek, as Romans 1–3 forcefully contends, then what has become of Israel's election? If Israel's election is to be understood as null and void, what does that imply about God? As Wayne Meeks notes, if God has abandoned the calling to Israel, then Gentiles have no reason to trust that God will not also abandon them.[27]

In response to this potentially disastrous conclusion, Paul crafts an argument about God's faithfulness. He insists that the "word of God" has not failed (9:6), that God has by no means rejected Israel (11:1). With Isaiah, he recalls that God has continually held out God's hands to Israel (10:21).[28] God is not fickle, but that does not mean that God is predictable.[29] This section of the letter does not permit the reduction of faithfulness to predictability; it is by no means clear that Paul's understanding of God's faithfulness would sit well with Matthew, for whom the events in Jesus' life fulfill quite specific passages of Scripture (e.g., 1:22–23; 2:17–18). In fact, Paul's argument on behalf of God's faithfulness actually rests upon some astonishing claims about God's freedom.

The most obvious assertion of God's freedom comes in 9:6–30, with its recital of Israel's history as the history of God's calling. The opening description of Israelites as people to whom belong "the adoption, the glory, the giving of the law, the worship, and the promises" (9:4) might suggest that these are Israel's *possessions,* but what follows permits no such conclusion. God *chose* to show mercy on Isaac, God *chose* to harden Pharaoh's heart. Pivotal to Paul's argument are the words of verses 11–12, which the NRSV regrettably confines to a parenthesis: "so that God's purpose of election might continue, not by works but by his call." The phrase "purpose of election" joins two nouns that do not otherwise appear together in the New Testament. Either of them might have served to make the point of God's initiative, but together they constitute a kind of exclamation mark that underscores God's role. The additional expression "not by works but by his call" highlights the entire statement; only God's choosing accounts for Israel's status with God.

If God chooses some and not others, that reflects only God's freedom and offers no basis for complaint (9:19–23). Indeed, God elects also "from the Gentiles" (11:24), a point Paul paradoxically reinforces by quoting Hosea's lines about the restoration of Israel. That God's freedom is at work here becomes even clearer when this passage is placed alongside other Jewish texts, as Neil Richardson has demonstrated. For example, the author of *Jubilees* introduces a note about the relative merits of Jacob and Esau prior to the pronouncement of blessing on Jacob by Abraham (*Jub.* 19:13–14; 22:10–24), and Philo emphasizes that God knows in advance what their behavior will only later reveal (*Legum allegoriae* 3.88–89). Although these and other authors comment on God's election, Paul is distinctive in his silence about any hint of merit.[30]

Another example of the freedom that characterizes God's faithfulness comes in Romans 9:32b–33, as Paul draws from Isaiah's language about the "stumbling stone." The complex questions about the text of Isaiah and its transmission and interpretation—not to mention the disputed identity of the stumbling stone in Romans itself—makes appeal to this passage intensely risky.[31] The point I am making, however, does not depend on resolving those questions. Having noted the paradox of Gentiles winning a race they were not running while the running Israel fails at the same race, Paul asserts that "they [i.e., Israel] have stumbled over the stumbling stone" (9:32b). He then introduces a modified form of the LXX of Isaiah 28:16, which depicts God laying a stone that will be fixed, secure, foundational. In the center of the quotation, however, he inserts a portion of Isaiah 8:14, and in so doing he replaces the foundation stone with a stone of stumbling. In other words, as Paul Meyer puts it, here Paul attributes to God an action of "placing in the midst of his people a base of security that is at the same time an obstacle over which they stumble."[32] By making what was to be a sound foundation into something that trips Israel up but can nevertheless be trusted (see the end of v. 33), God here becomes a trickster on behalf of Israel's redemption.

God's freedom again comes to expression in the argument about God's dealings with Israel and the Gentiles in chapter 11. As Paul understands events of the present and future, Israel's unbelief has led to salvation for the Gentiles, which will in turn prompt Israel's jealousy (11:11–12). A number of scholars connect Romans 11 with the "eschatological pilgrimage" tradition, according to which the last days will see the restoration of Israel, in response to which the Gentiles will stream into Jerusalem.[33] If that pilgrimage tradition is somehow in play here, then Paul attributes to God a complex inversion of the tradition. Here it is not Israel's triumph (its restoration) but Israel's failure (its rejection of the gospel) that invites the Gentiles to recognize God. In addition, in Romans 9–11, it is the Gentiles who lead Israel to its redemption rather than the other way around. Most important, many texts associated with the eschatological pilgrimage tradition are concerned with the vindication of Israel—its liberation from oppression by external powers, the return of the exiles (see, e.g., Isa. 60:1–22; Jer. 31:1–25; Ezek. 20:33–34; Zech. 8:1–23; 14:10–11; 1 Bar. 4:36–37; 5:1–9; *Jub.* 1:15–18). By contrast, Paul is less concerned with the vindication of Israel than with the vindication of God.

These indications of God's freedom do not exhaust either the possibilities or the problems of Romans 9–11. They may, however, suffice to undermine any notion that God's faithfulness can be predicted in advance, in the sense of being a "taken-for-granted." Even as God fulfills the ancient promises to Israel, God also cannot be restricted to a petty understanding of that fulfillment. To refer to Paul's own language about knowing in 2 Corinthians 5 may be helpful here. In that important passage, Paul distinguishes knowing *kata sarka* (NRSV: "from a human point of view") from knowing "now," in the light of God's apocalypse in Jesus Christ. Not only Christ but all people are understood differently, as is the cross itself (1 Cor. 1:18). By the same token, Romans 9–11 implies that God's faithfulness is not faithfulness that can be perceived *kata sarka,* in a merely human sort of way. For a writer who knows that the cross is God's power and wisdom but that not all have been granted the gift to see it, it would seem clear that God's faithfulness may also be perceived differently by those who have received the gift of sight. What looks like rejection or even fickleness is merely God's own brand of faithfulness. The blessing at the end of chapter 11 appears to underscore this very point, with its declaration of the unsearchability of God's judgments and inscrutability of God's ways.

GOD'S FREEDOM AND THE PROBLEM OF ETHICS

With the conclusion of Romans 11, Paul moves to the final section of the body of the letter, a section that is often designated as "ethical" or "paraenetic."[34] The assumption is that Paul has now turned from his exposition of God's activity to an exposition of the demands made on believers by that activity. There are numerous problems with such a schematization, not least of which is the way God's own activity continues to dominate in 12:1–15:13. As in chapters 1–11, in this section also God is "on the loose," here in the sense that God's demands cannot be confined to a single slice or portion of human life.

The two verses that open this section of the letter are generally understood as providing an overview of what is to follow. Recently, Stanley Stowers has described these verses as insisting that the Romans "are to renew their minds,"[35] but how exactly are the Romans to accomplish such an impressive feat? Paul opens with an appeal to "the mercies of God," a phrase that—at the very least— locates what follows in connection with God's merciful activity to humankind, activity first introduced as early as chapter 1 but recently recapitulated with reference to Israel and the Gentiles in chapters 9–11.

"By the mercies of God" is far more than an appeal to God's activity, as if God has now carried out the divine part of the bargain and it is up to human beings to take up their assigned portion so that the total task will be complete. "By" (*dia*) often refers to the means or instrumentality through which something takes place, not simply to attendant circumstances. It is by, and only by, God's mercies that human beings are able to undertake the life Paul evokes in

12:1–2. Not even the admonitions Paul offers can be fulfilled apart from God's continued intervention.

God's role does not disappear even in the admonition to "be transformed by the renewing of your minds." The passive voice ("be transformed") is essential, as human beings do not transform their own minds. Indeed, in 1:21–22 Paul has explicitly associated futile and senseless thinking with the problem of Sin from which humanity must be delivered. The passive voice here is almost certainly a divine passive, referring to God's renewal of the mind.

A glance at the next few chapters shows that this is not, for Paul, merely introductory chatter about God that serves to decorate the transition into a section that otherwise imagines the human being as an independent ethical agent.[36] It is God who assigns gifts (12:3), Christ's body that governs how members relate to one another (12:5), God's prerogative (and no one else's) to judge the dietary practices of fellow believers. The culminating pleas of 15:1–2 and 15:7 both end in prayers that understand God as the one who grants the gift of fulfillment for these admonitions:

> May the God of steadfastness and encouragement grant you to live in harmony with one another, in accordance with Christ Jesus, so that together you may with one voice glorify the God and Father of our Lord Jesus Christ. (15:5–6)

> May the God of hope fill you with all joy and peace in believing, so that you may abound in hope by the power of the Holy Spirit. (15:13)

There may be a sense of comfort in that reminder about God's role, but the remainder of 12:1–2 is apt to generate discomfort rather than comfort. As is widely recognized, Paul here employs language that usually has its home in cultic situations.[37] "Sacrifice" clearly belongs in the context of religious observance, but the Greek word translated "worship" (*latreia*) also is not a general term for obeisance to the divine but carries specific connotations of the cult.

In this context of cultic language, Paul urges Roman Christians to "present your bodies." The adjectives "living" and "holy" prompt readers to infer a critique against other sacrificial cults—that is, Paul implicitly identifies the Christian's sacrifice as superior to that of pagan rituals or even the sacrificial practices in Jerusalem. That critique certainly finds its place in Hebrews, but Paul's concern is to assert a positive claim about the comprehensive nature of the gospel's work. The "body" (*sōma*) includes the physical being, but it refers to the entire person. In addition, the phrase here is "your bodies" rather than the singular "your body," suggesting that the appeal is to a corporate body of believers rather than to solitary individuals. In a classic discussion of this passage, Ernst Käsemann articulated both features well, commenting that the body, in Paul, is the human

> capacity for communication and the reality of his incorporation within a world that limits him. God lays claim to our corporeality because he is no longer leaving the world to itself, and our bodily obedience expresses the

fact that, in and with us, he has recalled to his service the world of which
we are a part.[38]

The call then is for believers together to present themselves to God as their
appropriate form of worship. The text offers nowhere to hide. Here it is clear that
Paul has no place in his thinking for a distinction between Christian behavior
and the "rest" of life. The cultic language employed here cannot be confined to
cultic act. To present "your bodies" is to present all that there is. Again, Käsemann is helpful by insisting that there is no longer room for cultic thinking, since
the very use of cultic language in Romans 12:1–2 demonstrates paradoxically
how extensive is the upheaval in human life. There is no longer anything "pro-
fane" and there is no longer anything "holy" except "the community of the holy
people and their self-abandonment in the service of the Lord."[39] Here we find
Paul's version of the rending of the temple veil in Mark's Gospel. No place offers
safety from the God who reclaims the world for himself. God's demand is of all.

GOD IS "ON THE LOOSE"

In his reflection on the completion of the work of the Society of Biblical Literature's Pauline Theology Group, Paul W. Meyer observed that many participants
in the discussion had moved away from discussions of Paul's *theology* (as a fixed
content, even as a coherent set of ideas) and toward discussions of Paul's *theologizing* (as an ongoing activity). Meyer noted, however, that contributors to the
discussion often reflected the assumption that Paul began from a fixed point (his
theological convictions) and modified that fixed point as developments required
(theologizing). His own proposal was that the actual process was the reverse, that
Paul's theology or convictions were not his starting point but his end-product; in
other words, Paul revised and recast his convictions in the light of events.[40] Crucially, for Meyer, this discovery of Paul's theology does not reflect only changing
pastoral situations, much less some quirk in Paul's mental processes. Instead, this
fluidity in Paul's theology has to do with the gospel itself. It is nothing less than
the crucifixion and resurrection of Jesus that "*forces* the revision and recasting of
all the traditional language, concepts, convictions and categories."[41]

The preceding brief and very preliminary reflection on God's activity in Romans
confirms Meyer's suggestion. Paul's opening announcement about the gospel's
power for salvation (1:16) creates enormous ambiguities, as a glance at any critical
commentary will confirm. Only as the letter unfolds does it become clear that
God's power for salvation is all that is capable of defeating the enormous reign of
Sin and Death. God's power for salvation encloses the previously excluded Gentiles
and extends even to the present deafness of Israel, and God's power for salvation
enables and demands the total service of those who are "called to belong to Jesus
Christ" (1:6). The identity of this God is emphatically not a "taken-for-granted."
No less than the God of Mark's ending is the God of Romans' "on the loose."[42]

Notes

1. Donald H. Juel, *A Master of Surprise: Mark Interpreted* (Minneapolis: Fortress Press, 1994), 120 (see also above, p. 11).
2. Ibid., 35–36.
3. Ibid., 120 (see above, p. 11).
4. For a concise review of the problems involved in any such comparison, a cogent argument in favor of comparing the theologies of Mark and Paul, and an inviting example of that conversation, see C. Clifton Black, "Christ Crucified in Paul and in Mark: Reflections on an Intracanonical Conversation," in *Theology and Ethics in Paul and His Interpreters: Essays in Honor of Victor Paul Furnish*, ed. Eugene H. Lovering Jr. and Jerry L. Sumney (Nashville: Abingdon Press, 1995), 184–206.
5. For some orientation to the scholarly conversation, see Karl P. Donfried, ed., *The Romans Debate,* rev. and expanded ed. (Peabody, MA: Hendrickson Publishers, 1991); James C. Miller, "The Romans Debate: 1991–2001," *Currents in Research* 9 (2001): 306–49.
6. Nils Dahl, "The Neglected Factor in New Testament Theology," in *Jesus the Christ: The Historical Origins of Christological Doctrine*, ed. Donald H. Juel (Minneapolis: Fortress Press, 1991), 153–63. This essay originally appeared in *Reflections* 75 (1975): 5–8. An important exception to this comment about the neglect of God in the study of Romans is the work of Halvor Moxnes, *Theology in Conflict: Studies in Paul's Understanding of God in Romans,* Novum Testamentum Supplements 53 (Leiden: E. J. Brill, 1980). More recently, see Neil Richardson, *Paul's Language about God,* Journal for the Study of the New Testament: Supplement Series 99 (Sheffield: Sheffield Academic Press, 1999), esp. 26–94 and 308–15; and R. B. Hays, "The God of Mercy Who Rescues Us from the Present Evil Age," in *The Forgotten God: Perspectives in Biblical Theology*, ed. A. Andrew Das and Frank J. Matera (Louisville, KY: Westminster John Knox Press, 2002), 123–43.
7. J. D. G. Dunn, *The Theology of Paul the Apostle* (Grand Rapids: Wm. B. Eerdmans Publishing Co., 1998). On the privileging of Romans in discussions of Pauline theology, see esp. 25–26. Dunn earlier defended this methodological starting point in "In Quest of Paul's Theology: Retrospect and Prospect," in *Pauline Theology,* vol. 4, ed. E. Elizabeth Johnson and David M. Hay, Symposium Series (Atlanta: Society of Biblical Literature, 1997), 95–115. See also the trenchant critique by Steven J. Kraftchick, "An Asymptotic Response to Dunn's Retrospective and Proposals," in *Pauline Theology* 4:116–39.
8. Dunn, *Theology of Paul the Apostle*, 29.
9. Ibid., 185.
10. Ibid., 18, 713–16.
11. Ibid., 729–30.
12. Francis Watson, "The Triune Divine Identity: Reflections on Pauline God-Language, in Disagreement with J. D. G. Dunn," *Journal for the Study of the New Testament* 80 (2000): 99–124. See also the review by Douglas Campbell for an account of the implied "contract" view of Christianity in Dunn's view of Paul ("The DIAΘHKH from Durham: Professor Dunn's *The Theology of Paul the Apostle*," *Journal for the Study of the New Testament* 72 [1998]: 91–111). It is, of course, a sign of the importance of Dunn's work that it generates such extended critique and conversation.
13. Dunn, *Theology of Paul the Apostle*, 31–50.
14. To be sure, the promise to Abraham might render this move from promise to Israel to offering to the Gentiles less than startling, but it is interesting that Paul does not refer to Abraham here. The juxtaposition of Scripture's promise and the obedience of the Gentiles remains unexplained.

15. E. P. Sanders, *Paul and Palestinian Judaism: A Comparison of Patterns of Religion* (Philadelphia: Fortress Press, 1977), 442–47. As J. Louis Martyn has observed, Sanders's point was anticipated in Barth's *Church Dogmatics* (*Galatians,* Anchor Bible 33A [New York: Doubleday, 1997], 95).

16. Leander Keck, "What Makes Romans Tick?" in *Pauline Theology,* vol. 3, ed. David M. Hay and E. Elizabeth Johnson (Minneapolis: Fortress Press, 1995), 25. The following section owes much to Keck's analysis, although my attention is to God's actions more than to the spiral of human captivity.

17. The NRSV perpetuates the translation of *pistis Iēsou Christou* as an objective genitive, reflecting faith "about" or "in" Jesus Christ. Many contemporary scholars, myself included, favor translating the phrase here and elsewhere as a subjective genitive referring to the faithfulness or obedience of Jesus. The literature is extensive; see esp. George Howard, "On the 'Faith of Christ,'" *Harvard Theological Review* 60 (1967): 459–65; Luke T. Johnson, "Romans 3:21–26 and the Faith of Jesus," *Catholic Biblical Quarterly* 44 (1982): 77–90; Morna Hooker, "ΠΙΣΤΙΣ ΧΡΙΣΤΟΥ," *New Testament Studies* 35 (1989): 321–42; Richard B. Hays, "ΠΙΣΤΙΣ and Pauline Christology: What Is at Stake?" in Johnson and Hay, eds., *Pauline Theology* 4:35–60; J. D. G. Dunn, "Once More, ΠΙΣΤΙΣ ΧΡΙΣΤΟΥ," in Johnson and Hays, eds., *Pauline Theology* 4:61–81. Even if the phrase is taken as a subjective genitive, however, the next phrase quite explicitly concerns "all who believe."

18. On this passage and 2 Cor. 5:16–17, see J. Louis Martyn, "Epistemology at the Turn of the Ages," *Theological Issues in the Letters of Paul* (Nashville: Abingdon Press, 1997), 89–110.

19. An important exception to this generalization is Paul W. Meyer, who comments that "faith cannot mean some prerequisite condition to be fulfilled by human beings before God can act" ("Romans," *HarperCollins Bible Commentary,* ed. James L. Mays et al., rev. ed. [New York: HarperCollins, 2000], 1048). Meyer's elegant commentary on Romans is now available in Paul W. Meyer, *The Word in This World: Essays in New Testament Exegesis and Theology,* ed. John T. Carroll, New Testament Library (Louisville, KY: Westminster John Knox Press, 2004), 151–218.

20. Brendan Byrne, *Romans,* Sacra Pagina (Collegeville, MN: Liturgical Press, 1996), 127. For similar observations, see J. A. Fitzmyer, *Romans,* Anchor Bible 33 (New York: Doubleday, 1993), 342, 350; Douglas J. Moo, *The Epistle to the Romans,* New International Commentary on the New Testament (Grand Rapids: Wm. B. Eerdmans Publishing Co., 1996), 224–26.

21. Dunn, *Theology of Paul the Apostle,* 379.

22. See esp. M. Eugene Boring, "The Language of Universal Salvation in Paul," *Journal of Biblical Literature* 105 (1986): 269–92; and Richard H. Bell, "Rom 5.18–19 and Universal Salvation," *New Testament Studies* 48 (2002): 417–32. Both of these fine studies draw distinctions among various realms in Paul's discourse. Boring identifies statements regarding a limited scope of salvation as reflecting the image of God as judge and those regarding universal salvation as reflecting the image of God as king (see esp. 291). Bell understands the inclusive statements in Rom. 5 as reflecting a "mythical perspective," as distinguished from the historical framework employed in Rom. 11:25–32 (see esp. 430).

23. Charles B. Cousar, "Continuity and Discontinuity: Reflections on Romans 5–8," in Hay and Johnson, eds., *Pauline Theology* 3:203–4.

24. By contrast, see Stanley Stowers's claim that Rom. 5–8 has to do with the way in which Gentiles "obtain obedience," not with "a scheme of sin and salvation" (*A*

Rereading of Romans: Justice, Jews, and Gentiles [New Haven, CT: Yale University Press, 1994], 251).

25. Paul W. Meyer, "The Worm at the Core of the Apple," in *The Conversation Continues: Studies in Paul and John in Honor of J. Louis Martyn,* ed. Robert T. Fortna and Beverly R. Gaventa (Nashville: Abingdon Press, 1990), 62–84. This essay was reprinted in Meyer, *Word in This World,* 57–77.

26. The literature on Romans 9–11 is enormous. A few important recent works that address the question of God's faithfulness include: Paul Meyer, "Romans," 1060–66; E. Elizabeth Johnson, "Romans 9–11: The Faithfulness and Impartiality of God," in Hay and Johnson, eds., *Pauline Theology* 3:211–39; Douglas Moo, "The Theology of Romans 9–11," in Hay and Johnson, eds., *Pauline Theology* 3:240–58.

27. Wayne Meeks, "On Trusting an Unpredictable God," in *In Search of the Early Christians,* ed. Allen R. Hilton and H. Gregory Snyder (New Haven, CT: Yale University Press, 2002), 213.

28. On the manifold voice of Isaiah in Rom. 9–11, see the important recent work of J. Ross Wagner, *Heralds of Good News: Isaiah and Paul "in Concert" in the Letter to the Romans,* Novum Testamentum Supplements (Leiden: E. J. Brill, 2002).

29. Confidence and certainty are not the same thing, as Wayne Meeks notes: "The reader [of Rom. 9–11] is not allowed to think that confidence depends on knowing just how God will act in the future." ("On Trusting an Unpredictable God," 212).

30. Neil Richardson, *Paul's Language about God,* Journal for the Study of the New Testament Supplement Series 99 (Sheffield: Sheffield Academic Press, 1994), 26–94.

31. See esp. Wagner, *Heralds of Good News,* 126–57.

32. Meyer, "Romans," 1062.

33. To be sure, some Jewish texts anticipate not the redemption but the destruction of Gentiles as Israel's enemies. For an overview of the texts and related debates, see Terence L. Donaldson, *Paul and the Gentiles: Remapping the Apostle's Convictional World* (Minneapolis: Fortress Press, 1997), 69–74; E. P. Sanders, *Jesus and Judaism* (Philadelphia: Fortress Press, 1985), 77–119; idem, *Judaism: Practice and Belief 63 BCE–66 CE* (London: SCM Press, 1992), 291–92.

34. The scholarly literature on this section of the letter has given particular weight to deciphering the source of Paul's admonitions and the relationship (if any) between the content of this section and the situation at Rome. Such difficult questions necessarily lie outside the scope of this essay.

35. Stowers, *A Rereading of Romans,* 318.

36. On the problem of separating Pauline theology from Pauline ethics, see esp. J. Louis Martyn, "De-apocalypticizing Paul: An Essay Focused on *Paul and the Stoics* by Troels Engberg-Pedersen," *Journal for the Study of the New Testament* 86 (2002): 61–102.

37. Fitzmyer, *Romans,* 640; Moo, *Epistle to the Romans,* 750–51.

38. Ernst Käsemann, "Worship and Everyday Life," in *New Testament Questions of Today,* trans. W. J. Montague (Philadelphia: Fortress Press, 1969), 191.

39. Ibid., 192.

40. Paul W. Meyer, "Pauline Theology: A Proposal for a Pause in its Pursuit," in Hay and Johnson, eds., *Pauline Theology* 4:140–60. This essay was reprinted in Meyer, *Word in This World,* 95–116.

41. Ibid., 159.

42. I am grateful to Charles B. Cousar, J. Louis Martyn, and Patrick J. Willson for their comments on an earlier draft of this essay.

Chapter 7

Prophetic Surprise
in Romans 9–11
Thomas W. Gillespie

The thesis of this essay is threefold: (1) that Romans 9–11 is an instance of early Christian prophecy, (2) that its argument is undergirded by "a narrative substructure," and (3) that it entails a surprising story-ending of the kind that fascinated my friend and colleague Donald H. Juel in his Markan studies.[1]

I

Elsewhere I have proposed that early Christian prophecy, as attested by the apostle Paul, was extended Spirit-inspired discourse that interpreted the apostolic kerygma.[2] Briefly stated, the argument is that the prophets, second only to the apostles in the ecclesial economy ordained by God (1 Cor. 12:28), were the media of divine revelations (1 Cor. 14:6, 26, 31) that explicated the inherent meaning of the gospel (1 Cor. 2:1–13). In this latter text the apostle designates his initial preaching in Corinth as the proclamation of "the mystery of God" (*to mystērion tou theou,* v. 1) that has as its subject "Jesus Christ, and him crucified" (v. 2). He then places this message in the context of "the wisdom of God," which is itself "a

91

mystery" (*mystērion*) and thus "hidden" (v. 7). The mystery of God's hidden wisdom is materially specified by means of an unidentified scriptural citation in terms of "what no eye has seen, nor ear heard, nor the human heart conceived, what God has prepared for those who love him" (v. 9). Paul declares, however, that these things "God has revealed to us through the Spirit" (v. 10). For we have received "the Spirit from God," he explains, "so that we might understand the gifts bestowed on us by God" (v. 12). Here the participle *charisthenta* ("gifts bestowed') has its textual antecedent in "what God has prepared" (v. 9) and thus in "God's wisdom" (v. 7), which is the ground of the proclamation of "the mystery of God" (v. 1). In sum, the Spirit reveals the hidden wisdom of God that is inherent in the mystery of God proclaimed in the gospel of "Jesus Christ, and him crucified" (cf. 1 Cor. 1:23). Moreover, this understanding is expressed "in words not taught by human wisdom but taught by the Spirit" (v. 13). Although neither the word "prophet" nor its cognates "prophecy" and "prophesy" occur in this text, it is reasonable to infer that the subject matter under discussion is that inspired speech commonly denoted elsewhere in the apostle's letters by such terminology.

Given this profile of the function of early Christian prophecy, I have further argued that 1 Corinthians 15 may be identified as a canonical example of such extended utterances because of several formal characteristics.[3] First among these is the fact that the text is a clearly defined literary unit,[4] marked off by the strong Pauline opening transition marker "I would remind you, brothers and sisters . . ." (v. 1) and the clear closing marker "So then, my beloved . . ." (v. 58).[5] Secondly, it is extended discourse occasioned by the claim of "some" in Corinth that "there is no resurrection of the dead" (v. 12). The issue at stake is thus the eschatological implications of the undisputed kerygmatic claim in the cited gospel tradition "that he [Christ] was raised on the third day in accordance with the scriptures" (v. 4). Finally, the text interprets this phrase in accordance with the revealed "mystery" (*mystērion*) that the resurrection entails not merely an escape from the power of death but God's eschatological defeat of death itself and thus the future resurrection of dead bodies (vv. 51–57). The formal similarities between 1 Corinthians 15 and Romans 9–11 are striking.

Romans 9–11 is likewise an identifiable literary unit.[6] It begins with an oath, "I am speaking the truth in Christ" (9:1), and concludes with a doxology, "To him be the glory forever. Amen" (11:36). The evident integrity of these three chapters led C. H. Dodd to affirm that they were "originally a separate treatise," which the apostle introduced at this point in his letter.[7] Indeed, he contended, if we read these chapters by themselves "we get the impression that we are listening to Paul preaching." Thus he continues:

> Chaps. ix.–xi . . . have a beginning and a close appropriate to a sermon, and the preaching tone is maintained all through. It is the kind of sermon that Paul must often have had occasion to deliver, in defining his attitude to what we may call the Jewish question. It is quite possible that he kept by him a MS. of such a sermon, for use as occasion demanded and inserted it here.[8]

Commentators since have generally dismissed this conjecture, however, and stressed the integral relationship of chapters 9–11 to 1–8.[9] But estimates of the possible origin of a literary unit and its integral connection to what precedes it in the larger text are two different issues that need not be mutually exclusive. One can agree, for example, with C. E. B. Cranfield's assessment that chapters 9–11 should not be considered an "excursus" because they illumine many parts of the preceding text and contribute to the development of the letter's theme,[10] without prejudice to the possibility that the passage may have originated independently in prophetic discourse. Such an origin would not necessarily require the literary judgment that it is for that reason a digression. Thus, Dodd's inference that Romans 9–11 represents a "sermon" genre should not be dismissed out of hand.

A second common feature is that Romans 9–11 also represents an even more extended discourse on an issue of the gospel. This surfaces in the apostle's denial that "the word of God has failed" (9:6). Commentators tend to identify "the word of God" in this text with the divine promises to Israel in the Old Testament, but Paul uses the phrase only to refer to the gospel. It occurs six other times in the apostle's extant letters (1 Cor. 14:36; 2 Cor. 2:17; 4:2; Phil. 1:14; 1 Thess. 2:13 [two times]), and in each instance it designates the apostolic message. It is true that Paul believed "the gospel of God" is that which "he promised beforehand through his prophets in the holy scriptures" (Rom. 1:2; cf. Gal. 3:8). Indeed, the point of the gospel is that God is keeping "every one" of these promises in Jesus the Christ (2 Cor. 1:18–20). But "the word of God" is in Paul's parlance a synonym for the gospel of the Christ in whom God is doing all the things that he promised to Israel.[11] Thus, as 1 Corinthians 15 is occasioned by the claim of some that belief in the gospel of the risen Christ (v. 4b) does not entail the hope of a future resurrection of dead bodies (v. 12), so Romans 9–11 addresses the suspicion of still others that the gospel has failed because it has not achieved the conversion of Israel (9:6; cf. 10:1, 16; 11:7, 28). At issue then is whether the apostle's claim that the gospel is "the power of God unto salvation to everyone who has faith, *to the Jew first* and also to the Greek" (Rom. 1:16), can be sustained in view of the widespread Jewish resistance to it in Paul's time. In 1 Corinthians 15 it is one aspect of the gospel that requires prophetic clarification, while in Romans 9–11 it is the gospel itself in its relation to Israel that needs interpretation. Thus, as J. D. G. Dunn aptly puts it, Romans 9:6 is "the text or thesis to be expounded."[12]

The third common characteristic of these two passages is their respective appeals to divine revelation. In Romans 9–11 it appears, as in 1 Corinthians 15, at the conclusion of the discussion in the introduction of a "mystery" (11:25–32). That talk of a "mystery" assumes divine revelation is implicit in the lexical meaning of the Greek term. Louw and Nida define *mystērion* as "the content of that which has not been known before but which has been revealed to an in-group or restricted constituency." Yet they caution:

> There is a serious problem involved in translating *mystērion* by a word which is equivalent to the English expression "mystery," for this term in English

refers to a secret which people have tried to uncover but which they have
failed to understand. In many instances *mystērion* is translated by a phrase
meaning "that which was not known before," with the implication of its
being revealed at least to some persons.[13]

The point is that a mystery is known by revelation from within, not discovery
from without. Thus, Fitzmyer is on target when he explains that for Paul
mystērion "denotes a secret knowledge about a decision hidden in God from of
old, now revealed in and through Jesus Christ for the salvation of all humanity,"[14]
with the proviso that the immediate medium of such revelation is the Spirit.
Hence, the "telling" (1 Cor. 15:51) and the "making known" (Rom. 11:25) of a
"mystery" involves speaking "in words not taught by human wisdom but taught
by the Spirit" (1 Cor. 2:13).

Admittedly, the three formal characteristics shared by Romans 9–11 and 1
Corinthians 15 do not require that these discrete passages be identified as examples
of prophetic speech, despite the remarkable match between their literary form and
the functional profile of early Christian prophecy I have proposed. But one further
feature of Romans 9–11 does argue for such a genre identification. Consider the
phrases "in Christ" (*en Christō*) and "in the Holy Spirit" (*en pneumati hagiō*) in the
opening oath (9:1). The tendency is to interpret both as appeals to moral integrity
with regard to the apostle's ensuing declaration that he could almost wish to be himself accursed and cut off from Christ for the sake of his own people (9:2).[15] Dunn,
however, senses that this is the language of inspiration in Paul, particularly the
phrase "in the Holy Spirit," which he rightly contends is "essentially charismatic in
force, expressing a sense of basic inspiration informing and determining his conscience *and the whole process of witness bearing.*"[16] This is equally true of the claim
to be "speaking in Christ." That personal integrity in preaching and divine inspiration are related issues for Paul is evident from his defense of his preaching ministry in 2 Corinthians, where he identifies himself and his colleagues as "persons of
sincerity" rather than "peddlers of God's word," who are sent from God and in his
presence speak in Christ (2:17; cf. 12:19). This "speaking in Christ" is in fact the
converse of Paul's claim that "Christ is speaking in me" (2 Cor. 13:3, where the
Greek syntax is literally "the in me speaking Christ").[17] If the "in Christ" and "in
the Holy Spirit" phrases in Romans 9:1 are understood as claims to divine inspiration, and thereby also to personal integrity, then they introduce both the apostle's
oath in verse 2 and the testimony of chapters 9–11 in its entirety. The "truth" Paul
speaks in Romans 9–11 is "the mystery" of the gospel in relation to Israel as revealed
by the Spirit that "searches everything, even the depths of God" (1 Cor. 2:10).

II

The second part of my thesis is that the prophetic "sermon" of Romans 9–11 is
informed by a "narrative substructure" of the kind introduced into Pauline studies some twenty years ago by Richard B. Hays.[18] His broad thesis is that "the

framework of Paul's thought is constituted . . . by a 'sacred story,' a narrative structure."[19] In arguing his case, he makes two important distinctions. The first is between *story* ("the ordered series of events which forms the basis for various possible narrations") and *narrative* ("explicitly articulated narrations").[20] The second, following Northrop Frye, is between the Aristotelian terms *mythos* (the plot of a literary work, the linear sequence of events depicted) and *dianoia* (the theme or pattern or meaning of such a work).[21] Hays argues that Paul's "sacred story," although never narrated in his letters, is nonetheless about Jesus Christ and entails both *mythos* and *dianoia*. Thus, his specific thesis is that the kerygmatic summaries that are embedded in Galatians 3:1–4:11 are "recapitulations of the gospel message" that "express the *dianoia* of the gospel story" and thereby "provide some clues to its shape."[22]

In the introduction to the recently published second edition of his seminal work, Hays observes that the focus of the initial volume on discerning the form of Paul's "sacred story" about Jesus inevitably raises the further question of how this story fits into "the wider story of Israel, the story of election and promise told in the Old Testament."[23] Others have already begun addressing this issue and have even expanded the investigation into the possibility of a Pauline metanarrative that extends from the creation to the eschaton.[24] Not surprisingly, much of the ensuing discussion has focused on the theoretical adequacy of the literary categories *story* and *narrative*, *mythos* and *dianoia*.[25] For the purposes in this brief essay, I will use the distinctions Hays proposes as a heuristic device to identify the narrative substructure in Romans 9–11 that shapes Paul's response to the suspicion that "the word of God has failed." It is visible not in "kerygmatic summaries," as in Galatians 3:1–4:11 according to Hays, but in the apostle's allusions to and citations of Israel's scriptures in the course of his prophetic "sermon."

Beginning with the list of divine blessings that Paul attributes in Romans 9:1–5 to the "Israelites," his "own people," his "kindred according to the flesh," it is clear that the enumeration is crafted in such a fashion that it serves the rhetorical purpose of producing "the impression of extensiveness and abundance by means of an exhausting summary (polysyndeton)."[26] What is less obvious is the fact that "the adoption, the glory, the covenants, the giving of the law, the worship, and the promises" plus "the patriarchs" all allude to acts, events, and people foundational to Israel's life and attested in Israel's scriptures. Later in this text Paul will speak of these benefits as "the gifts of God" (*ta charismata tou theou*, 11:29), each actually given at a time and place, and intimating thereby that there is a story line here that connects them in an ordered series of events that begins with the patriarchs, continues through the exodus, and concludes with the wilderness wanderings—the latter including the giving of the law. In other words, the list represents "the sacred story" of Israel as actually narrated in the Pentateuch and demonstrates the apostle's basic understanding of the nature of the Torah (Greek: *ho nomos* ["the law"]).

On this topic, James A. Sanders has persuasively argued two points. The first is that the Torah "is best defined as a story (*mythos*) with law (*ethos*) embedded in it."[27] The second is that this applies whether the Torah is limited to the Penta-teuch, as was the case in Paul's day, or extended to the Hexateuch or even to the Tetrateuch[28] (the "Primary History" of Israel[29]). The point to be scored is that Paul viewed the Law (Torah) as primarily a story that is open-ended and teleo-logical. For out of the gifted history and blessed lineage of the Israelites "comes the Messiah" (9:5). Paul's "sacred story" of Jesus, as postulated by Hays, is here grounded squarely in the Torah story of Israel. What follows in Romans 9–11, therefore, is best understood as the apostle's understanding of the *dianoia* of that story.

Foundational for Paul in regard to the meaning of the Torah story is the insight that it is driven by God's *purpose*. This comes to expression in a paren-thetical remark he makes in regard to the story of Rebecca, who, being pregnant by Isaac with twin boys (Esau and Jacob), was told by God before they were born, "The elder shall serve the younger" (9:10–13, citing Gen. 25:23). The reason given for this divine decision is that it enables "God's purpose" (*hē prothesis tou theou*) to continue "[according to] election" (*kat' eklogēn,* 9:11b). While election is specified here as the mode of God's purposeful activity, the important thing to note is that it is goal oriented. The same applies to the preceding reference to the election of Isaac, the child of promise by Sarah, instead of Ishmael, a child of the flesh by Hagar (9:7–9). But it applies also to the charismatic gifts bestowed upon Israel. For it is not only the patriarchs who are elected to serve God's purpose but the adoption, the glory, the covenants, the legislation, the worship, and the promises as well. As Robin Scroggs summarizes the point, "Paul is conscious of being a part of an ongoing history in which God, the central actor, relates to a people with an ultimate aim."[30]

How God relates to elect Israel is by *mercy*. In response to the imagined inter-locutor who objects that God's elective activity is a divine injustice (9:14), Paul refers to the Torah story of Moses and Pharaoh from the time of the exodus to make the point that election is a matter of mercy, not justice: "For [God] says to Moses, 'I will have mercy on whom I have mercy, and I will have compassion on whom I have compassion'" (9:15, citing Exod. 33:19). While justice requires deserved equal treatment, mercy transcends justice by giving what is unearned, unmerited, and undeserved. That is why God's elective activity "depends not on human will or exertion, but on God who shows mercy" (9:16). Here Paul picks up on a theme he introduced initially by the observation that God's purpose of election occurs "not by [human] works but by his call" (9:12a), indeed a theme he will develop throughout Romans 9–11 in order to interpret the *dianoia* of the story (cf. 9:32; 10:3; 11:6, 31). And, as Hays reminds us, the "theme" or "mean-ing" of the story is not "something abstracted from the narrative" but rather "an organic property of the narrative."[31] This is the way it is told because this is the way it happened in the story.

God's merciful purpose can be resisted, however. This too is a point of the story of Moses and Pharaoh as told in the Torah (Exod. 7–12). It is important to note that in Romans 9:14–18, Pharaoh is not an analogous figure to Ishmael and

Esau. Paul pointed up the difference between Abraham's two sons and Isaac's twins in order to show that "not all Israelites truly belong to Israel, and not all of Abraham's children are his true descendants" (9:6b–7). But the story of Moses and Pharaoh contributes nothing to that argument. Rather, it introduces the corresponding notion that God "has mercy on whomever he chooses, and he hardens the heart of whomever he chooses" (9:18). In the Torah narrative, Pharaoh is hardened because he resists God's purpose to deliver Israel from its Egyptian bondage. For Paul, he serves as a type of anyone, including the Israelite, who does the same at any time and under other circumstances. The apostle needs this typology because after Jacob the argument that there is an Israel within Israel must be made on other than genealogical grounds. In order to maintain such a distinction within the lineal descendants of Jacob (Israel), the apostle turns to the theme of "hardening." Genealogy remains important to him because it contributes to Israelite identity. "I myself am an Israelite," he affirms, "a descendant of Abraham, a member of the tribe of Benjamin" (11:1). In the next breath, however, he distinguishes between "the elect [*hē eklogē*]" in Israel and "the rest [*hoi loipoi*]" who were "hardened" (11:7). Pharaoh represents this latter condition in Israel's sacred story.

That this sacred story of God's merciful elective purpose extends beyond the Pentateuch for Paul into the "Primary History" of Israel is implicitly attested by a variety of scriptural citations in Romans 9–11, particularly those from the prophets who are located historically in the time of the kings.[32] But it surfaces explicitly in his citations from the account of Elijah in which the prophet pleads with God against Israel because of its idolatry (Rom. 11:2b–5, citing selectively 1 Kgs. 19:10–18). In his exhaustive study of the apostle's use of Scripture in Romans, J. Ross Wagner has shown that in citing specific biblical texts Paul is "tapping into" the larger literary (and in some instances narrative) contexts from which such texts derive.[33] In Romans 11:2b–5, he notes, "Paul turns to the episode in the story of Elijah where, after Elijah's dramatic victory over the prophets of Baal and his subsequent ignominious flight to the desert in fear and despair, the prophet encounters God on Mt. Horeb."[34] Assuming that his readers are familiar with this story, at least in its broad outline, Paul focuses on the dialogue between the prophet and God. Elijah claims to be the last of the true Israelites (11:3), but the divine voice replies that God has kept for himself "seven thousand who have not bowed the knee to Baal" (11:4). From this Paul infers, "So too at the present time there is a remnant [*leimma*], chosen by grace [*kat' eklogēn charitos gegonen*]" (11:5), adding by way of explanation that "if it is by grace, it is no longer on the basis of works, otherwise grace would not be grace" (11:6). Wagner notes that here the apostle "appeals again to the principle enunciated earlier by means of the story of Jacob and Esau in Romans 9:11–13," demonstrating thereby that the grace given to the remnant in Elijah's day corresponds to the divine mercy at work in Israel's initial election.[35] Put simply, the *dianoia* of the story remains constant as it unfolds in accordance with God's purpose.

For Paul this purpose is being worked out beyond the sacred story of Israel (narrated in the Primary History) in both the story of Jesus and of the church. In those sections of Romans 9–11 where he develops this point, it becomes evident that what God purposes through his merciful and elective activity is *righteousness*. In Romans 9:19–29, for example, Paul uses the metaphor of the potter and the clay to defend God's freedom not only to call some and not others within Israel to serve his purpose but also his right to call Gentiles together with Jews to the same end. In a sentence that begins with a hypothetical "What if God . . ." (*ei . . . ho theos*) and ends up an anacoluthon, Paul rescues his convoluted syntax by speaking of those in his own time whom God has in fact "called" (*ekalesen*), namely, "us . . ., not from the Jews only but also from the Gentiles" (v. 24).[36] Consequently, according to Romans 9:30–33, "Gentiles, who did not strive for righteousness, have attained it, that is, righteousness through faith" (v. 30), while Israel as a whole failed in its pursuit of "the law of righteousness [*nomon dikaiosynē*]"[37] because it conducted its quest as though righteousness were not based on faith but on works (9:31–32).

In Romans 10:1–4, Paul bears witness that Israel's failure on this point is occasioned not by a lack of zeal for God but of knowledge (10:2). For being ignorant of "the righteousness of God" (*hē dikaiosynē tou theou*), he explains, Israel seeks to establish its own righteousness and thereby fails to submit to "the righteousness of God" (10:3). Byrne speaks of the "bi-polar" nature of this phrase in Paul, with one pole being the divine and the other the human.[38] In terms of the first pole, it can denote (1) the righteousness God demonstrates (by his covenant faithfulness to Israel); (2) the righteousness God gives (by his mercy toward Israel); and (3) the righteousness God requires (of his covenant partner Israel). At Israel's end of the polarity, righteousness is the status attained before God by obedience to the law (whether that be understood in terms of "covenantal nomism" or the more traditional "Lutheran" view of "works righteousness").[39] Clearly it is this human effort Paul has in mind here when he speaks of Israel seeking to establish its own righteousness, or when he affirms that God's elective purpose is based not on "works" (*ergon*) but on "the one who calls" (*ek tou kalountos*) (9:12), or when he emphasizes that God's election depends not on "human will and exertion" but on "God who shows mercy" (9:16). It is the same human effort he critiques when he explains that Israel failed to attain "the law of righteousness" because it pursued it not on the basis of "faith" but of "works" (9:32). That being the case, "the righteousness of God" in Romans 10:3 is a reference to God's righteousness—the righteousness he demonstrates by giving mercy, the mercy that requires faith as a proper response.

The apostle explains the righteousness of God by affirming that "Christ is the end [*telos*] of the law unto righteousness to all who believe" (10:4).[40] What the logical connection is between the righteousness of God and Christ is unstated, at least here. The missing link is provided in Romans 3:21–26, however. In this passage, all three nuances of the divine pole of the phrase are related to Christ: (1) God "discloses" and "proves" that he is himself righteous by putting forward

Christ Jesus as "a sacrifice of atonement by his blood" that effects redemption; (2) God's act in Christ is a gift of grace; and (3) God's gift is received through faith in Jesus. It is in this sense of purposeful accomplishment rather than termination that Christ is to be understood as "the end [goal] of the law." Thus, the sacred story of Israel includes for Paul "the coming of the Messiah" (9:5), and belief in him now becomes the criterion for distinguishing between "elect" Israel and "the rest" who are hardened.

In Romans 10:5–21, Paul develops how God is presently effecting righteousness in human life under the rubrics of "the word of faith that we proclaim" (v. 8b) and "the word of Christ" (v. 17). With regard to the Israel of Paul's day, his point is that despite the apostolic mission to the Jews, "not all have obeyed the good news" (v. 16a). This, of course, is the situation that has occasioned the suspicion that "the word of God had failed" (9:6). Paul points out that in Israel's sacred story this is nothing new, as the complaint of the prophet attests, "Lord, who has believed our message?" (10:16b, citing Isa. 53:1). Indeed, the Scriptures document Israel's perennial resistance to its God, a fact the apostle makes clear by a collage of citations (vv. 18–21) from the Psalms (19:4), the Law (Deut. 32:21), and the Prophets (Isa. 65:1–2)—the latter including the divine lament, " 'All day long I have held out my hands to a disobedient and contrary people.' "[41]

This is not universally the case, of course, because Paul is himself a believer in Jesus Christ precisely as "an Israelite, a descendant of Abraham, a member of the tribe of Benjamin" (11:1). In this faith he is joined by others of his people "in the now time" (en tō nyn kairō), who constitute the present remnant, chosen by grace (11:5). But it is true of "the rest" of Israel, who in their unbelief have been "hardened" and are presently "enemies of God" with regard to the gospel (11:28). It is at this point in the sacred story of Israel that Paul writes his letter to the Romans. But the story is not over, "the word of God" is not finished with its work, and God's merciful elective purpose is not yet fully realized. How then will it all end?

III

According to Paul, this is to be the end of the story: "all Israel will be saved" (11:26). Such a claim comes as a surprise to the reader who has taken seriously the apostle's views on ethnic Israel up to this point of the argument (cf. 9:8, 27–29, 31–33; 10:3, 16, 18–21; 11:7–10, 20). Yet it cannot come as a total surprise in view of other statements that leave open the question of the ultimate destiny of "the rest" in distinction from "the elect" in Israel. "They have stumbled over the stumbling stone" (9:32), but they have not "stumbled so as to fall" (11:11). "Not all have obeyed the good news" (10:16), but "God has not rejected his people whom he foreknew" (11:2). Branches of the olive tree have been broken off because of their unbelief, but "God has the power to graft them in again" (11:17–24). Now Paul boldly asserts in the context of Romans 11:25–32 that "all Israel [pas Israēl] will be saved" (v. 26).

The basis for his apostolic claim is nothing less than divine revelation. For this is "the mystery" (*to mystērion*) Paul communicates to the understanding of his readers. Stated fully it reads: "I want you to understand this mystery: a hardening has come upon part of Israel, until the full number of the Gentiles has come in. And so all Israel will be saved" (11:25b–26a). These may be "words not taught by human wisdom but taught by the Spirit" (1 Cor. 2:13), but they are not for that reason without some ambiguity. Exegetical controversy over this text swirls around several grammatical questions: (1) Should the phrase *pōrōsis apo merous tō Israēl gegonen* be translated "a partial hardening has come upon Israel" or "a hardening has come upon a part of Israel"? (2) Is the "Israel" mentioned in verse 25 identical with "all Israel" in verse 26, and what is the scope of the latter? (3) What is meant by "the full number of the Gentiles" (*to plērōma tōn ethnōn*)? (4) Should the adverb *houtōs* in verse 26 be translated modally ("thus") or temporally ("then")?

Briefly, the answers are as follows: (1) The term *pōrōsis* denotes the kind of hardness associated with petrification, and thus it is as difficult to imagine a "partial hardening" as it is "a soft rock." The reference here is to that "part" of Israel that has been "hardened" by its unbelief in Christ.[42] (2) It seems most natural to take the phrase "all Israel" as the sum of the two parts previously designated "the elect" and "the rest" (11:7), although many commentators like to hedge their bets on whether the phrase includes each and every Israelite or merely designates a general group.[43] Either way the distinction between "Israel" in verse 25 and "Israel" in verse 26 is that between the part and the whole, suggesting that the "part" that has experienced "hardening" is within the scope of the "all" who will be saved.[44] (3) Whatever may be the scope of the phrase "the full number [*to plērōma*] of the Gentiles," it is clearly a parallel expression to the "full inclusion [*to plērōma*]" of Israel (11:12), which also takes its meaning from the distinction between "the elect" and "the rest" (11:7). Thus, if the "full inclusion" of Israel is the equivalent of "all Israel," then "the full number of the Gentiles" might well connote, as Cranfield suggests, "something like 'the Gentile world as a whole.' "[45] (4) The adverb *houtōs* is clearly modal ("and *thus* all Israel will be saved"), although the temporal sense is not excluded because all Israel will be saved only when the time of the hardening of a part of Israel has ended, and that will not occur "until" (*achris*) the full number of the Gentiles has come in.

From the perspective of the end of the story, Paul sees the divine purpose taking strategic form. In his explanation of the mystery (11:28–32), he writes, "Just as you were once disobedient to God but have now received mercy because of their disobedience, so they have now been disobedient in order that, by the mercy shown to you, they too may now receive mercy" (vv. 30–31). This picks up on a theme introduced earlier: "But through their stumbling salvation has come to the Gentiles, so as to make Israel jealous. Now if their stumbling means riches for the world, and if their defeat means riches for Gentiles, how much more will their full inclusion mean!" (11:11b–12). Accordingly, Paul glorifies his ministry in order to activate jealousy among his own people, "and thus save some of them. For if their rejection is the reconciliation of the world, what will their acceptance be but life from the dead!" (11:14–15). The return to this well-developed theme in the explanation of the mystery is one indication that the apostle was well aware of this revelation from the beginning of Romans 9–11.[46] In fact, I would argue that the revealed knowledge that "all Israel will be saved" controls Paul's entire argument in its apology against the suspicion that "the word of God had failed" (9:6).

Just how big a surprise this revelation occasions comes to expression in Paul's final word of explanation: "For God has imprisoned all [*pantas*] in disobedience so that he may be merciful to all [*pantas*]" (11:32). Here linguistic ambiguity gives way to clarity. It may be the case that it is "impermissible to argue that 'Israel' cannot change its referent within two verses," as N. T. Wright asserts with regard to Romans 11:25 and 26,[47] but surely it is also impermissible to contend that the term *pantas* ("all") *can* change its sense in the space of but one sentence. Louw and Nida locate the adjective in two semantic domains, that of *totality* and that of *completive degree*. In the first, it denotes "the totality of any object, mass, collective, or extension—'all, every, each, whole.' "[48] In the second, it specifies "a degree of totality or completeness—'complete, completely, totally, totality.' "[49] If lexicography is ignored on the *mercy* side of the equation, then there must be exceptions to "all" on the *disobedience* side as well. But that would be unthinkable for one who charged that "all, both Jews and Greeks, are under the power of sin, as it is written: 'There is no one who is righteous, not even one' " (Rom. 3:9–10, citing Ps. 14:3). The surprise then is total. "All Israel will be saved" means precisely "all Jews," and if "all Israel" is the equivalent of the "full inclusion" of Israel and that phrase is parallel to the "full number of the Gentiles," then the mystery reveals God's mercy to everyone in the end of the story. Jews and Greeks are "imprisoned in disobedience" without exception because they are equally "under the power of sin." According to the mystery revealed to Paul, they are also the objects of divine grace. The *dianoia* of the story is true to the end.

How God will achieve this goal is through "the Deliverer" (*ho hruomenos*) who will come "out of Zion" to "banish ungodliness from Jacob" and to "take away their sins" (11:26b, citing Isa. 59:20–21 and Isa. 27:9 in a conflation).[50] The mystery here, as in 1 Corinthians 15, is mediated through Scripture.[51] The traditional identification of this agent of eschatological deliverance with Christ is hotly contested by scholars who contend that in Romans 9–11 Paul attests to a redemptive *Sonderweg* ("special way") for Israel apart from belief in Jesus.[52] On the grounds that "Christ" does not appear again in the text after Romans 10:17, it is argued that the coming "redeemer" refers simply to God. But the point is moot in view of Paul's identification of the Messiah as the one "who is over all, God blessed forever" (9:5).[53] The redeemer whom Paul expects "out of Zion" (*ek Ziōn*), in accordance with Isaiah 59:20–21, is none other than the scandalous rock God has laid "in Zion" (*en Ziōn*), in accordance with Isaiah 28:16 (Rom. 9:33). The connection between this rock and Christ is made explicit when Isaiah 28:16 is again cited with reference to the confession of Jesus as Lord (10:9–11). Yet as Wagner wisely observes:

To press for a sharp distinction between a "christological" and a "theological" reading of Isaiah 28:16 would be profoundly unfaithful to the structure of Paul's own thought, in terms of which such a dichotomy is incomprehensible. . . . For Paul, to identify the stone with Christ is not to push God off center stage; it is rather to specify more exactly the manner in which God has become a stumbling stone to some in Israel. The irreducible polyvalence of Paul's metaphor is thus rooted ultimately in his theological and christological convictions.[54]

Although Paul does not envision God achieving the divine purpose apart from the Messiah, "the end of the law" (10:4), the Messiah comes out of Israel (9:5) and thus stands in the line of those who are "the true descendants" of Abraham (9:7).[55]

With reference to the Second Gospel and yet with relevance to Romans 9–11, Professor Donald H. Juel wrote: "Mark's Gospel, *as the rest of the New Testament,* can be read as promising only if the God who plays such a major role in the story can be trusted. If God does not keep promises to Israel, there is little reason for Gentiles to expect anything."[56] Paul's prophetic sermon says the same. The sacred story of Israel is interpreted in the light of the mystery that reveals the end of the story in the salvation of "all Israel" as well as "the full number of the Gentiles." Throughout the story, from beginning to end, the *dianoia* of its narrative substructure is shaped and formed by the mercy of God, who purposes righteousness in human life and thereby the hope of salvation. As for the suspicion that "the word of God has failed," Don Juel would say that it is too early to tell, for the story is not over. Or, as Jesus puts it in Mark's Gospel, "The end is still to come" (Mark 13:7).

Notes

1. See esp. "A Disquieting Silence: The Matter of the Ending," in this volume.
2. Thomas W. Gillespie, *The First Theologians: A Study in Early Christian Prophecy* (Grand Rapids: Wm. B. Eerdmans Publishing Co., 1994).
3. Ibid., 199–235.
4. Hans Conzelmann, *1 Corinthians,* Hermeneia (Philadelphia: Fortress Press, 1975), 249, calls it "a self-contained treatise on the resurrection of the dead."
5. For stylistic transition and conclusion markers in Paul, see Jonas Holmstrand, *Markers and Meaning in Paul* (Stockholm: Almquist & Wiksell International, 1997).
6. Brendan Byrne, S.J., *Romans,* Sacra Pagina (Collegeville, MN: Liturgical Press, 1996), 282, speaks for the consensus: "These three chapters clearly do form a unit within the letter."
7. C. H. Dodd, *The Epistle of Paul to the Romans* (New York: Harper & Brothers, 1932), 148.
8. Ibid., 149.
9. An exception to this scholarly consensus is Douglas Moo, "The Theology of Romans 9–11," in *Pauline Theology,* vol. 3, ed. David M. Hay and E. Elizabeth Johnson (Minneapolis: Fortress Press, 1995), 248 n. 13, who agrees that the passage is not "an excursus or an afterthought" and reveals "many specific textual and thematic contacts with chaps. 1–8." Nonetheless, he argues, "the very number of these contacts suggests that chaps. 9–11 form a *discrete argument,* relating gener-

ally to the argument of chaps. 1–8 without being tied to any one text or theme" (emphasis mine).

10. C. E. B. Cranfield, *The Epistle to the Romans*, International Critical Commentary (Edinburgh: T. & T. Clark, 1979), 2:445.
11. For the important point that promises are "kept" rather than "fulfilled," see Nils Alstrup Dahl, "Promise and Fulfillment," in *Studies in Paul: Theology for the Early Christian Mission* (Minneapolis: Augsburg, 1977), 121–36.
12. James D. G. Dunn, *Romans 9–16* (Dallas: Word Books, 1988), 518.
13. Johannes P. Louw and Eugene A. Nida, eds., *Greek-English Lexicon of the New Testament Based on Semantic Domains* (New York: United Bible Societies, 1988), 1:345.
14. Joseph A. Fitzmyer, *Romans,* Anchor Bible (New York: Doubleday, 1992), 621.
15. Thus, Cranfield, *Epistle to the Romans*, 2:451–53 writes that "in Christ" means "with a due sense of [Paul's] accountability" and "in the Holy Spirit" is a qualification of the apostle's conscience in terms of its "being renewed and illumined by the Holy Spirit."
16. Dunn, *Romans 9–16*, 523 (emphasis mine): The *en* phrase is not local but "more instrumental ('inspired by')."
17. Victor Paul Furnish, *II Corinthians,* Anchor Bible (New York: Doubleday, 1984), 570: "More literally, 'the Christ who speaks in me,' but here the *en* ('in') is surely instrumental, 'by means of' or 'through.' Cf. especially 2:17." See also Rudolf Bultmann, *Der zweite Brief an die Korinther* (Göttingen: Vandenhoeck & Ruprecht, 1976), 244–45.
18. Richard B. Hays, *The Faith of Jesus Christ: An Investigation of the Narrative Substructure of Galatians 3:1–4:11* (Chico, CA: Scholars Press, 1983).
19. Ibid., 5.
20. Ibid., 17.
21. Ibid., 21–22.
22. Ibid., 29.
23. Richard B. Hays, *The Faith of Jesus Christ: The Narrative Substructure of Galatians 3:1–4:11*, 2nd ed. (Grand Rapids: Wm. B. Eerdmans Publishing Co., 2002), xxxv.
24. See Bruce W. Longenecker, ed., *Narrative Dynamics in Paul: A Critical Assessment* (Louisville, KY: Westminster John Knox Press, 2002), 1–16.
25. Ibid., 19–24, 45–54.
26. Robert Funk, Friedrich W. Blass, and Albert Debrunner, *A Greek Grammar of the New Testament and Other Early Christian Literature* (Chicago: University of Chicago Press, 1961), par. 460.
27. James A. Sanders, *From Sacred Story to Sacred Text* (Philadelphia: Fortress Press, 1987), 15.
28. James A. Sanders, *Torah and Canon* (Philadelphia: Fortress Press, 1972), 9–15.
29. So designated by David Noel Freedman, *The Unity of the Hebrew Bible* (Ann Arbor: University of Michigan Press, 1991), 6–7, who also appraises this Primary History as "the first and perhaps the most important and influential prose narrative ever written."
30. Robin Scroggs, "Salvation History," in *Pauline Theology*, vol. 1, ed. Jouette M. Bassler (Minneapolis: Fortress Press, 1991), 215.
31. Hays, *Faith of Jesus Christ*, 2nd ed., 23.
32. An example is Romans 9:27–28, where the apostle cites a prophecy of Isaiah from the time of the Assyrian crisis in the eighth century BCE which promises that despite the impending judgment upon Israel for its unfaithfulness, "the remnant [*hypoleimma*] shall be saved" (Isa. 10:22–23). God's merciful purpose continues its elective activity in Isaiah's time.

33. J. Ross Wagner, *Heralds of Good News: Isaiah and Paul "In Concert" in the Letter to the Romans* (Leiden: E. J. Brill, 2002), 5–19.

34. Ibid., 232.

35. Ibid., 236–37.

36. Charles H. Cosgrove, *Elusive Israel: The Puzzle of Election in Romans* (Louisville, KY: Westminster John Knox Press, 1997), 35: "Paul's 'What if . . . ?' is a hypothetical that does not assert what God has done but invites Paul's audience to consider what God has a right to do." This is correct so far as vv. 22–23 are concerned. The aorist verb *ekalesen* ("he has called") in v. 24, however, is declarative of what God has done in Paul's day by calling both Jews and Gentiles into one church.

37. An instance of hypallage, the rhetorical reversal of the expected syntactic relation between two words; *nomon dikaiosynē* is thus the equivalent of *tēn dikaiosynēn tēn ek nomou* in Rom. 10:5.

38. Byrne, *Romans*, 314. Cf. 57–60 for a succinct survey of canonical and extracanonical usage of the phrase.

39. For a critique of "covenantal nomism" as an adequate concept of first-century Judaism, see D. A. Carson, et al., eds., *Justification and Variegated Nomism*, vol. 1, *The Complexities of Second Temple Judaism* (Tübingen: Mohr Siebeck, 2001).

40. The *gar* ("for") is explanatory.

41. That the apostle is not alone in his criticism of Israel is demonstrated by David Noel Freedman, *The Nine Commandments: Uncovering the Hidden Pattern of Crime and Punishment in the Hebrew Bible* (New York: Doubleday, 2000), who points out that the Primary History of Israel, from the giving of the Mosaic law in Exodus through Kings, tells the story of the serial breaking of the "nine" commandments—"one by one, book by book—until they run out of both books and commandments" (xi).

42. Otto Hofius, " 'All Israel Will Be Saved': Divine Salvation and Israel's Deliverance in Romans 9:11," in *The Church and Israel*, Supplementary Issue, no. 1, *The Princeton Seminary Review* (1990): 34 n. 86: "The prepositional phrase *apo merous* is adnominal to *pōrōsis* and has a quantitative (numerical) sense."

43. Thus Ernst Käsemann, *Commentary on Romans* (Grand Rapids: Wm. B. Eerdmans Publishing Co., 1980), 313: "*pas Israēl* is a fixed Jewish formula" that "does not designate the sum of individuals but the people which establishes the individuality of its members."

44. N. T. Wright, *The Climax of the Covenant: Christ and the Law in Pauline Theology* (Edinburgh: T. & T. Clark, 1991), 250, contends that the context precludes "all Israel," meaning "all Jews." But the point of the mystery is not only *how* but *that* "all Israel will be saved."

45. Cranfield, *Epistle to the Romans*, 2:575–76.

46. Dunn, *Romans 9–16*, 679: "[T]he revelation of the mystery was no doubt given to Paul some time before he wrote this letter and was in part at least the reason for the fervency of his work as 'apostle to the Gentiles.' "

47. Wright, *Climax of the Covenant*, 250.

48. Louw and Nida, *Greek-English Lexicon*, 1:59.23.

49. Ibid., 1:78.44.

50. Wagner, *Heralds of the Good News*, 280, speaks of "a rather deft conflation of two texts widely separated from one another within the book of Isaiah" that nonetheless demonstrate "a remarkable correspondence . . . both in theme and in syntactical structure."

51. David E. Aune, *Prophecy in Early Christianity and the Ancient Mediterranean World* (Grand Rapids: Wm. B. Eerdmans Publishing Co., 1983), 251, notes the

first-century belief that divine mysteries were commonly concealed in, among other things, "texts such as the OT." Dunn, *Romans 9–16*, 679, points out that the means by which the mysteries were unveiled were various: "at Qumran characteristically by interpretation of scripture."

52. See Lloyd Gaston, "Israel's Misstep in the Eyes of Paul," in Karl P. Donfried, ed., *The Romans Debate* (Peabody, MA: Hendrickson Publishers, 1991), 309–26; cf. also John G. Gager, *Reinventing Paul* (Oxford: Oxford University Press, 2000), 43–75.

53. In support of the NRSV translation of this contentious text, see Cranfield, *Epistle to the Romans,* 2:464–70.

54. Wagner, *Heralds of the Good News,* 157.

55. E. Elizabeth Johnson, "Romans 9–11," in Hay and Johnson, eds., *Pauline Theology* 3:238. "Yes, the Christ is from Israel and the redeemer comes from Zion (Rom. 9:5; 11:26); Israel's salvation is without question achieved by means of Christ's death and resurrection, as is the redemption of the whole world. But for Paul those affirmations are of a piece with his claim that Abraham trusted the God who justifies the ungodly, raises the dead, and creates out of nothing, and is thus the rightful ancestor of all who believe (4:5, 17, 24)."

56. Juel, *Master of Surprise,* 144 (emphasis mine).

Chapter 8

Baptism as Change
of Lordship
Michael Welker

In his book *A Master of Surprise: Mark Interpreted,* Don Juel offers a powerful reading of Mark's account of Jesus' baptism.[1] He observes that Mark does not use the term for the "opening" of the heavens used by Luke and Matthew. "Mark uses *schizō*, which means 'tear' or 'rip' " (34; see Mark 1:10). The same term is used for the tearing of the temple curtain at the moment of Jesus' death. When the heavens are torn apart, he observes, the Spirit comes down and the voice of God declares, "You are my beloved son!" The moment the temple curtain is torn apart a pagan centurion declares, "Truly this man was God's Son!" (Mark 15:39).

Juel comments that at least for Mark, "Jesus' confirmation is a surprise, a shock; it occurs as part of a baptism of repentance for the forgiveness of sins. The Christ, the Son of God, opens his ministry where he is not expected, with outcasts in some desert place. When the expected one appears he does not meet expectations" (39). He speaks of "the one in whose ministry God comes frighteningly close" (42). These observations and insights can open an illuminating perspective on baptism in general, a perspective all too easily lost in our baptismal practices with the sweet little babies, children holding flowers and candles, and the images of Jesus' open arms and his gentle invitation: "Let the little children come to me; do not stop them" (Mark 10:14). Juel's observations on the aspects of shock and surprise in Jesus' baptism according to Mark can open our eyes to the fact that baptism is a dramatic change of lordship.

Don Juel himself was, and indeed in his readings and writings continues to be "a master of surprise" also. Matthew Skinner, a former student of his, looks back on Juel's reflections on Mark 15:39 in the classroom:

> Like a critic who delights in investigating and revealing the secrets behind magicians' illusions, Don dissected people's biblical exegesis, often wondering aloud why so much knowledge about texts and their histories prevented us from actually reading the texts. Likewise, he eagerly exposed students' hermeneutical assumptions, not necessarily to invalidate them but always to impel us to acknowledge and examine them. His sarcastic reading of the centurion's "confession" in Mark 15:39 best illustrates this practice. While reading the passion narrative aloud, he would voice "Sure this was God's son!" with acerbic scorn. He clearly enjoyed the effects of the reading as much as he believed it a faithful rendering of Mark's account. His bold interpretation sounded alarms among students, driving us to the text to examine its contours for evidence to support various readings.[2]

What are we left with in Juel's reading of Mark's account of Jesus' baptism— and maybe our own baptisms too—as a dramatic change of lordship? Or Jesus' inauguration in his baptism and death—and maybe also our own fellowship— as events constantly open to doubt, disbelief, and even sarcasm? Or is it both a change of lordship and an event open to severe doubt? And why and how so?

The biblical texts that speak about baptism certainly do not witness to an easy triumph of God. Like the inauguration of Holy Communion, which reaches into the depth of the night of betrayal—sustaining, comforting, and rescuing the disciples of Christ in the midst of their endangerment and self-endangerment under the power of sin and evil—baptism is a change of lordship that does not tell a simple story of God's victory won without labor and beyond any doubt. In the following essay, I would like to show that in different traditions the New Testament witnesses to baptism keep this strange double perspective, noticed and highlighted by Don Juel. I will try to demonstrate this with respect to John the Baptist, to Jesus' baptism, and to the voices of Paul and Luke.

THE BAPTISM OF JOHN: A REVOLUTIONARY EVENT

The baptism of John comes as a dramatic, provocative, even revolutionary event. Mark speaks of the astounding resonance of this man "crying in the wilderness": "And people from the whole Judean countryside and all the people of Jerusalem were going out to him and were baptized by him in the river Jordan, confessing their sins" (Mark 1:5). He invokes the authority of Isaiah: "See, I am sending my messenger ahead of you, who will prepare your way; the voice of one crying out in the wilderness: 'Prepare the way of the Lord, make his paths straight' " (1:2–3).

In order to understand its revolutionary impact, it is important to see that the baptism of John is a double provocation: It is a provocation for the Roman superpower present in Israel because it challenges the political status quo and prepares for the advent of a savior, and it is a provocation for the authorities of Israel's religion, particularly for the temple establishment and its taking care of sins via sacrifices. Over against these two powers, John with his proclamation points to a third and higher "way of the Lord." His baptism invites "people from the whole Judean countryside and all the people of Jerusalem" to become cleansed in order to salute the Lord and to follow his ways. Here is more than a great, if struggling, tradition, and here is more than a worldly superpower.

The proclamation of the coming Lord does not occur in a palace or in the temple, but in the wilderness. The gathering crowd does not come to welcome the Lord directly, to sing and praise and jubilee—but to repent their sins. It is important to notice that the biblical notion of sin goes far beyond personal guilt and moral weakness. It includes the suffering under a desperate situation and the inability to do anything against it. Rome is too mighty and the law of God and the temple are simply not powerful enough. The Lord himself has to come.

The next move of surprise in Mark is that—although John seems to set the stage for Jesus so impressively—Jesus does not go on stage but rather joins the crowd. By asking to be baptized himself he joins his fellow humans who ask and seek and cry for God's presence in the middle of earthly regulations, laws, and powers. He joins those who want to discern their entanglement in earthly rules and powers—partly helpless, partly deserved—who above all would love to live under the rule and power of God, under God's righteousness and justice, under God's guidance. Come, repent and be cleansed! In this situation, John's baptism comes as a revolutionary message: The Lord is near, prepare the way for him. But then the Lord they meet joins them in their poverty and frailty. This change of lordship is vulnerable and open to doubt, disbelief, and even derision. What a dramatic surprise.

JESUS' BAPTISM AND HIS AUTHORIZATION FROM "ON HIGH"

The stories in the New Testament of Jesus' baptism speak in more or less dramatic and violent ways about the "opening of the heavens." For the biblical traditions, the opening of the heavens is not just an event in nature. To be sure, sunlight and water, warmth and cold come from heaven. Natural powers from "on high" shape all life in decisive ways. But for biblical thinking, "the heavens" are also the place from which normative cultural and historical powers determine life on earth. Powers of the past and of the future are seen to be assembled "in heaven" or "in the heavens." Like the sun and rain, storm and hail, and other natural forces, these powers "overcome" life on earth in ways that are very hard to predict and most difficult, if not impossible, to control, to direct, and to manipulate. When Jesus in his own baptism joins the people from Judea and Jerusalem who seek cleansing and repentance, the heavenly realm of power opens upon him, or becomes torn apart. The unconditionally good, creative, life-supporting, and saving power of God, the Holy Spirit, descends on him. He becomes empowered by the divine power par excellence.

The fact that John's provocative baptism is thus confirmed is further strengthened by the following: The cult and the sacrifices in the temple of Jerusalem, now challenged and replaced by John's baptism, came to their annual climax on Yom Kippur, the great day of general atonement. Only on this day was the name of the Lord pronounced. Only on this day did the high priest go behind the temple curtain to bring about atonement for the sanctuary and for all of Israel through a blood rite. Only on this day did the high priest step in front of the ark of the covenant, the place of the encounter of heaven and earth, the encounter between God and the world. About the preparation of the high priest for the day of the direct encounter with God Leviticus 16:4 says: "He shall put on the holy linen tunic. . . . He shall bathe his body in water."

The story of Jesus' baptism, the story about the transparency between the heavens and the earth, about the direct encounter with God and God's powers from on high clearly alludes to Yom Kippur, to the great Day of Atonement. But no longer are this feast and this day and no longer are the high priest and the temple the temporal and spatial instances of this great encounter. The dramatic opening of the heavens and the encounter with God's power and God's voice occur after Jesus bathes his body in the water of Jordan. The second New Testament story about Jesus' authorization "from above," the story about Jesus' "transfiguration" (Mark 9:2–10 par.), obviously also alludes to Yom Kippur when it says that Jesus' "clothes became dazzling white." Cleansing bath, holy garment, dazzling white—in both cases the high priest and Yom Kippur seem to be associated. Does this mean that the theophany and the authorization of Jesus by the Holy Spirit and the Word of God point to a change of the religious authorities and of the representative of God?

These perspectives on baptism can be met with reserve or even sarcasm. Christian supersessionism, the ugly and brutal ideology of the substitution of the church for Israel, easily comes to mind. As soon as one imagines Israel's struggle against the Roman Empire in Jesus' days, the ambivalence over against this change of authority and lordship may even increase. Do we here just witness one religion pushing its key figure in the place of the other religion's main cultic event and representative? The continuity of the God of Israel and Jesus' stepping down to the repenting and confessing people in search of God help ease the deep irritation. But it is by no means easy to understand the high priest imagery and the message: Through baptism you are all brought into Jesus' place as witnessed to by Mark; you all become directly authorized by God's Word and by the power of the Holy Spirit. Even today, Christianity itself is divided over these promises and perspectives. Do we believe in the holy priesthood of all who are baptized? "Sure they are . . ."?

". . . BURIED WITH CHRIST BY BAPTISM INTO DEATH" (ROM. 6:4): BAPTISM TEARS US AWAY FROM THE POWERS OF THIS WORLD

To become the child of the creative and saving God through baptism does not mean entering into a cozy religious relation with my "inner other" or with my romantic religious dream partner. Against many tendencies in current church life toward self-secularization and self-banalization, this has to be made clear time and again. The creative, sustaining, saving, and ennobling God establishes a relation to us through baptism, by guiding us through death into life. In a way that sounds very strange and appalling to most ears, this is thus expressed by Paul:

> Therefore we have been buried with him [Christ] by baptism into death, so that, just as Christ was raised from the dead by the glory of the Father, so we too might walk in newness of life. For if we have been united with him in a death like his, we will certainly be united with him in a resurrection like his. We know that our old self was crucified with him so that the body of sin might be destroyed, and we might no longer be enslaved to sin. (Rom. 6:4–6)

For the current consciousness, even a religiously literate one, these remarks of Paul's are very hard to take, particularly since they seem to express a certain hostility toward the bodily existence, a hostility we hardly want to share. In any case, they seem to stand in a deep conflict with the practice of child baptism. Who could dare to associate the sweet newborn babies with sin, cross, and death? Who could dare to name them "our old self" that should go, even symbolically, through death in order to gain the postbaptismal relation to God and to enjoy the change of lordship? Acceptance as a child of God seems in accord with child baptism. "Buried with Christ by baptism into death," however, seems to mirror a sinister theology that most people would rather like to dismiss, at best leaving it to mature and religiously experienced persons who are able to work it through.

However, behind Paul's words there is not only a deep understanding of the saving work of Christ but also the insight that the powers and ties of the world, including our bodily existence, can become forces that enslave us, forces that bring us under the powers of sin and evil, that distance us from God and from the life intended for us by God in the divine creativity and grace. Paul and other New Testament traditions therefore understand baptism as a symbolic act, full of indication, by which we are freed from these powers, ties, and bondages. God wants us to have a share in God's own life, in the divine and eternal life. In baptism we symbolically go with Christ through the abyss of death in order to become prepared for our participation in his resurrection; already here and now we become involved in God's eternal life. The deuteropauline Letter to the Colossians sees this similarly to Paul: "When you were buried with him [Christ] in baptism, you were also raised with him through faith in the power of God, who raised him from the dead" (Col. 2:12).

Baptism is an act of renewal, an act in which we become children of God and are drawn away—indeed, torn away—from the principalities and powers of this world. This act can certainly happen at any phase of a human life. There is no good reason why it should not happen and be celebrated at the beginning of a human life. Already at its beginning this earthly and finite life should become connected, involved, and kept in the eternal life—the life with God, in God, and from God. This life with God, in God, and from God cannot be accessed and gained by education or maturity, nor through a conscious decision and attitude of faith or the best spiritual knowledge and practice. This entering into the new life with God is connected with such a radical disconnection from the principalities and powers of this world that only the talk about death—indeed, death on the cross—can capture the radicality and uniqueness of this change of lordship.

Jesus Christ was crucified in the name of religion, in the name of two laws (the Roman and the Jewish law), in the name of politics, even world politics and in the name of public opinion. Even his disciples and followers leave him and flee. At the cross, the total lostness of the world under the power of sin is revealed. Jews and Gentiles, friends and foes, residents and foreigners—the whole representative world is under this power of sin. Only a new creation out of chaos can overcome this situation.

The baptism in the name of Jesus Christ and in the name of the triune God enacts and witnesses such a radical change in human life. Through baptism we become filled by the saving powers of God that create new life in the midst of and out of death, despair, and chaos.

"YOU WILL RECEIVE POWER WHEN THE HOLY SPIRIT HAS COME UPON YOU; AND YOU WILL BE MY WITNESSES . . . TO THE ENDS OF THE EARTH" (ACTS 1:8): BAPTISM WITH THE HOLY SPIRIT ELEVATES US TO PARTICIPANTS IN CHRIST'S LORDSHIP

The baptism with water by John is a preparation for the presence of Jesus Christ in whom "all flesh shall see the salvation of God" (Luke 3:6). Jesus, over whom the heavens open or are torn apart, on whom the Spirit descends and who is designated "Son of God," does himself not baptize with water but rather "with the Holy Spirit" (Mark 1:8 par.). He gives the power of the Spirit that awakens faith, love, hope, and many other spiritual gifts in human beings, thus working against their enslavement by the principalities and powers of this world, their endangerment and self-endangerment under sin and evil.

Baptism with the Holy Spirit is not a numinous or even a fantastic and magic enterprise. It is shaped by Jesus' personhood and presence, by his proclamation and his life. The baptized persons become shaped by the identity of Jesus, by his life, his cross, and his resurrection. Therefore, they call themselves "Christians." They take on Christ's name. Baptized by the Spirit, endowed with the spiritual gifts, Christians participate in Christ's power and reign. They are "sent" and they are granted a "missionary existence." This missionary existence finds expression in their witness, teaching, festive living together, loving care, help and support, and many other forms of life. Through the sacraments, through teaching and their witness, Christians remind themselves and others of the danger that all good norms and institutions, even religion and their very own faith and spiritual life, can fall prey to the power of sin. The baptism in the name of Jesus, the orientation on his life, and proclamation and the remembrance of his cross and resurrection counter this danger time and again.

According to the first chapter of Acts, Jesus appears before his disciples during the forty days after his resurrection. He speaks of the coming reign of God and asks them in their table fellowship to wait in Jerusalem for the pouring of the Holy Spirit: "John baptized with water, but you will be baptized with the Holy Spirit not many days from now. . . . You will receive power when the Holy Spirit has come upon you; and you will be my witnesses in Jerusalem, in all Judea and Samaria, and to the ends of the earth" (Acts 1:5, 8). Baptism is not a saving act or a change of lordship that just restores past states of affairs. Those who are baptized are enabled to grow in faith, to become Christ's witnesses "to the ends of the earth."

You will be my witnesses! You will become bearers of the Holy Spirit! You will be a new creation! You will participate in a new life, in eternal life! These are different perspectives on the same event, inaugurated in and through baptism. A great event of sustenance, rescue, and ennoblement occurs here. The human beings who are baptized are not only brought under a new lordship, under the lordship of Christ. They become participants, bearers, mediators, representatives of this lordship. In their fragile and finite lives, they are to witness to this lordship, this new and eternal reign of God. This, of course, opens God's mighty working among the creatures to all sorts of confusion, skepticism, and derision. The surprise of this freeing and ennobling lordship is not to be experienced without voices of disbelief and doubt.

The power of the resurrection does not annihilate the incarnation of Christ. It rather draws those who bear witness to it deeper and deeper into his life incarnate. The heavenly seed goes into the ground. More and more human lives become connected with his life and presence. Through baptism they are not only elevated and glorified and empowered by the great gifts from "on high." Through baptism they are also drawn into the labor and the misery of his earthly life, even buried with Christ into death.

Don Juel saw these aspects of the gospel's message. He saw both its comforting and its haunting dimensions. He saw the whole range of possible reactions to the Christ event in the voice of the pagan centurion: "Truly this man was God's Son!" / "Sure, this was God's son!" He had sensitivity for the actual and the potential witnesses from the right and from the left side of God, from on high and from the deep. This opened to him and this has opened to his students, colleagues, and readers a great sensitivity to the many ways the Holy Spirit works through the witness of the Bible and the life of the church. This also gave him a great sensitivity to the frailty and the dignity of human voices echoing what the centurion had to say when the temple curtain was torn apart.

Notes

1. Donald H. Juel, *A Master of Surprise: Mark Interpreted* (Minneapolis: Fortress Press, 1994). This book will be quoted in the text with page numbers in parentheses.
2. Matthew L. Skinner, "Marking a Life: A Tribute to Don Juel," *inSpire* 8, no. 1 (2003): 33.

Chapter 9

The End of the Beginning: Genesis 50

Patrick D. Miller

The beginning has to come to an end at some point. The biblical story has a clear beginning, and that beginning has a clear ending in the final chapter of the book of Genesis (= the book of Beginning). It is the end of the era of the ancestors of Israel. But the beginning is much larger than that, for the beginning that Genesis depicts is the beginning of everything, the world and all that is therein. There is no abrupt conclusion to the universal history recounted in the first eleven chapters of Genesis. There is clearly a movement from Genesis 11 into the beginning of Genesis 12 that may be recognized as a movement from universal history into the story of God's way with Abraham and his seed. That movement, however, is already anticipated in Genesis 11 with the recounting of the line of Terah, which is itself a continuation of the preceding genealogies of Noah and his sons, more specifically, the genealogy of Shem.[1] So there is no clear ending to the story of the creation of the world and its creatures, the beginning of culture, languages, and nations. There is a kind of seamless mix of genealogy and narrative until one realizes as one moves further into the book that the narrative now dominates. The focus of attention continues to be the family whose genealogy began in Genesis 1–11, but now it is much more concentrated, and God's attention is directed toward the family of Noah-Shem-Abraham, though the reader is told early on that that focus has to do with God's intentions in and with the whole of creation and humanity (Gen. 12:1–4a).

THE BEGINNING IS OVER

When one comes to the end of Genesis, however, there are various ways in which the experience of ending is manifest even as the story goes on. Genesis 50 serves to effect the ending even as it leaves the door open to the future.[2] The most obvious and explicit dimension of ending is in the elaborate report of the death of Jacob, which occurs at the end of chapter 49, and then in the extended report of the mourning, embalming, and burial of Jacob in the ancestral burial ground at Machpelah, back in Canaan. When one adds the final blessing of Jacob upon his sons (Gen. 49:1–27) to this report of his death and burial that begins near the end of chapter 49 and carries through much of chapter 50, it is clear that great emphasis is being placed upon the end of Jacob's life. What is being signaled by this extended report on Jacob's end is the end of an era, more specifically the end of the era of the ancestors of Israel. In 50:24, Joseph refers to the land that God swore to "Abraham, Isaac, and Jacob." This is the first time that the three names occur together in Scripture, but they become a kind of cliché for the ancestors and their era in Israel's history. Thus, the God who continues on in the biblical story is henceforth known as the God of "Abraham, Isaac, and Jacob" (e.g., Exod. 3:6, 15–16; 4:5; 6:2), the covenant is known as a covenant made with Abraham, Isaac, and Jacob (Exod. 2:24), and the promised land is the land that the Lord swore to "Abraham, Isaac, and Jacob" (Exod. 6:8; 33:1; Num. 32:11; Deut. 1:8; 6:10). The time of the three ancestors is now over, and the death and burial of the last one, narrated at some length and in much detail, reinforces the end of the beginning.

That ending in death is then underscored further by the last verses of Genesis 50, which record the charge and death and burial of Joseph (vv. 22–26). A large part of this last chapter, therefore, has to do with the end in the literal sense of the death of the ancestors. Joseph's place is somewhat ambiguous. He does not belong to the triad of ancestors, yet he is one of Jacob's children. His disappearance from the scene, however, is reflected not only in his death but in his disappearance from the tribal contingent of Jacob's sons in favor of his own sons, Ephraim and Manasseh. The ancestors are gone by the end of Genesis 50, and the twelve sons and tribes are left. The beginning is over. The story continues now, without end, into the story of these twelve tribes and their families, and their land, and their seed. While some weight is placed upon different ones of these, judgments in fact already having been made about some of them (see Gen. 49), the beginning is clearly over and the rest of the story now goes on, without Joseph as either part of the ancestral triad or as a tribe.

JOSEPH'S DEATH AS OPENING TO THE FUTURE

The great weight of this final chapter is on the end of the beginning. But there are also indications that even in the end, the door is open to a new beginning. That is evident already in the elaborate account of the taking of Jacob back to the ancestral grave in the promised land, an anticipation of Israel's return. As Leon Kass has put it:

> Thanks to Jacob's forethought, his funeral becomes the occasion for an enor-
> mous pilgrimage from Egypt to the Promised Land, described in the last chap-
> ter of Genesis—a prefiguring of the Exodus four hundred years later. Joseph
> has gotten Israel into Egypt and inadvertently taught Pharaoh how to keep
> them there. It will take Moses, with plenty of divine assistance, to get them
> out. Jacob will die trying. His final efforts, although insufficient to effect more
> than a temporary physical return, are not politically or spiritually fruitless.[3]

The opening to the future at the end of the beginning is evident especially in the final section (50:22–26). There is a kind of ending in verse 21, a reso-lution that concludes the Joseph story (see below), but the death of Joseph is as much an opening as it is an ending. The less explicit indication of the open-ing to the future is in the embalming and keeping of the bones of Joseph so that there is no final settlement in Egypt. This is the only place in the Old Tes-tament where there is reference to embalming. The custom of embalming, which may be accounted for in this context by the Egyptian setting and is already anticipated in the first part of the chapter with the embalming of Jacob, is much more than a particular custom coming into play because of the setting. The embalming of Jacob makes it appear that Joseph is simply following well-known Egyptian practice. The payoff, however, is in the *second* embalming, which is much more than simply a custom. It is the preservation of the bones of Joseph so that there is no burial of the Israelite ancestors in Egypt. There is a future for this people, but it is not in Egypt even if Egypt seems at the moment like the best place to be. The embalmed and preserved Joseph is an indication there can be no permanent settlement in Egypt. The importance of that will become more evident when we look at verses 15–21 in light of the whole of the Joseph story.

The more obvious opening of Genesis 50 to the future, to an era beyond the end of the ancestors, is in the explicit words of Joseph to his brothers as he nears death. His brief speech to them is in two parts:

> I am about to die; but God will surely come to you, and bring you up out of
> this land to the land that he swore to Abraham, to Isaac, and to Jacob. (v. 24)

> When God comes to you, you shall carry up my bones from here. (v. 25)

The text forms a clear bridge to the exodus, both in its content and in the specific language that it uses.[4] The formula "bring you up" (*ʿālâ*) is one of the primary technical terms for the exodus delivery and is used over forty times to refer to that event. Furthermore, Joseph uses the same verb for the brothers carrying his bones with them when that time comes. His participation in the exodus from Egypt is anticipated beyond his death. So Joseph's death is the end of Joseph and the ancestors, but it is not the end. With all the focus and weight of the text on Jacob's embalmed body being carried back to Canaan for burial at the grave of the ancestors in Machpelah, there is surely some self-consciousness about the fact that Joseph does *not* ask to be taken back to Canaan for burial, and that is not done. The story of the ancestors is at an end. The door to the future has to do with the "children of Israel/Jacob," and Joseph, who is one of those, will be among them. The bridge to the book of Exodus and the deliverance from Egyptian slavery is connected at this point when Moses not only carries Joseph's bones out as the people leave Egypt but quotes Joseph's charge in doing so (Exod. 13:19).

Joseph's announcement and subsequent charge repeat a second verb that has roots in the exodus context. The NRSV translation of the verb *pāqad* as "come to you" is a very bland and somewhat deceptive translation in that it conceals its significant nuance. While the verb is indeed often translated as "visit," its force is "to pay attention," "to notice." But that is never simply the action of a neutral observer; it is a regard that is either positive and caring or negative and judging. In this context, it is anticipatory of the future plight of the Israelites. The emphatic construction in verse 24, "God will surely take notice of you," implies that in the future this family will be in dire straits but God will take note of that and deliver them. Joseph's words thus do not simply imply a future for his brothers beyond his death. The door to the future that is present in his words has an ominous dimension to it but also a gracious one. His words *imply* a predicament, but they *promise* divine care and attention.

What is signaled here becomes thematic in the book of Exodus. The specific and compassionate attention of God is what evokes the whole exodus event. The verb *pāqad* appears twice in contexts that make this point:

> Go and assemble the elders of Israel, and say to them, "The LORD, the God of your ancestors, the God of Abraham, of Isaac, and of Jacob, has appeared to me, saying: I have given heed [*pāqad*] to you and to what has been done to you in Egypt. I declare that I will bring you up out of the misery of Egypt, to the land of the Canaanites, the Hittites, the Amorites, the Perizzites, the Hivites, and the Jebusites, a land flowing with milk and honey. (Exod. 3:16–17)

> The people believed; and when they heard that the LORD had given heed [*pāqad*] to the Israelites and that he had seen their misery, they bowed down and worshiped. (Exod. 4:31)

The evocation of the delivery from Egypt out of the Lord's taking notice and caring is not confined to these two uses of the verb *pāqad*. The beginning of the exodus from Egypt really begins with these words that precede the call of Moses:

> After a long time the king of Egypt died. The Israelites groaned under their
> slavery, and cried out. Out of the slavery their cry for help rose up to God.
> God heard their groaning, and God remembered his covenant with Abra-
> ham, Isaac, and Jacob. God looked upon the Israelites and God took notice
> of them. (Exod. 2:23–25)

Furthermore, twice in the call of Moses the Lord tells of having observed the
plight of the Israelites and of having heard their cry (3:7, 9).

Later, in an oracle to the prophet Jeremiah, the Lord promises to take note
(*pāqad*) of the Judean exiles when their time of captivity is over and bring them
back to the land. In the Psalter and elsewhere, the verb *pāqad* becomes part of
the petition that the person in need prays to the Lord, who is merciful and compassionate (Pss. 80:14 [Heb. 80:15]; 106:4), and in Psalm 8:4 (Heb. 8:5) the
psalmist sees the attention God pays to human beings as a marvelous and astonishing fact.[5] The verb even seems to appear in an ancient Hebrew inscription as
a cry for God's attention and help.[6]

JOSEPH AND HIS BROTHERS: RESOLUTION AS
ENDING AND BEGINNING

Between the death, embalming, and burial of Jacob (Gen. 50:1–14) and the
death and embalming of Joseph (vv. 22–26), between the closing of the door on
the ancestral era and the door left open to the future, there is a signal event, which
is itself a crucial piece of ending that also opens things up in different ways. In
verses 15–21, we hear of the resolution of the conflict between Joseph and his
brothers, a conflict that turns out to have been much more than they intended
or recognized, though it was also all that they intended and recognized:[7]

> When Joseph's brothers saw that their father was dead, they said, "What if
> Joseph were to bear a grudge against us and return to us in full all the wrong
> that we did to him!" So they sent word to Joseph, "Before his death, your
> father commanded: 'Thus you shall say to Joseph: Ah now, forgive, I pray
> you, your brothers' transgression and their sin; they indeed did you wrong!'
> Now, therefore, please forgive the transgression of the servants of the God
> of your father." Joseph wept when they spoke to him. Then came his broth-
> ers also and fell before him, and said, "Here we are as your servants." But
> Joseph said to them, "Do not be afraid, for am I in the place of God? Now
> *you* reckoned to do wrong to me; *God* reckoned it for good so as to do as he
> has done this day to preserve alive a great people. Now, therefore, do not be
> afraid; *I* will provide for you and your little ones." And he reassured them,
> speaking kindly to them. (author's trans.)

The death of Jacob has not quite brought the beginning to an end. Indeed, if
this text is taken seriously, the father's death has heightened the primary tension
and conflict of the Joseph story, namely, the conflict between Joseph and his
brothers and the effects of that on both parties.

Family Conflict Threatens the Future

The conflict between brothers is a familiar dimension of the story of the beginning, reaching all the way back to Cain but evident especially in the conflict between Jacob and Esau. If the story is taken at its literal level, Joseph and his brothers know of a significant precedent for their long-lasting grudge in the immediately preceding generation. The one other place where the verb *śātam*, "bear a grudge," appears in Genesis is in the report that Esau bore a grudge against Jacob for stealing the blessing (Gen. 27:41). The animosity in that instance leads to the desire to kill Jacob and the eventual flight of Jacob to his uncle's home in order to escape Esau's revenge. The "dwelling together of brothers in unity" (Ps. 133:1) is one of the primary biblical themes, one that begins at the beginning and runs through the biblical story. The only possibility for this family to be the means of God's blessing among the families of the earth (Gen. 12:3) is if they are able to survive in this world, which means finding a way of living together. The door to the future is threatened by the fratricidal instinct, the hostilities that begin between brother and brother(s). Closure of this era cannot happen if the possibility of the children of Jacob destroying each other is not precluded. That the brothers' fear of Joseph is a misapprehension does not mean the matter can be ignored any more than in the case of Jacob and Esau. In both generations, brotherly harm has been done; the endangerment of the family's survival beyond fraternal conflict is a real issue. There is a sense therefore in which any future beyond the ancestral era, beyond the beginning and the story of Abraham, Isaac, and Jacob, is seen to depend upon the capacity of this generation of brothers, the generation that will define the future,[8] to live together. The beginning does not end until the threat, or, in this case, the fearfulness before an unreal threat, is tended to. That is what these verses are about.

The problem between Joseph and his brothers, however, would seem to have been resolved back in Genesis 45:1–15 when Joseph first made himself known to them. Indeed, his response earlier is not far different from what happens here: Joseph weeps, reassures the brothers, lets them know that he means them no harm and that, on the contrary, he is there to take care of them in the difficult circumstances of the famine in the land. What has happened to create fear in the hearts of Joseph's brothers after this earlier reassurance?

It would seem to be the ending of the ancestral era. The precipitating cause is laid out in the text: "When Joseph's brothers saw that their father was dead . . ." The new thing in the picture is the death of Jacob. It is as if the brothers believe the only thing that has stood between them and Joseph's revenge has been their father. With him out of the picture, there is nothing holding Joseph back, and he has the power to do them in very easily.

Misreading the Past and Present

That sense of Joseph's power or status is a key aspect of the way in which the brothers approach him. Their response is revealing. Their first move is to play the only card they have, which is Joseph's very evident love for their father. So they send a message indicating that before he died Jacob left word for Joseph that he should forgive the brothers the wrong they did to him long ago. There is certainly no indication that Jacob in fact left such a message. It may well be a pure construct on the part of the brothers, and at least some of its specific formulation would seem to suggest that (see below). Their assumption is that the only reason Joseph has not come at them before now is because he knew what that would do to his father. That assumption turns out to be a gross misreading of Joseph's intentions and at a deeper level of the whole situation, a misreading that Joseph's response corrects on the way to a resolution of the long-standing tension and conflict.

A further significant misreading of Joseph is indicated by the way the brothers shape the (presumed) paternal request and their actions and words when they come to him. The father's request begins, "Ah now, forgive, I pray you," a somewhat stilted translation of the very succinct and rhyming sequence 'ānnā' śā' nā' (v. 17a). The two particles surrounding the imperative śā' (forgive) are clearly strong particles of entreaty, seeking to give weight and urgency to the request. But there is more going on than simply that, or at least more is implied in the particular particle 'ānnā'. The particle occurs thirteen times in the Old Testament. In every other use, it is a particle of entreaty addressed to God. Only this instance is an exception. But is it really an exception? While it is difficult to conceive of Jacob addressing his son as if he were God, the language and actions of the brothers following this request tend to suggest that that is exactly how *they* regard Joseph. They identify themselves twice as "servants/slaves" ('ăbādîm), once as "servants of the God of your father" and once as "your servants." The juxtaposition of those two expressions creates a resonance and some confusion. Are these two different statuses, or is it that they are servants of God who now in some sense stands before them in all his power in the form of Joseph? A further confirmation of that possibility is in their falling down before Joseph (v. 18). There is nothing unusual about that. Joseph is in some sense a ruler or governor (śālît, Gen. 42:6), and they have prostrated themselves before him on each occasion of their encounter in Egypt (Gen. 42:6; 43:26). But such practice has served to reinforce their sense of Joseph's power and control of the situation, his capacity to do whatever he pleases.

If the reader of the story is not sufficiently aware of what is going on in the words and actions of the brothers, Joseph certainly is. That is consistent, of course, with his role in the story throughout, his wisdom and discernment when all around him are clueless or acceding to his greater wisdom.[9] In this instance, Joseph says directly and bluntly to his brothers, "Am I in the place of God?" That is, he recognizes immediately all the indications that they are treating him as God or, to use Joseph's own language, as standing in the place of God. This misunderstanding is at the heart of the story, and its clarification brings about resolution, the ending of the beginning and the possibility of an opening to the future for this family.

The Hiddenness of God's Providence

There is one other feature of the text that indicates the brothers regard Joseph as in some sense in the place of God, and that brings us to the heart of the matter, to the problem that has to be dealt with before the beginning can come to an end. It is the brothers' wrong against their brother, the *rā'â* they have done to him, which they now confess as a sin and a transgression. The problem that needs resolving is not the threat of Joseph's revenge but the reality they fear will evoke that revenge: the *rā'â*.[10] The language is vivid. The fear of the brothers is that Joseph will pay them back—to put it literally, turn the wrong back against them. What they seek is forgiveness of the wrong or, to put it literally once more, a lifting or taking up of the *rā'â*. It is as if the wrong sits there, a tangible, vibrant reality. Something is going to be done with it. It cannot be ignored forever. Either Joseph will throw it back at them with great vehemence,[11] or he will lift it up— the literal meaning of the Hebrew verb *nāśā'*, properly translated as "forgive"— and take it away. These are the presumed or "natural" alternatives when human beings wrong each other. The wronged one will either wrong back—and probably with greater vehemence—or will let the wrong go. Joseph has the power to do both things as far as his brothers are concerned. Their only hope is that a father's love will bend the power in a particular direction.

The brothers assume that the love of Jacob and the power of Joseph are the operative factors in this situation. Joseph lets them know that the love and power at work to deal with the wrong are of another order. He responds in neither way they had anticipated. He does not deal with the *rā'â* as they feared, but neither does he do as they requested and hoped. In this story, revenge for wrong and forgiveness of wrong are not the only options. Rather, Joseph's response is an indication of what the story has made clear in Genesis 45: The *rā'â* of the brothers has already been dealt with. That is the point of the crucial and climactic verses 20–21. In his response, Joseph discerns what is going on and what role each of the parties plays or has played in the larger scheme of things. The brothers assume that the issue of the wrong is between Joseph and them. Joseph lets them know that there is a third party involved when "sin" and "transgression" have taken place.[12] His challenge to the ways in which his brothers put him in the place of God has one more target: the assumption that it is up to Joseph to forgive the wrong. But forgiveness of sin and transgression is a divine act.[13] Rarely in the Old Testament is forgiveness an act of a human being toward another human being.[14] But Joseph goes further than simply informing them that it is not his place to forgive sin. Neither will he turn the wrong back against them. The *rā'â*, the wrong, has been dealt with by God in another way altogether. There is no escaping or ignoring the wrong. That has happened, and Joseph has suffered greatly from it—sold into slavery, taken to a foreign land, put in prison, cut off from family. All of that is real and cannot be glossed over. Sin and wrong have happened. What the brothers reckoned or planned to do to Joseph they did—and to his great harm.

There has been, however, another reckoning or intentionality at work in all this. "*You* intended wrong"—that's a fact; now here's another fact—"*God* intended it for good so as to do as he has done this day to preserve alive a great people."[15] The bad, the wrong, the harm is there. But alongside that is another reality, a good, which is manifest and fully visible in the way in which Joseph's presence in Egypt has worked to keep a lot of people alive in the face of a great famine—even his own family from whom he had been taken away. In the providence of God, the intended and accomplished wrong has become a powerful good.

The assumption that wrong can only be dealt with by some form of reprisal or some form of removal, by revenge/judgment or forgiveness, is set aside in this story. It is thus an important report about one of the critical features of the human story, the reality of sin and more particularly the sin of brother against brother. What does God do about sin? The alternatives of judgment or forgiveness are not the only ones. Neither thing happens here. The brothers do not get their wish, but they also do not see their fear realized. Joseph neither forgives nor condemns but sees the matter in a wholly different manner. As the beginning started with an account of God's creative and providential work, it ends with another instance of that providential intention of God. Once more humankind is provided for in the most literal sense possible—food and sustenance to keep persons alive. And that has happened by God's mysterious reckoning of the brother's evil to God's good.

The Mystery of God's Providence

One must be careful at this point. Gerhard von Rad has pointed to the sparseness of Joseph's formulation. There is no conjunction between the two statements "You intended harm" and "God intended it for good." We are not really told how these two contrary analyses of reality can fit together. If there were a conjunction here, one would have some leeway to understand or propose how the two clauses relate to each other—for example, "You intended harm . . . *but* God intended it for good." That is, God worked out a providential good over against the wrong of the brothers. Or perhaps a conjunction might suggest the possibility that God's providential care happened somehow in and through the harmful event, through or by means of the harm that the brothers did. However we might speculate about the way in which God does good with the brother's harm, the text remains mysteriously open and does not try to provide some way of harmonizing these contrary facts. Gerhard von Rad's formulation perhaps says it as well as can be expressed:

> [T]his guidance of God is only asserted; nothing more explicit is said about the way in which God incorporated man's evil into his saving activity. The two statements "you meant . . ." and "God meant . . ." are ultimately very unyielding side by side. . . .
> The reader must remember, however, that Joseph's statement in ch. 50.20 expresses something extreme by its downright abrupt separation of

divine and human activity. It relegates God's activity to a radical secrecy, distance, and impossibility of recognition.[16]

But because God has dealt with the brother's *rāʿâ,* even if not in one of the expected modes of response, Joseph, who is the wise one able to discern what is going on, draws the proper conclusion (v. 21). It is twofold: The brothers need not be afraid, and they and others will be provided for. That is what God's good is all about. The absence of forgiveness does not mean that the brothers must remain fearful about what Joseph might do. In God's good, Joseph's part is to be the one who brings that good about. Joseph's "now therefore" (v. 21) thus corrects the "now therefore" of his brothers (v. 18). The logic of divine providence counters the restricted logic of human reason. The outcome is reassurance and comfort rather than fear.

Walter Brueggemann has called attention to the repeated *ʾal tîrāʾ,* "do not be afraid" (vv. 19, 21).[17] It is the characteristic "oracle of salvation," the divine response to the human cry or prayer for help.[18] As it is elsewhere spoken by the prophet or by the priest, here it is spoken by the wise man, appropriately so inasmuch as he is the one who discerns how God has dealt with the cause of the brother's fearful petition and is the one whom they perceive as a threat. God's voice is as strangely absent from the Joseph story as God's providence is mysteriously present. The reassuring word is given through Joseph as, indeed, are all the interpretive and revelatory words of this story. Joseph is brother, interpreter, and provider. He is the future only through his sons and his bones. Joseph now closes the door on the beginning; his brothers and his children will carry the story into the future.

The Open Door

The "great people" (v. 20) whom Joseph preserves alive is an intimation of that future, for the presupposition of the exodus story is the fulfillment in the brothers and their descendants of the creation promise to be fruitful and multiply and fill the earth (Gen. 1:28). Exodus 1 tells how that promise has come to pass, but its fulfillment has not produced blessing. When Joseph is gone, the "great people" become perceived as a threat to the Egyptians, and the "good" that God provided through Joseph's leadership in Egypt is turned into wrong. The land of provision has become a place of exile. It would seem that we are back where we began, and indeed we are—in a kind of strange reversal. Now the good that God intended stands alongside the harm that Pharaoh does against the Israelites. The door that remains open at the end of Genesis leads into darkness, into oppression, misery, and suffering. Perhaps this time, the God whose involvement in this story is so mysterious—discernable only to the wise and understanding Joseph—will have to become more directly, personally, and compassionately involved. The end of the beginning suggests that will be the case, that God will indeed take notice of this "great people" (v. 24).

Notes

1. As many have observed, one might make a better case for the closure of the Primeval History with the end of Gen. 8 than the end of Gen. 11, but even there the story continues quite directly in Gen. 9 without any literary conclusion at the end of Gen. 8.

2. The metaphor of the door as a feature of narrative ending is central to the interpretive strategy of Donald Juel in his interpretation of the ending of Mark. The ambiguity inherent in the metaphor is crucial. The door may be a bar to the future or it may provide an opening into the future. The way in which Gen. 50 provides a door that is both shut and open is an avenue into the interpretation of this crucial chapter that Juel's strategy has led me to see and to describe in these pages.

3. Leon Kass, *The Beginning of Wisdom: Reading Genesis* (New York: Free Press, 2003), 638.

4. See Claus Westermann, *Genesis 37–50: A Commentary* (Minneapolis: Augsburg, 1986), 209.

5. In Job 7:17–18, however, this attention is experienced in a highly negative and unpleasant fashion. On the interplay of Ps. 8 and Job 7 at the point of God's attention, see P. D. Miller, "What Is a Human Being? The Anthropology of Scripture," in *What about the Soul? Neuroscience and Christian Anthropology*, ed. Joel Green (Nashville: Abingdon Press, 2004), 63–73.

6. See P. D. Miller, "Psalms and Inscriptions," in *Congress Volume: Vienna 1980*, Supplements to Vetus Testamentum 32 (Leiden: E. J. Brill, 1980), 330–32. This essay was reprinted in Miller, *Israelite Religion and Biblical Theology: Collected Essays*, Journal for the Study of the Old Testament Supplement Series 267 (Sheffield: Sheffield Academic Press, 2000), 228–31.

7. On this part of the chapter, see esp. Gerhard von Rad, *Genesis*, Old Testament Library (Philadelphia: Westminster Press, 1972), 431–40; and Walter Brueggemann, "Genesis 50:15–21: A Theological Exploration," in *Congress Volume, Salamanca, 1983*, Supplements to Vetus Testamentum 36 (Leiden: E. J. Brill, 1985), 40–53.

8. As their name indicates: *běnê ya'ăqōb*, "the sons of Jacob" (= "the children of Israel").

9. For ways in which this narrative reflects and does not reflect sapiential features, see Brueggemann, "Genesis 50:15–21."

10. One should note that the expressed fear of the brothers—"What if Joseph were to . . ."—is preceded by the particle *lû*, which in all other instances precedes an unreal condition, that is, it states a case that has not been or is not likely to be realized. Thus, the brothers seem to be evoking an improbability. Their words and deeds, however, suggest they are genuinely afraid of what Joseph now may do.

11. The verb is in an emphatic mode.

12. Consider Levinas's notion of the "third party" in the moral community. For brief discussion and reference, see P. D. Miller, "The Good Neighborhood: Identity and Community through the Commandments," in *Character and Scripture: Moral Formation, Community, and Biblical Interpretation*, ed. William P. Brown (Grand Rapids: Wm B. Eerdmans Publishing Co., 2002), 55–72.

13. The discussion here is an argument in support of Brueggemann's suggestion: "Perhaps the earlier rhetorical question is honored, i.e., only God can forgive" ("Genesis 50:15–21," 50).

14. When that does occur, the human being is usually a representative of the deity, such as Moses (Exod. 10:14) or a prophet (1 Sam. 15:25), and the sin is against

the person as a representative of God. In 1 Sam. 25:28, David receives Abigail's petition to "forgive" her transgression, though in this case the transgression is really an act of boldness and temerity rather than a sin. The apparent exceptions to the general understanding of God as the forgiver of sin that are cited here all have to do with the use of the verb *nāśā'*. The even more common word for forgive, *sālah,* is always of God. For the interpretation of this latter verb, see Walter Brueggemann, "The Travail of Pardon: Reflections on *slh,*" in *A God So Near,* ed. Brent A. Strawn and Nancy R. Bowen (Winona Lake, IN: Eisenbrauns, 2003), 283–97. See in this regard the important first chapter of Donald W. Shriver Jr., *An Ethic for Enemies: Forgiveness in Politics* (New York: Oxford University Press, 1995), though his claim that the Joseph story is an exception to the apparent confinement of forgiveness to divine-human interaction is difficult to sustain. The point of the discussion in this essay is that forgiveness does *not* in fact take place in this story. Something else altogether happens.

15. The italicized words are emphatic in the Hebrew text. Joseph's statement serves to identify what each party is responsible for in all that has happened, including himself, as is evident in the emphatic *I* of verse 21—"*I* will provide" (cf. Gen. 45:11; 47:12).
16. Von Rad, *Genesis,* 432, 438–39.
17. See Brueggemann, "Genesis 50:15–21."
18. See P. D. Miller, *They Cried to the Lord: The Form and Theology of Biblical Prayer* (Minneapolis: Fortress Press, 1994), chap. 4.

Chapter 10

Between Disappointment and Hope at the Boundary: Moses' Death at the End of Deuteronomy

Dennis T. Olson

The Gospels report that the women came to the tomb on that first Easter morning to prepare a human corpse for its final rest, hoping temporarily to mask the odor of death with a few fragrant spices. In Mark's version, the white-robed messenger announces Jesus' resurrection to these startled women and instructs them to go and tell the disciples that Jesus was no longer in the tomb, that he had been raised from the dead, and that the disciples would see him in Galilee just as Jesus promised. But the Gospel ends enigmatically as it concludes with the women's reaction: "And they said nothing to anyone, for they were afraid" (v. 8). Donald Juel argues that the enigmatic and unsettling character of this ending needs to be preserved and not interpreted away:

> Interpretations must respect the two impressions with which the story concludes: disappointment and anticipation. The temptation is to resolve the tension and choose one or the other mood. A few bold interpreters have compared Mark to modern existentialist writers whose point is that life is endlessly disappointing. . . . The most we can hope for, as one author so eloquently puts it, is a "glimpse . . . before the door of disappointment closes on us." [1]

Juel acknowledges there is disappointment in this ending, but there is something more. Yet that "something more" is not grounded in what the human disciples or subsequent readers of Mark's Gospel might accomplish. Some interpreters try to argue that the ending of Mark leaves the conclusion to the reader, "to an act of faith to accomplish what the disciples could not."[2] But Mark's story provides no basis for such confidence, as even the closest disciples repeatedly do not seem to understand what Jesus is all about. "There is hope only because Jesus is no longer imprisoned in the tomb—and because God can be trusted to finish what has been begun."[3]

Is this unsettled ending to Mark, situated between disappointment and anticipation, peculiar to Mark when compared to the many endings of other biblical narratives or books? Or is this tension between hope and distress a more frequent and pervasive posture that finds echoes in the conclusions of other biblical literature? The thesis of this essay is that Juel's description of the end of Jesus' earthly existence as described in Mark's Gospel finds an important echo in the story of the death of Moses in Deuteronomy 34. The narrative of Moses' death is an echo that resonates within a variety of biblical and other rhetorical contexts. Like the end of Mark, Moses' death scene at the conclusion of Deuteronomy urges in multiple ways the simultaneous holding together of these two seemingly opposed and incompatible dispositions in the life of faith: disappointment and hope. We will examine samples of that interplay of dispositions with Deuteronomy 34 in dialogue with the book of Deuteronomy itself as well as with the narrative of the death of King Josiah at the end of the Deuteronomistic History.

THE DEATH OF MOSES IN DEUTERONOMY 34

Deuteronomy 34 recounts the story of Moses' death at the boundary of the promised land of Canaan. At this critical boundary, Moses was allowed to see the land from afar, but he himself was not able to enter it. Actual entry into Canaan was reserved only to a new generation whom Moses had been teaching and preparing throughout the book of Deuteronomy (Deut. 1:34–40; 3:23–28). Moses faithfully led the Israelites out of slavery in Egypt and through the chaos and trials of the forty years of wilderness wandering. Moses had experienced a lifetime of self-doubt, struggle, deprivation, disappointment, and conflict along with a life of unparalleled human access to God, a closeness and even friendship with God that was unique among human beings (Exod. 33:11; Num. 12:6–8; Deut. 34:10–12). As portrayed in Exodus–Deuteronomy, Moses' life embodied the unsettling coexistence of deep disappointment and profound hope. The scene of Moses' death captures in one final crescendo this uneasy juxtaposition of frustration and expectation that characterized the career of Moses in his life and also in his death.

Deuteronomy 34 divides into three sections: verses 1–6, verses 7–9, and verses 10–12. Verses 1–6 are set on top of Mount Nebo on the eastern side of the Jordan River. God allows Moses to look west and survey the land of Canaan from its northern extremity in Dan to the southern reaches of the Negeb. This is the land God had promised to Israel's ancestors long ago—"to Abraham, to Isaac, and to Jacob" (v. 4; cf. Exod. 32:13). At last, Moses' eyes can take in the reality of the homeland of Canaan, a homeland for which he had yearned his whole life. Moses had named his first son "Gershom," for he said, "I have been an alien [*gēr*] residing in a foreign land" (Exod. 2:22). The scene is a fulfillment of God's earlier promise in Deuteronomy 3:27 and 4:22 that Moses would indeed one day see with his own eyes the promised land. But the fulfillment is only a distant sight, a bittersweet glimpse of a promised home that would also elude him. God proclaims, "I have let you see it with your eyes, but you shall not cross over there" (34:4).

With that, Moses dies in the land of Moab "at the LORD's command." It is not a "natural" death but a premature and divinely imposed limit on Moses' life. The Hebrew then literally reads, "He buried him." Who is the "he" who buries Moses? Moses and God had earlier been alone on another mountaintop (Exod. 19–34), and they are once again alone here on Mount Nebo. Thus, the only one available to bury Moses is God. Many translations avoid the straightforward implication of the divine burial by translating the verb simply as a passive: "He was buried" (so NRSV). But the next clause in the sentence underscores the absence of any other humans: "No one knows his burial place to this day." Only God knows. And so God is the one who buries Moses in an unmarked grave on a mountaintop in a foreign land. Thus, Moses' grave cannot become the site of a shrine for worshiping a dead human ancestor, a practice prohibited by Deuteronomy's own laws (Deut. 14:1; 18:11; 26:14). Moses is a "servant of the LORD" to be remembered but not a god to be worshiped.

The second scene in chapter 34, verses 7–9, is often considered a later Priestly or Deuteronomistic supplement to the chapter. The scene begins with a notation that Moses was 120 years old at his death, a long human life but not an exception in the biblical tradition (cf. Gen. 25:7; 47:28; 50:26). Unlike his ancestor Isaac in Genesis 27 who was feeble and blind in his old age, Moses at 120 remains strong and clear sighted: "His sight was unimpaired and his vigor had not abated" (34:7). The Hebrew word for "vigor" is associated with the fresh, moist property of young trees and fresh fruit. At 120, Moses remains strong, young, and supple. This description is somewhat at odds with the more feeble Moses of Deut. 31:2, as Moses confesses there, "I am no longer able to get about." While perhaps the product of two different editorial hands, these portraits have the effect of holding together the feeble and typically human Moses with Moses the strong hero and legendary leader. Given this tension, Moses' death is both a product of inevitable human mortality but also a divinely imposed and premature demise.

Verses 8–9 recount the thirty days of the people's grieving over Moses' death, the usual period for mourning the dead. But then the "period of mourning for Moses was ended" (34:8). Respect, love, and memory remain, but the community of Israelites must move on as a new generation under the leadership of

Joshua, a leader "full of the spirit of wisdom" and one on whom Moses had laid his hands (Deut. 31:7–8, 14–15, 25; cf. Num. 27:12–23). Joshua, however, is not simply a new Moses, as the next scene will underscore. When Moses lays his hands on Joshua in Numbers 27, God instructs Moses to give Joshua "some" of his authority, implying not all of it. A new dimension and model of leadership emerges: The human leader Joshua will be guided and judged by the wisdom and teaching of the book of the *torah* of Moses (Deut. 31:24–29; Josh. 1:7–8). Scripture, a book, has power alongside human leaders in guiding the people of God forward.

Verses 10–12 are commonly judged by scholars to be among the latest editorial additions to the book of Deuteronomy and the Pentateuch as a whole. Verse 10 testifies to Moses' incomparability as a prophet: "Never since has there arisen a prophet in Israel like Moses." That uniqueness stems in part from the unparalleled intimacy between God and Moses: God "knew" Moses "face to face," a description that is used of no one else in the Old Testament. Moses' uniqueness derives not only from his closeness to God but also from his unmatched and powerful "signs and wonders" done in Egypt and "all the mighty deeds and all the terrifying displays of power" that Moses did for all Israel (Deut. 34:11–12). What is remarkable is that this cluster of vocabulary includes technical terms that Deuteronomy elsewhere consistently attributes to God alone (4:34; 6:22; 7:19; 11:3; 26:8; 29:3). Moses had testified to the incomparability of *God's* mighty deeds earlier in Deuteronomy: "O LORD God, you have only begun to show your servant your greatness and your might; what god in heaven or on earth can perform deeds and mighty acts like yours!" (Deut. 3:24). The narrator in Deuteronomy 34 returns the favor and praises *Moses* and his great deeds with similar words. In functional terms, Moses and God become mirror images of one another: Moses is the human instrument of divine activity. Moses' life, actions, and words mediate the activity and words of God. Moses has been a unique vehicle for God's saving activity on behalf of Israel, even as the inevitability of his limits, death, and failures is acknowledged. Moses embodies the rich complexity of the struggle of human life lived in relationship with a purposeful God who is both intimately near and infinitely far. In his life and death, Moses experiences great accomplishment and sinful failure, dramatic hopes and frustrated dreams, heroic sacrifice and painful tragedy, a unique human life but also a death like all mortals.

THE DEATH OF MOSES IN THE CONTEXT
OF THE BOOK OF DEUTERONOMY

The death of Moses is more than just the last scene or chapter in the book of Deuteronomy. Moses' death casts a crucial interpretive shadow over the entire book of Deuteronomy. In each major section of Deuteronomy, the reader encounters important allusions to the imminent death or absence of Moses. On one hand, Moses' death outside the promised land of Canaan functions negatively but realistically as a central metaphor for human finitude in both its individual and corporate experience. A full experience of the promised land would always in some way be under threat and repeatedly be beyond the grasp of individual Israelites, leaders, and the nation as a whole. Individual suffering, group conflict, national division, the attack of enemies, natural disasters, and the exile of north (722 BCE) and south (587 BCE) undermined Israel's sustained settlement and enjoyment of God's gift of the land of Canaan. Moses' death beyond the Jordan River rings true to the necessary and inevitable losses and limits of human life and faithfulness before God (Deut. 32:48–52).

On the other hand, Moses' death functions positively as a teaching paradigm of a life of sacrificial giving and letting go for the sake of others. In God's mysterious economy, Moses' death before he has reached his goal of Canaan opens the path for the rebellious Israelites to continue their journey to the promised land (Deut. 1:37–40; 3:26–28; 4:20–22). This last act of sacrifice, divinely imposed, is emblematic of Moses' dedication to God throughout his whole life and to his leading and shaping the people of God throughout their wilderness journey from Egypt to Canaan. Moses' death outside the promised land in chapter 34 functions both negatively as a metaphor for human limitation and frailty as well as positively as a paradigm of a life lived and given for others. This is evident throughout the major sections of Deuteronomy.

Deuteronomy 1–4 and the Death of Moses

Chapters 1–4 begin Moses' catechetical address to the new generation of Israelites, a generation born in the wilderness and about to enter the promised land. These opening chapters consist largely of Moses' teaching through selected key stories of Israel's past journey through the wilderness. The first narrative in Deuteronomy is a brief account of Moses giving up some of his authority by appointing tribal heads to help lead the people (1:9–18; cf. Exod. 18; Num. 11). This earlier sharing of leadership responsibilities prefigures Moses' transferal of leadership to Joshua at his death in chapter 34, an act of relinquishing and letting go, an acknowledgment of limits and a kind of dying.

The next major narrative recounted by Moses is the spy story from Numbers 13–14, retold in Deuteronomy 1:19–2:25. The spy story narrates the refusal of the old exodus generation of Israelites to enter the land of Canaan because of the spies' report of the strength of the Canaanite military might. The Israelites refuse to trust that God will bring them safely into Canaan as God had promised. As a result, God condemns the old generation to forty years of wilderness wandering during which all the old generation will die in the wilderness; only the new generation of those born in the wilderness will be allowed to enter the promised land of Canaan. On one hand, Moses' death outside the promised land in chapter 34 is in part woven into the negative judgment on the old generation of Israelites (1:37; 3:23–27; cf. Deut. 32:48–52; Num. 20:10–13). On the other, Moses' death outside the land in some way positively opens up the possibility that a new generation will be able to enter the land (Deut. 4:21–22). Deuteronomy 4:25–31, however, also warns all subsequent generations that Moses' fate of dying outside the land remains a continuing possibility into the future.

Deuteronomy 5–11 and the Death of Moses

Chapter 5 narrates the giving of the Ten Commandments at Mount Horeb (also known as Mount Sinai). In the face of the divine theophany with its terrifying thick darkness, cloud, and blazing fire on top of the mountain, the Israelites beg Moses to go up the mountain in their stead: "Why should we die? . . . If we hear the voice of the LORD our God any longer, we shall die. . . . Go near, you yourself, and hear all that the LORD our God will say" (5:25–27). Such close encounters with God risk death for any human, and so the people commission Moses to stand in the place of death as a mediator for the sake of the people.

Chapters 6–11 form an extended commentary on the first commandment: "You shall have no other gods before me." The major teaching narrative is the story of the golden calf recounted in Deuteronomy 9:8–10:11 (cf. Exod. 32). Moses recalls how God had angrily resolved to destroy all the Israelites after their idolatrous worship of the golden calf. God promised Moses that once Israel was destroyed, God would in effect make Moses a new Abraham, the father of a new nation: "I will make of you [Moses] a nation mightier and more numerous than they [the rebellious Israelites]." Moses resists the temptation and lets his own ambitions die. In a unique detail added in Deuteronomy's retelling of the golden calf story, Moses assumes a posture resembling death and lies prostrate before God for forty days and forty nights. He eats no bread and drinks no water, denying himself the basics of life (9:18). Moses intercedes for the people of Israel, and remarkably God listens to Moses and allows the Israelites to live (9:19, 20; 10:10).

Deuteronomy 12–28 and the Death of Moses

Moses' address in these chapters is filled with "statutes and ordinances" that function as an expansive explication of the Ten Commandments presented in Deuteronomy 5. The Hebrew word for "death" or "dying" (*mwt*) saturates these chapters, occurring thirty-two times in chapters 12–26. This concern over issues of life and death weaves the laws of Deuteronomy into the larger tapestry colored by the distinctive theme of the death of Moses. The positive thread that weaves its way in and out of these many statutes and ordinances is the call to a life of letting go, giving away, dying to self. In his study *Law and Theology in the Book of Deuteronomy*, J. G. McConville observes that many laws in Deuteronomy

> are in some way costly to the one who obeys. . . . The principle involved is in fact a paradox. Enjoyment of the land and its benefits depends upon a readiness to relinquish them. We have noticed that blessing was promised for the act of self-denial involved in slave release or the remittance of debts.

> But it is actually a regular principal that where blessing is promised it is in the context of self-restraint.[4]

Obedience in the statutes and ordinances of Deuteronomy is often portrayed as letting go or giving away a portion of what God has already given (money, property, crops, power, life, freedom, time, space), all as an acknowledgment of human limits and dependence on God. Such giving away or letting go in chapters 12–28 is done in relation to *God* (e.g., tithes, sacrifices, sacred space and time, purity restrictions, singular devotion to God above all other loyalties), to *neighbor* (e.g., release of debts and slaves, no bribes, justice for the widow and the orphan, crops left for the needy to glean, restrictive boundaries of clean and unclean in regard to a host of relationships and practices), and to *nature* (e.g., saving lost or stolen animals, not muzzling an ox, letting the mother bird go while only taking the young, restrictions on cutting trees). Obedience is learning to let go of the gifts God has given. Such dying to self-interest for the sake of God and others results in a life of true joy for the gifts God has given (Deut. 12:7, 12, 18; 14:26; 16:11, 14, 15; 26:11; 27:7). Disobedience is grasping and clinging to God's gifts, making objects or self into idolatrous objects of ultimate concern, desire, and trust. Israel's disobedience would eventually lead to its own death and exile outside the promised land (Deut. 27:45–68).

One other important reference specifically to Moses' death occurs among the statutes and ordinances in Deuteronomy 18:15–19. Moses promises that God will raise up a new "prophet like me" in the future after Moses is gone. Among the later Old Testament prophets, Jeremiah emerges as a clear example of such a "prophet like Moses." Like Moses, Jeremiah complained of his human limitations and inadequacy to be a prophet, but he then received God's assurance that God would provide what he needed (Jer. 1:6–8; cf. Exod. 3:11–12). Like Moses, Jeremiah suffered years of pain and persecution as a mediator between God and the rebellious people of Judah (Jer. 11, 15, 20). Like Moses, Jeremiah ended up dying against his will outside the promised land; he was taken forcibly out of Judah to Egypt and presumably died there (Jer. 42–43). Jeremiah's suffering as a prophet and intercessor for his people ended not only with his own exile to Egypt but also Judah's exile to Babylon. However, Jeremiah holds on to the promise and hope that God would one day return a future generation back home to the promised land (Jer. 30–33). Like Moses, Jeremiah ends his life as a prophet with a mixture of disappointment and hope.

Deuteronomy 29–33 and the Death of Moses

Moses introduces in Deuteronomy 29–32 a new covenant at Moab "in addition to" the covenant made at Horeb with the Ten Commandments (29:1 [Heb. 28:69]). The new covenant of Moab divides into three sections. Chapters 29–30 offer a covenant-making liturgy that moves through the future exile and death of the community to the promise of restoration and God's shaping the people into obedient doers of God's will. The obedience and love of God that the people were unable to achieve before will in the future become *God's* act of "circumcising the heart" and *God's* creating the obedience that the laws alone could not do (Deut. 30:6; cf. Deut. 10:16).

The second section, chapter 31, makes provision for the vacuum of leadership that will be left by the imminent death of Moses (31:2, 14, 15, 27, 29). The unique Moses will be replaced by a combination of human leaders (Joshua, the elders, Levites, parents who catechize the young), a written book of Moses' teaching (the *torah* of Moses—a form of Deuteronomy itself), and a song (the Song of Moses in chapter 32).

The third section, chapter 32, is the Song of Moses, which recounts the movement of Israel through judgment and death to life and hope. The Song proclaims God's sovereign power over life and death as God proclaims:

> There is no god beside me.
> I kill and I make alive;
>   I wound and I heal;
>   and no one can deliver from my hand. (32:39)

But this divine power seeks to move Israel through death to life. Divine love and compassion will come when human pretensions and powers are relinquished:

> Indeed the LORD will . . . have compassion on his servants,
>   when he sees that their power is gone,
>   neither bond nor free remaining. (32:36)

For Israel, life will come out of death, deliverance out of exile, hope out of judgment.

Moses' prayer to God to bring blessings upon the twelve tribes in Deuteronomy 33 are the last words that we hear from Moses. This final act of intercessory prayer, a kind of deathbed blessing, signifies that Moses is about to die and that Israel's future no longer lies in Moses' hands but in God's. The prayer testifies to the limits of human control and to the limitless mercy of God who alone transcends the boundaries and limits of human power and mortality. The blessings of the tribes are followed immediately by the actual narration of Moses' death in Deuteronomy 34.

DISAPPOINTMENT AND HOPE AT THE BOUNDARY: THE DEATH OF MOSES AND THE DEATH OF KING JOSIAH AT THE END OF THE DEUTERONOMISTIC HISTORY

We have seen that the account of Moses' death resonates in varied ways throughout the book of Deuteronomy. We now widen our lens further out to consider the role of the death of Moses at the end of the book of Deuteronomy in light of the larger Deuteronomistic History (Joshua–Kings) to which, following Martin

Noth, it is related. What meaningful connections, if any, might we discern between the death of Moses outside the land at the conclusion to Deuteronomy and the death of Josiah in 2 Kings 23 at the conclusion of the Deuteronomistic History (2 Kgs. 22–25)? What are the similarities or differences in the presentation as we compare the fate of Moses and the fate of King Josiah? What implications might we draw from such a comparison? Alongside the death of King Josiah, what might the closing scene of the Deuteronomistic History with Judah's King Jehoiachin eating at the Babylonian king's table in exile (2 Kgs. 25:27–30) contribute to the theme of disappointment and hope at the conclusion of a major biblical corpus of literature?

King Josiah reigned in the southern kingdom of Judah from 640 to 609 BCE, just a few decades before Babylon's destruction of Jerusalem and exile of much of the population of Judah in 587. The Deuteronomistic Historian presents Josiah in 2 Kings 22–23 as a consistently positive and faithful leader who engaged in reforms of Judah's religious life and worship. In fact, many scholars assume that much of the Deuteronomistic History and some form of the book of Deuteronomy received at least one phase of its definitive shaping and editing during the time of King Josiah's reign in the seventh century BCE. Another stage in the editing likely occurred after the exile of 587.[5] Among other additions, this exilic edition included: (1) the account of the death of King Josiah in the encounter with Pharaoh Neco at Megiddo (2 Kgs. 23:28–30); (2) the note that Josiah's faithful reforms were not sufficient to prevent the imminent conquest and exile of Judah that could be traced to the sins of the previous king, Manasseh (2 Kgs. 23:26–27; cf. 2 Kgs. 21); (3) the account of Babylon's victory over Judah and the exile of its population (2 Kgs. 24–25); and (4) the enigmatic note at the very end of 2 Kings about Judah's King Jehoiachin being released from prison in Babylon and being allowed to eat at the table of the Babylonian king.

Some notable resonances emerge when the figures of Moses and Josiah are placed alongside one another. They are both celebrated leaders who seek to reform rebellious Israelites into a truer worship of the one God. Josiah discovers the "book of the *torah*" that is associated with Moses. They are both praised as unique and incomparable leaders.[6] "Never since has there arisen a prophet in Israel like Moses, whom the LORD knew face to face" (Deut. 34:10). The narrator's assessment of Josiah is similar. Before Josiah, "there was no king like him, who turned to the LORD with all his heart, with all his soul, and with all his might, according to all the law of Moses; nor did any like him arise after him" (2 Kgs. 23:25). The other major similarity is that Moses and Josiah both die somewhat prematurely and enigmatically without achieving what seems to be their full destiny and promise.

In a 1968 article, Stanley Frost observed how the "recalcitrant fact" of the tragic and premature death of King Josiah is never interpreted or explained in the Deuteronomistic History itself or in any prophetic or other biblical book. Frost labeled it a biblical "conspiracy of silence."[7] The account is simply narrated:

> In his days Pharaoh Neco king of Egypt went up to the king of Assyria to
> the river Euphrates. King Josiah went to meet him; but when Pharaoh Neco
> met him at Megiddo, he killed him. His servants carried him dead in a char-
> iot from Megiddo, brought him to Jerusalem, and buried him in his own
> tomb. (2 Kgs. 23:29–30)

Josiah was only thirty-nine years of age at his death. He was remembered as a
great reformer, instituting the proper worship of the LORD in accordance with
"the book of the law" of Moses, presumably some version of the book of
Deuteronomy:

> Josiah put away the mediums, wizards, teraphim, idols, and all the abomi-
> nations that were seen in the land of Judah and in Jerusalem, so that he
> established the words of the law that were written in the book that the priest
> Hilkiah had found in the house of the LORD. (2 Kgs. 23:24; cf. 2 Kgs.
> 22:8–20)

This same "book of the law" (Deuteronomy) and the Deuteronomistic History
itself are often seen as infused with a theology of just retribution by which God
acted in history. "If you obey the commandments of the LORD your God . . . ,
then you shall live and become numerous. . . .But if your heart turns away and
you do not hear, . . . I declare to you today that you shall perish; you shall not
live long in the land" (Deut. 30:16–18). Frost argues that this theology of retribution was unable to account for Josiah's tragic death. The note about the greatness of Manasseh's sin overwhelming Josiah's faithfulness was "the deuteronomic
historians' rather halfhearted attempt to deal theologically with Josiah's death,"
and Frost contends that it "just will not do."[8] Frost concludes:

> We are left then with a general conspiracy of silence on the subject of the
> death of Josiah because, given the OT premises, no one could satisfactorily
> account for it theologically. The fact is that the death of Josiah promised to
> be the relatively small but sharp-edged rock on which the OT concept of
> divinely motivated history foundered.[9]

We can agree with Frost that the premature and tragic death of an obedient
and faithful king would seem to contravene a simplistic theology of retribution
in which blessings and long life are the rewards for obedience, curse and death
the consequences for disobedience. But by including the account of Josiah's death
in the exilic edition of the Deuteronomistic History, the notion of a "divinely
motivated history" did not founder as much as it became deeper, richer, and more
complex. A general order of act and consequence may be operative in a loose
moral weave in reality, but it does not apply rigidly or exhaustively. Elements of
complexity, mystery, and paradox remain in human understandings of the
divine. Josiah's tragic and premature death seems in part in contradiction to the
prophet Huldah's earlier promise to Josiah and in part in fulfillment of it. Because
of Josiah's faithfulness and humble heart, Huldah proclaims, Josiah would be
spared from seeing the destruction of Jerusalem: "Therefore, I will gather you to

your ancestors, and you shall be gathered to your grave in peace; your eyes shall not see all the disaster that I will bring on this place" (2 Kgs 22:20). To die so young in the encounter with Pharaoh Neco hardly seems like going "in peace," and yet it spared Josiah from witnessing the destruction of Jerusalem and the temple he sought to reform.

Alongside this enigmatic story of Josiah's death is the final scene in the Deuteronomistic History. Judah's captive King Jehoiachin is released from jail and kept under a kind of house arrest in the Babylonian king's palace, where he dines at the king's table (2 Kgs. 25:27–30). What does this concluding episode convey? For Martin Noth, this was just the last nail in the coffin for exilic Israel, the end of a string of disasters, the last gasp of Israelite kingship. The narrative recounts the "simple fact" that "the history of the Israelite and Judean monarchy was over."[10] Gerhard von Rad, in contrast, argued that the final scene is a hopeful sign that the embers of Judah's royal Davidic line remain intact, even if glowing dimly; God's promise of a Davidic king "forever" in 2 Samuel 7 remained in force. Walter Brueggemann rightly suggests that perhaps we must hold both Noth and von Rad together on this text:

> Given the uncertainty about the meaning of this text, we may entertain the thought that the paragraph offered both here and in Jeremiah 52:31–34 [also forming the conclusion to the MT version of that prophetic book], ends the royal narrative and is intentionally enigmatic because more could not be said. The narrator observes that the royal line is in jeopardy, but tells us no more than that. Thus whatever hope is offered here is unspoken—no blueprint, no firm design, no fixed assurance, but only "the conviction of things not seen" (Heb 11:1). The paragraph might do nothing more than confirm the flat verdict of v. 21: still in exile, still out of the land. But it might not![11]

CONCLUSION: BETWEEN DISAPPOINTMENT AND HOPE

The death of Moses at the end of Deuteronomy closes the Pentateuch on a note of disappointment and hope. God denied Moses his wish that he could set foot in the promised land of Canaan. But somehow Moses' death made possible the forward march of the next generation into the promised land (Deut. 1:37; 3:23–28; 4:21–22). At the same time, Moses' death outside the land was also the result of his own humanity and a momentary lapse of faith (Deut. 32:48–52; cf. Num. 20:10–13). The exilic editors of Deuteronomy sought in this mixture of tragedy and comedy to communicate the experience of faith with a God who defies final resolutions, easy endings, or smooth conclusions. As one commentator notes, "Deuteronomy suspends Moses' audience and all subsequent readers in between end and beginning."[12]

The same is true at the end of the Deuteronomistic History, where Josiah's death and the final scene of Judah's king eating at the Babylonian royal table leave the reader in unresolved tension, a space between disappointment and hope. But it is precisely in that uneasy space of the recognition of human limits, frustrations, disappointments, mortality, and failure that we may turn away from ourselves to another—"because God can be trusted to finish what has been begun."

Notes

1. Donald Juel, *Mark*, Augsburg Commentary on the New Testament (Minneapolis: Augsburg, 1990), 233. The "one author" to whom Juel alludes is Frank Kermode, and the quotation about the "door of disappointment" is from Frank Kermode, *The Genesis of Secrecy* (Cambridge, MA: Harvard University Press, 1979), 145. A more extended engagement of Juel with Kermode over the interpretation of Mark 16 may be found in Juel's essay in this book.
2. Juel, *Mark,* 234.
3. Ibid.
4. J. G. McConville, *Law and Theology in Deuteronomy,* Journal for the Study of the Old Testament: Supplement Series 33 (Sheffield: JSOT Press, 1984), 15, 17.
5. The two-redaction theory (Josianic and exilic) of the growth of the Deuteronomistic History was proposed by Frank Cross, "The Theme of the Book of Kings and the Structure of the Deuteronomistic History," in *Canaanite Myth and Hebrew Epic* (Cambridge, MA: Harvard University Press, 1973), 274–89. Cross's thesis differed from Noth's, which maintained that the entire Deuteronomistic History was written as a unified exilic composition. Cf. Martin Noth, *The Deuteronomistic History,* Journal for the Study of the Old Testament: Supplement Series 15 (Sheffield: JSOT Press, 1981). Other proposals have also been made. See the review in Antony Campbell and Mark O'Brien, *Unfolding the Deuteronomistic History: Origins, Upgrades, Present Text* (Minneapolis: Fortress Press, 2000).
6. A helpful study of the incomparability formulae in the Deuteronomistic History is Gary N. Knoppers, " 'There Was None Like Him': Incomparability in the Books of Kings," *Catholic Biblical Quarterly* 54 (1992): 411–31. Moses, Solomon, Hezekiah, and Josiah are all described as unique and incomparable, but this is not a contradiction. Their incomparability is only in terms of specific traits or roles: Moses as prophet (Deut. 34:10), Solomon's wealth and wisdom (1 Kgs. 5:10; 10:23–24), Hezekiah's trust (2 Kgs. 18:5–6), and Josiah as reformer king (2 Kgs. 23:25).
7. Stanley Brice Frost, "The Death of Josiah: A Conspiracy of Silence," *Journal of Biblical Literature* 87 (1968): 369–82.
8. Ibid., 380.
9. Ibid., 381.
10. Noth, *Deuteronomistic History,* 12, 98.
11. Walter Brueggemann, *1 and 2 Kings,* Smith & Helwys Bible Commentary (Macon, GA: Smith & Helwys, 2000), 606.
12. Thomas W. Mann, *Deuteronomy,* Westminster Bible Companion (Louisville, KY: Westminster John Knox Press, 1995), 167.

Chapter 11

Doors Thrown Open and Waters Gushing Forth: Mark, Ezekiel, and the Architecture of Hope

Jacqueline Lapsley

OF ENDINGS AND ARCHITECTURE

Perhaps not surprisingly, the vast majority of novels written by women in the nineteenth century feature a woman as the central character. Furthermore, nearly every one of these novels ends with either the marriage or death of this heroine. "Once upon a time, the end, the rightful end, of women in novels was social—successful courtship, marriage—or judgmental of her sexual and social failure—death."[1] Not infrequently, the endings to these works feel odd and disjunctive—the heroine shows enormous spunk throughout the tale, challenging gender stereotypes and social limitations, only to be married off at the end, her feisty spirit domesticated, her defiance reined in. Order and convention are reasserted, and the threat to the status quo is defused. Or if the heroine is especially unruly and marriage becomes an incongruous, literally unbelievable option (or if the author cannot stomach the imposition of the necessary constraints to the character), then the heroine suffers a tragic demise.[2] Female *Bildung*, or quest, narratives, so characteristic of novels with male heroes in the nineteenth century, were incompatible with the romance narrative that was the only appropriate story

139

line for female characters. So while *Bildung* narratives often dominate the middle part of these novels, for the most part that aspect of the story must be suppressed in the end.[3] These endings of marriage or death thus often feel "tacked on," the seams where they have been attached to otherwise well-crafted tales too obvious. Yet it is precisely the disjunction between the tales themselves and the triumph of convention at the end that discloses the social, especially gender, turmoil roiling beneath the surface of the West in the nineteenth century. These novels offer closure, their endings trying to tamp down the chaos of momentous social change, to stuff the genie unleashed in the bulk of the novel back into the bottle as best they can. But the artistic cost and the cost to truth are high. The endings of these novels attest, rather desperately but poignantly, to the idea that art "can achieve meaning . . . only at the expense of truth."[4] In this case, endings purchase socially acceptable meaning at the expense of truth.

Don Juel has shown us, persuasively and compellingly, that this is precisely what Mark's Gospel, in its shortest form, refuses to do. Both the appended endings, whether long or short, are akin to the happy marriage of the heroine in a nineteenth-century novel—they wrap up the untidy bits, "meaning" is sustained, and chaos is kept at bay. But the mute terror of the women in Mark 16:8 rejects closure and thus artistic and theological "meaning" in the usual sense. The truth is that God's power in Jesus cannot be contained by any version of artistic closure, and Jesus is, as Juel observes, "on the loose."[5] Two aspects of Juel's reading of Mark are of particular interest to me in my reading of a very different book of the Bible—Ezekiel. The first concerns the attention to endings. Juel's attention to Mark's ending, with Kermode in the background, will help to illumine certain aspects of Ezekiel's ending, and especially how Ezekiel's ending relates to what precedes it in the same book. Secondly, the attention that Juel gives to the door of the tomb in Mark's Gospel leads me to consider the preponderance of architectural imagery in Ezekiel's ending. The book of Ezekiel is replete with two quite distinct types of "bodies": Most frequently clean, closed, smooth surfaces find expression in the temple structure, in architecture properly speaking, whereas disruption and disorder are represented on human bodies. The way this contrast plays itself out in the ending of the book offers an intriguing window into Ezekiel's theological struggles.[6]

It is impossible to understand the function of an ending if we do not have an adequate understanding of what precedes it. Endings function only in relation to the rest of a work; an ending responds to the beginning and the middle, either by offering closure through resolution of tensions permeating the work, or by refusing closure and allowing the tensions to remain unresolved. Before turning our attention to the ending of Ezekiel, we need to have a better sense of what kinds of tensions characterize the rest of the book. Since that is of course an enormous task, beyond what can be accomplished here, we will briefly focus on one aspect: the tensions present in Ezekiel's use of a different form of "architecture," namely, the human body. Once we have a basic sense of the human body as a peculiar site of tension in the book, we will be in a better position to grasp how Ezekiel's ending, the move to more conventional architecture, responds to those tensions.

OTHER FORMS OF ARCHITECTURE: THE HUMAN BODY

Reading Ezekiel is a disorienting experience, yet in this case, disorientation is not a sign of incompetent reading. On the contrary, the rhetoric of the book hopes to disorient its hearers/readers in order to clear the ground for a radical reorientation to reality. For Ezekiel, that reality is an accurate and unflinching understanding of human nature and of God's nature, and of how the two can and should be in relationship to each other. Human sinfulness is a problem for all the prophets, but this is especially true for Ezekiel. The depth of human sin confounds Ezekiel and becomes for him a nearly insurmountable problem, given his fierce commitment to the holiness of God. Ezekiel's torturous struggle to imagine a way forward, a viable future in which this holy God and this sinful people might continue in relationship, is played out throughout the book. The disorientation forces the reader to "bottom out," to realize that she or he does not know which way is up or down, theologically speaking (which of course is to speak of all of reality), and so to be open to Ezekiel's efforts to redescribe that reality. But this purposiveness does not mean that the book does not disclose a number of unresolved tensions. One such tension, as I have discussed elsewhere, concerns the capacity of human beings to make appropriate moral decisions.[7] But another tension can be perceived in Ezekiel's writing about bodies, or more specifically, his writing *on* bodies.

The human body appears throughout Ezekiel as the site of conflict; it is both the means of communication for, and subject of, the divine message of punishment and salvation. The body is the site of the many sign-acts in Ezekiel, from the consumption of dung-smoked food (chap. 4) to the famously regenerated bodies (chap. 37), and as such it becomes both *medium* for the message and the *subject* of both punishment and deliverance. The human body itself communicates God's word; it is the necessary means of expressing the divine message. Yet a deep ambivalence attends the body, for the body is not infrequently punished in Ezekiel for its association with transgression. Metaphorically (e.g., in his use of sexual imagery for apostasy) and perhaps also literally, Ezekiel identifies the body as both the source and the site of sin. Frequently, therefore, the body is punished even as it delivers the divine word (e.g., chaps. 16, 23). Yet elsewhere deliverance is written onto the body (e.g., chap. 37); Israel will be saved in and through their bodies, just as they are punished in and through their bodies, apparently, in some deep, mysterious way, for the sin of their bodies. The human body thus functions as an ambivalent and ambiguous sign throughout much of the book.

Jeremy Schipper has recently argued that the numerous bodies and body parts in Ezekiel can be profitably understood through the lens of the grotesque.[8]

Broadly speaking, the grotesque (a Renaissance word) describes an artistic style that "incorporated animal and human bodies into various decorative designs. This unnatural mixing was greeted by 'serious' art critics as a travesty against the 'classical body' and, thus, against the true, mimetic function of art."[9] Schipper profits from the lengthy attention Russian theorist Mikhail Bakhtin devotes to the grotesque in his study of Rabelais. Bakhtin vividly defines the grotesque in opposition to the "classical body" of the Renaissance, with its smooth and precise lines:

> The new bodily canon, in all its historic variations and different genres, presents an entirely finished, completed, strictly limited body, which is shown from the outside as something individual. That which protrudes, bulges, sprouts, or branches off (when a body transgresses its limits and a new one begins) is eliminated, hidden, or moderated. All orifices of the body are closed. The basis of the image is the individual, strictly limited mass, the impenetrable façade.[10]

In contrast to this, the grotesque body bulges, sprouts, and protrudes, and functions not only negatively, as a satire of the inappropriate, but also positively, blurring the boundaries between life and death and affirming life-giving qualities. It is the grotesque body that reveals the innate organic connection between death and life, and insists that life springs out of death. The "classical body" attempts to deny this connection, but the growing, dynamic, grotesque body affirms it by calling into question the separation between life and death (the "order of things") that the classical body tries to uphold. The grotesque body is an ambivalent sign, as Schipper observes, calling "into question the very structure or order of things (life, truth, dominant ideologies, and so on) by externalizing conflicting ideologies in a single irresolvable image."[11]

Schipper considers the way the accumulation of grotesque body images in Ezekiel serves both to disorient the reader and to lay the groundwork for the new message, the reorientation to the reality of the sovereign and transcendent God who still acts to deliver Israel despite a sinful past. (This despite the very real possibility that the people may not even be capable of living in right relationship to God.[12]) The vision in chapter 1 begins the trend of conjuring images that both disorient the reader and create something new. In this case, fused human and animal bodies are forever indefinable, largely indescribable, and without clear boundaries; they forge something radically new that is neither human nor animal but divine.[13] Even salvation will be effected by means of a grotesque image: the heart of stone removed, replaced by a heart of flesh (36:26). This body, the people's body, is not a closed, finite, impenetrable body, but one that is, as Schipper observes, "in the act of becoming, a body in transition. This image . . . [expresses] competing ideas about humanity by locating and externalizing [Ezekiel's] ambivalent notion of human moral identity."[14]

The ultimate image of bodies in a state of becoming is, of course, the description of the dry bones brought to life in chapter 37. Because the inner and outer features of the body (sinews, flesh, bone, and skin) coalesce in this image, it fits Bakhtin's understanding of the grotesque.[15] Yet the people do not perceive the possibility of new life; they say, "Our bones have dried up, our hope has perished; we are doomed" (37:11).[16] When they see the dry bones, the people are confined by their notions of limited, closed, complete bodies, and think therefore that death is always only death. But the grotesque body of the dry bones blurs life and death; death becomes the occasion of new life (as is clearly the case with Rabelais's grotesque bodies). Schipper explains, "Through this image, Ezekiel is able to hold together the old, divinely punished Israel and another new, divinely saved Israel in an irreducible and extended metaphor."[17] In sum, one way in which Ezekiel creatively articulates the many tensions in the book is to write them onto grotesque bodies, which can simultaneously communicate both the depth of human sinfulness and the depth of God's intent to deliver them.

ENDING EZEKIEL: MAKING THE WORLD SAFE FOR GOD

So then, we might ask the same question that readers of nineteenth-century novels ask: What happens to all of these tensions in the end? Are they resolved or suppressed, or like unraveling threads, left to dangle untidily throughout the ending? On the one hand, the ending of Ezekiel flows quite naturally from what has preceded it. The book as a whole is structured by the three related visions of the *kabod* of YHWH (chaps. 1–3; chaps. 8–11; chaps. 40–48). The first vision of the *kabod* attests to the mobility of God, the theological implications of which are profoundly unsettling to an audience accustomed to the temple as God's earthly abode. The second vision describes the even more unsettling departure of the divine presence from the temple, driven out by the shameless abominations of a clueless, unrepentant people. In this context, the final vision in chapters 40–48 functions to bring the *kabod* full circle, as it returns to the new, completely holy temple where, Ezekiel tells us, God will abide forever (43:7; 48:35). Taken as the third vision in this series, this final vision makes sense, and completes the structure of the book. The ending does what Kermode says an ending often does—it wraps up loose ends, comforts us with the resolution of deep and disturbing conflict, and thereby achieves a satisfying closure.[18] It is meant to settle, not unsettle.

But does it settle everything? Certainly Ezekiel's ending tries to achieve closure, to make us feel secure that the chaos of the exile and the disorder described in the first half of the book have been rectified, brought under control by a God who in the end wills an ordered relationship between God and God's people. But a number of features of the final vision suggest a different, less pat reading. Juel's attention to Mark's ending alerts us to the possibility that Ezekiel's ending may reveal more than the prophet's evident interest in creation traditions[19] or cosmogonic reality.[20] Endings require particular scrutiny because they invariably must either attempt to "tie up" what has gone before, or deliberately avoid closure; either choice discloses significant meaning. And, as Blau DuPlessis observes, the ending is often the site where hermeneutic "untidiness" reveals itself most clearly: "Any resolution can have traces of the conflicting materials that have been processed within it. It is where subtexts and repressed discourses can throw up one last flare of meaning; it is where the author may sidestep and displace attention from the materials that a work has made available."[21] Ezekiel's world had much untidiness to sweep up; one of the enduring problems of the book is the gap between the severity of the problems he articulates (the most graphically described apostasy and transgression in any biblical prophet), and the glories of the new temple vision. The book is rather vague about how we can actually make the move from the morass of human sinfulness to the glorious new temple, overflowing with God's presence. The end of the book does not successfully resolve this tension, but its attempts to do so reveal the depth of the problem in intriguing ways.

One of the striking features of the temple vision in chapters 40–48 is the relative absence of human beings. At first, one may not be apt to notice this absence, given the overriding concern for measuring the temple and disseminating the new temple laws. But considered against the rest of the book and Ezekiel's prolonged struggle to deal with sinful humanity, the absence of people suggests that despite his best efforts to describe the rebirth of human identity (esp. in chap. 37), human beings continue to pose a threat to the holiness of God, and that the problem of how a holy God can dwell in the midst of a sinful people has not been fully addressed. Ezekiel's "solution" to this problem is to offer a decidedly regulated architecture of hope, in which people have only a limited and highly scripted role (see, e.g., 46:1–10).[22] The extent of the detail in the temple measurements indexes a certain anxiety about the future; this is most emphatically not Mark's open-ended future where God is "on the loose." There is an anxious quality to what even those with a profound appreciation of the theological depth of Ezekiel's vision consider the maddening detail with which Ezekiel narrates his vision of the temple.[23] The anxiety undergirding Ezekiel's ending derives from his fear that despite God's unilateral initiative to forge a new human identity, the people's sinfulness will somehow reassert itself and God will be driven once again out of the temple—even this visionary temple.[24]

Given the ways in which grotesque bodies become the site of such creative reflection on the relationship between sin and salvation, between death and life, in the body of the book, the nearly complete absence of bodies in the end, grotesque or otherwise, provides a startling contrast. The "body" of the temple is a "classic" one in Bakhtinian terms: smooth, precise, limited, complete, closed. Bakhtin continues the description of the "new bodily canon" cited above: "The basis of the image is the individual, strictly limited mass, the impenetrable façade. The opaque surface and the body's 'valleys' acquire an essential meaning as the border of a closed individuality that does not merge with other bodies and with the world. All attributes of the unfinished world are carefully removed, as well as all the signs of its inner life."[25] The contrast between the Ezekielian grotesque bodies earlier in the book, and the ending, which eliminates all grotesque bodies—all *bodies* altogether, all bulges, sprouts, unruly protrusions—is stark. The literal elimination of these bodies symbolizes their metaphorical elimination from the future. Prior to the ending, the grotesque body *articulated* significant theological tensions, and the ending responds by attempting to *eradicate* those tensions through elimination of the bodies that bear them. By clearing out the grotesque, the ending seeks to clean up the mess of conflict and ambiguity that human bodies represent.

THE ARCHITECTURE OF HOPE

Having found human bodies so theologically problematic (even as they generate enormous theological energy), Ezekiel transfers the medium of his message from the human body to a different kind of body: the temple. Architecture is a more precise, reliable, and stable metaphor than the human body. Crushed in and by the traumatic environment of the exile, Ezekiel pins all his hope for the future on the architecture of the envisioned temple. That the temple should dominate Ezekiel's ending occasions no surprise, for as Daniel Smith-Christopher observes, "[A]s an exilic construct, it is clear that the temple is part of the architecture of exilic identity and is part of the postexilic theology of recovery and identity."[26] The prophet is given a tour of the temple, in order that he might take in the theological significance of the architectural details and so that he may pass it on to the people:

> Now, mortal, explain the temple to the house of Israel, so that they may be ashamed of their iniquities. Let them measure the perfection, and if they are ashamed of all that they have done, make known to them the plan of the temple, its arrangement, its exits and its entrances, and its entire plan. . . . And write it down in their sight, so that they may observe and follow the entire plan and all its ordinances. (Ezek. 43:10–11)

Ezekiel's underlying hope is that this new temple will mediate a successful divine-human relationship, if the people can be convinced to digest inwardly the details of its perfection. Yet some of those same architectural details disclose a concern that even now this future is not assured. I want to focus on two architectural details as emblematic of the larger anxiety that the divine-human relationship is still imperiled. The first is a wall; the second, a door.

In the midst of his tour of the temple, Ezekiel sees the *kabod* of YHWH appearing out of the east, and moments later, YHWH speaks to the prophet, promising that in this temple, "I will reside among the people of Israel forever" (43:7). Immediately after this, YHWH mentions a problem in the architecture of the previous temple, namely, that the divine name was defiled by generations of both kings and regular folk, and by the "corpses of their kings at their death."[27] The reference has been variously interpreted as either royal burials quite close to the temple, or as royal memorial steles in the temple precincts, commemorating deceased kings.[28] The former evokes the specter of corpse contamination, which in the priestly worldview is, of course, unreservedly defiling, but in either case, the proximity of human kings is contaminating. The key for our purposes lies in what follows: "When they placed their threshold by my threshold and their doorposts beside my doorposts, *with only a wall between me and them,* they were defiling my holy name by their abominations that they committed" (43:8). The problem is not here limited to corpse contamination, that is simply an extreme case of a larger, more general problem, which is that the impurities generated by human sinfulness must not "touch" holiness (cf. 42:20). The priestly tradition is known for its peculiarly spatial articulation of the problem of sin.[29] The inherent sinfulness associated with the human dwelling (palace) was simply too close to the inherent holiness associated with the divine dwelling (temple). The apartment walls were too thin to sustain such disparate neighbors.

As for Mark, doors are a particular concern for Ezekiel. The prophet presciently envisions the need for traffic control and prescribes which doors foot traffic will use during major festivals (46:9–10), as well as legislates the times for the opening and closing of various gates and doors (e.g., 46:1). One door, the outer east gate of the sanctuary, is to remain closed permanently: "YHWH said to me, 'This gate shall remain shut; it shall not be opened, and no one shall enter by it; for YHWH, the God of Israel, has entered by it; it shall remain shut'" (44:2). This sealed door recalls Bakhtin's evocation of the "new bodily canon," with its "impenetrable façade" that contrasts so sharply with the imperfect protrusions of the grotesque body. Yet for Ezekiel the closing of this door symbolizes the fulfillment of God's promise to reside among the people forever; its sealing means that God will never again depart from the temple; the closed door is a potent architectural sign of the hope at the core of Ezekiel's temple vision.

For both Ezekiel and Mark, the promises of God sustain the hope embodied in the architectural imagery they offer; God's salvation is disclosed in the definitive closing of doors on the one hand, and the bursting open of heavy doors on the other. Corpse contamination is an extreme case of a larger problem for Ezekiel; for Mark it is the environment out of which hope is born. In contrast to Mark, for whom a tomb door thrown open forms the architecture of hope, for Ezekiel hope lies in sound architectural plans, good construction, precise directions for building use, and, crucially, really thick walls. For Mark an empty tomb—absence—fulfills the divine promises for salvation, whereas for Ezekiel it is the fullness of divine presence that signifies salvation. Perhaps the most obvious contrast concerns the temple: For Ezekiel precise, even obsessive, temple architecture embodies hope, whereas hope in Mark is signaled by the destruction of the temple.[30] These biblical writers share a conviction that God is at work in the world, fulfilling the divine promises for the deliverance of God's people, but the architectural imagery they employ to express that conviction could not be more different. For Mark, God's power and promise are attested in the open door, in Jesus having opened the door that could not be opened. Juel observes: "Jesus is out, on the loose, on the same side of the door as the women and the readers."[31] In Ezekiel's temple vision, the blurring of the boundaries of death and life, of God and humanity, would have been inconceivable. Mark's God is not constrained by death or contained by a tomb or a closed door, whereas for Ezekiel God's power and promise are reflected in the closed door, in the thick walls that allow God to be present amid the people.

The collision of priestly theology with the historical realities of the exile present Ezekiel with anthropological and theological problems that Mark simply did not face. The temple vision is a sustained effort to address those problems without losing sight of either the holiness of God or the proven sinfulness of human beings. Ezekiel's concern with architectural precision and solidity reflects a powerful impulse to get the mobile God of the prophet's vision in chapter 1 securely back into the temple at the end of the book (brooking no further departure). Ezekiel strains to offer a hermetically sealed ending, in which all possibility for unscripted activity is proscribed. Paradoxically, however, it is precisely this effort to regulate the future so precisely that reveals unresolved issues in the book. The strained precision of Ezekiel's ending discloses his continuing ambivalence over human identity, his doubt that even God's action can recreate people in such a way that the threat to the holiness of God, and thus to the continuation of the divine-human relationship, can be adequately defused. In a way reminiscent of the nineteenth-century novels mentioned above, the tidiness of Ezekiel's ending belies the unresolved conflicts that characterize the rest of the book. He wants everything to be wrapped up neatly in a "happy marriage" between people and deity.[32] But the reader has not forgotten the unruly, creative energy loosed in the earlier parts of the book, in those paradoxically death-inducing and death-defying bodies. Where these bodies articulate underlying conflicts, the temple vision seeks to contain and ultimately eliminate them.

The desire for completion in so much of Ezekiel, and especially in the temple vision, evokes the Bakhtinian "new bodily canon," in which "all orifices of the body are closed." This style of "classical" architecture (in the Bakhtinian sense) embodied in the temple exists in a tensive relationship with the grotesque architecture of the human bodies in the book. The dynamic forces and tensions present in the grotesque imagery earlier in the book burst the linguistic and imagistic confines of convention, and so they must be addressed by an ending that *does* something about them. The ending of Ezekiel tries to stuff the genie back into the bottle, tries to offer a contained, controlled resolution (a resolution that affirms the "classical" body) to the chaos unleashed in the rest of the book. Some of that chaotic energy is negative, but much of it toward the end is positive, life-giving energy (e.g., the dry bones) that, once unleashed, will alter Israel's future through the transformation of its very identity. Yet the power of these images cannot be left uncontained at the end. In this sense, the constraint of Ezekiel's ending is reminiscent of the endings to those nineteenth-century novels where the heroine leads an unconventional life, bursting out of social limitations and gender roles, only to be married off sweetly in the end.

WATER ON THE LOOSE

Yet this is not the whole story. In nineteenth-century novels by women, the conventional ending of marriage or death tried to repress the struggle of social change, but frequently the traces of the tensions prevalent in the book appear subtly in those endings; they cannot be entirely suppressed.[33] Similarly, the ending of Ezekiel is not only about containment, about reasserting the "classical" body. In the midst of so much static imagery, one extremely dynamic image bursts forth: the water that flows from the sanctuary itself, bringing life to everything around it (47:1–12).[34] This crucial aperture in the temple contrasts sharply with the otherwise restricted space and movement in this exact and exacting structure.[35] Not surprisingly, given the role of measurements in the rest of the vision, the first half of the passage describes the mysterious guide's efforts to measure the water, with prophet in tow. The guide measures in cubits, but the telling measurements of depth are made with reference to the body. Again the human body is set over against that which is made with human hands: Here it is the body that provides an approximate account (until it is beyond measuring) of the depth of the water. The measurements suggest that the water begins gently—the disruption of the closed sanctuary surface is only a small one—but it gathers tremendous force once outside of the sanctuary.[36] At first, the guide measures off one thousand cubits (about 1700 feet), at which point the water is only ankle deep. Then two thousand are measured, and it is knee deep, then three thousand and waist deep, and then four thousand plus and too deep to cross; one would have to swim. The impassibility is repeated twice in one verse: "I wasn't able to cross for the waters had risen. The water was at swimming height—a river that cannot be crossed" (47:5). The depth of this water is described not only by its being above the human head, and so beyond human capacities to contain or control, but also by being immeasurable. The water is the only thing in the temple vision that cannot be measured; this symbol of the power of God, initially just a trickle,[37] gushing forth from the temple to revivify the land, is simply too powerful to be appraised by a yardstick (so to speak). At this point the guide speaks to the prophet: "Do you see, mortal?" (47:6) Do you see that what God is doing now can neither be contained nor measured by instruments or calculations? This is God's healing power "on the loose," unleashed from the temple, now on the same side of the temple wall as the people.[38]

The second half of the passage conveys the way the river revivifies both land and sea—"everything will live wherever the river[39] goes" (47:9). The creation vocabulary of Genesis is prominent here; a withered world is recreated by the life-giving water, in much the same way the withered bones were recreated by the life-giving breath/wind/spirit of God in chapter 37. I will not dwell on the creation language here but simply note the lush fecundity that the river nourishes wherever it goes.[40] Of particular interest at present is the way in which the images of growth are described as being beyond measure. The effects of the river's surge are first described in verse 7: "When I returned, I saw upon the banks of the river a great abundance of trees" (*eṣ rav měʾod*). The indefiniteness of this expression of superabundance, *rav měʾod*, gestures toward the infiniteness of the renewal taking place—it is beyond measuring or calculating. This phrase denoting unquantifiability is repeated twice more to describe the resultant abundance of fish (47:9, 10). Measurements cannot express the immense hope unleashed by the torrent of the life-giving river. The phrase also occurs in chapter 37 to describe the infinite number of dry bones (37:2). Once they have been revivified by the breath (*ruaḥ*) of God, the immeasurability of their numbers is depicted by a repetition of *měʾod*: They constitute a "vast multitude" (*ḥayil gadol měʾod měʾod*).

The salvific action of divine water and breath cannot be quantified; the imprecision of their description indexes the power of God, in much the same way that the imprecise language of Ezekiel's vision of God in chapter 1 discloses the divine power and transcendence. Ezekiel's ending thus contains and reveals some of the same tensions stirring under the surface of the rest of the book; hope for the future is manifest in the controlled environment of the temple but also in the dynamic power of God to burst through the temple walls and heal both land and people with an incalculable flow. This tension echoes that between, in Bakhtin's lexicon, the classical body and the grotesque body, each bearing its own form of hopefulness. The hope embodied in the quantifiability of the temple measurements thus stands in some tension with the unquantifiable power and reach of both the healing water (chap. 47) and the life-giving breath (chap. 37).

BEYOND THE ENDING: THE PROMISES OF GOD

Perhaps the most unsettling aspect of the book of Ezekiel is the way in which God's power—both of fierce judgment and of gracious deliverance—is written out on the human body. The body is the source of death but also, in Ezekiel, of life. It is through the body—bumpy, bulging, grotesque as it is—that God offers the people a sustainable future. For a Christian tradition that continues to struggle with the embodiedness of existence, and with the ecologic interrelationships of a bumpy, bulging, incomplete creation, this is unsettling. For Ezekiel, as for us, there is no resolution to the tension between the "classical" architecture of the temple and the grotesque architecture of the human body. It may seem that much of the theological energy of the book resides in these human bodies, and perhaps less in the efforts to quantify holy space, but perhaps the most unsettling thing about reading Ezekiel is the realization that the tension exhibited in the book is the one we too must live in. God's power as manifested in the dry bones and in the life-giving waters is immeasurable (*měʾod měʾod*), yet we must try to measure it—this is the human condition that Ezekiel exemplifies for us. Ezekiel's ending discloses this fundamental conundrum even as it tries to repress it.

Both in Mark's Gospel and in Ezekiel, it is the promises of God that carry one beyond the ending. In Mark's case, Juel shows us how the promises made in the Gospel carry us beyond the mute terror of the women: "The story cannot contain the promises. Its massive investment in the reliability of Jesus' words becomes a down payment on a genuine future."[41] In Ezekiel's case hope rides out, irreversibly and uncontrollably, into the world on an increasingly powerful flow of healing water.[42] Juel's attention to the ending of Mark, to its unsatisfying nature, and to what that ending reveals about God and about us through our response to it—for all this we must be indebted to him. Moreover, one of the many fruits of Juel's engagement with Kermode is what it reveals about the possibilities of bringing literary theory into conversation with biblical studies and theology more broadly. Meaning—theological meaning—is borne only secondarily, and weakly at that, by propositional statements; rather, meaning is powerfully woven into the literary fabric of the Bible, into its figures, images, metaphors, and even genres.[43] Don Juel knew this far better than most of us.[44] We are indebted to him for delving into Kermode's work and weaving it into his own, for he found in Kermode an excellent lamp for reading Mark's Gospel, a lamp by which he deftly illumines aspects of the Gospel previously shrouded in darkness. That the fruits of this marriage between literary theory and biblical studies have proved to be theological testifies to the still only partially tapped richness of literary study for our theological understanding of the Bible.

It is a privilege to contribute this essay to this volume in memory of Don Juel. In the five years I knew him, Don taught me (and many, many others) much about how to be a faithful scholar, a passionate teacher, and a gracious colleague, however imperfectly I realize those lessons in my own life. Don was also a delightful and caring neighbor and friend. We miss him, even as we continue to cherish Lynda's friendship. In Ezekiel 43:8 God complains that the apartment walls between temple and palace were too thin; "only a wall between me and them" is not enough distance to sustain the relationship. Our house in Princeton is a duplex, the Juels on one side, my family on the other side. From our point of view the walls were never too thin, and Don and Lynda were polite enough to say the same, though Don would occasionally ask if our toddler "enjoyed" moving all the furniture around. Many who saw Don during the last, difficult months of his life testify that, in the midst of his profound suffering and the knowledge of his impending death, the integrity of his faith became ever more transparent as death approached. His witness to the power of the gospel and the promises of God, even beyond the ending, is something that I will never forget.

Notes

1. Rachel Blau DuPlessis, *Writing beyond the Ending: Narrative Strategies of Twentieth-Century Women Writers* (Bloomington: Indiana University Press, 1985), 1. Blau DuPlessis sees both of these endings as "romantic," and indeed the tragic end of those heroines who die has a strong "romantic" quality. I restrict these observations for the most part to Anglophone novels, although much the same can be said of French novels of the period (e.g., George Sand's *Indiana*).
2. A good example of this is George Eliot's *The Mill on the Floss,* in which the unbri-

dled, unconventional Maggie Tulliver abruptly dies in a flood at the end of the novel. She is too wild a character to marry, and there being no other alternatives, she must die, despite the apparent disjunction of such an ending with the rest of the novel (prevalent water imagery notwithstanding).

3. "In nineteenth-century fiction dealing with women, authors went to a good deal of trouble and even some awkwardness to see to it that *Bildung* and romance could not coexist and be integrated for the heroine at the resolution, although works combining these two discourses in their main part (the narrative middle) are among the most important fictions of our tradition. This contradiction between love and quest in plots dealing with women as a narrated group, acutely visible in nineteenth-century fiction, has, in my view, one main mode of resolution: an ending in which one part of that contradiction, usually quest or *Bildung*, is set aside or repressed, whether by marriage or by death" (Blau DuPlessis, *Writing beyond the Ending*, 3–4).

4. Donald H. Juel, *A Master of Surprise: Mark Interpreted* (Minneapolis: Fortress Press, 1994), 117 (and see above, pp. 8–9). The citation appears in a discussion of Frank Kermode's understanding of the relation between art and truth.

5. Juel, *Master of Surprise*, 120 (and see above, p. 11).

6. I am interested here in the way the book of Ezekiel as a whole functions, especially how the end relates to what precedes it. Traditional questions of authorship and composition are not in view at present.

7. Jacqueline E. Lapsley, *Can These Bones Live? The Problem of the Moral Self in the Book of Ezekiel*, Beihefte zur Zeitschrift für die alttestamentilche Wissenschaft 301 (Berlin: Walter de Gruyter, 2000). Another tension that has recently been explored concerns gender identity. See S. Tamar Kamionkowski, *Gender Reversal and Cosmic Chaos: A Study on the Book of Ezekiel*, Journal for the Study of the Old Testament: Supplement Series 368 (Sheffield: Sheffield Academic Press, 2003).

8. Jeremy Schipper, "Bakhtin's Notion of the Grotesque Body and Ezekiel," unpublished paper, 2003. I am wholly indebted in this section on the grotesque to the ideas Schipper articulates in this excellent paper.

9. Fiona C. Black, "Beauty or the Beast? The Grotesque Body in the Song of Songs," *Biblical Interpretation* 8 (2000): 309. While the coinage dates to the Renaissance, the phenomenon is ancient. On this see Johanna Stiebert, "Shame and Prophecy: Approaches Past and Present," *Biblical Interpretation* 8 (2000): 270. Stiebert also observes that while the grotesque is clearly present in Ezekiel, the comic dimension often associated with the grotesque is missing in Ezekiel.

10. Mikhail Bakhtin, *Rabelais and His World*, trans. H. Iswolsky (Bloomington: Indiana University Press, 1984), 320.

11. Schipper, "Bakhtin's Notion."

12. See Lapsley, *Can These Bones Live?* esp. 67–107.

13. Schipper, "Bakhtin's Notion." Schipper rightly notes, with relevant citations, the ancient Near Eastern cultural predecessors of this vision.

14. Schipper, "Bakhtin's Notion."

15. See Bakhtin, *Rabelais and His World*, 318. See also Schipper, "Bakhtin's Notion," 17.

16. Translations are mine unless otherwise noted.

17. Schipper, "Bakhtin's Notion."

18. Juel, *Master of Surprise*, 110 (and see above, p. 4).

19. On this topic, see Jon Levenson, *Theology of the Program of Restoration of Ezekiel 40–48*, Harvard Semitic Monographs 10 (Missoula, MT: Scholars Press, 1976).

20. See Susan Niditch, "Ezekiel 40–48 in a Visionary Context," *Catholic Biblical Quarterly* 48 (1986): 208–24.

21. Blau DuPlessis, *Writing beyond the Ending*, 3.
22. For a more sustained discussion of these issues, as well as relevant bibliography, see Lapsley, *Can These Bones Live?* esp. 173–83.
23. Levenson acknowledges that to many the great temple vision in chaps. 40–42 has seemed to be an "indulgence in pedantry" (*Theology of the Program of Restoration,* 1).
24. The nature of the vision is not my concern here. For a useful summary of views, see Kalinda Rose Stevenson, *The Vision of Transformation: The Territorial Rhetoric of Ezekiel 40–48,* Society of Biblical Literature Dissertation Series 154 (Atlanta: Scholars Press, 1996), 125–42.
25. Bakhtin, *Rabelais and His World,* 320.
26. Daniel L. Smith-Christopher, *A Biblical Theology of Exile* (Minneapolis: Fortress Press, 2002), 114–15.
27. The apostasy of the kings is mentioned first, but is not our concern here. The translation of the end of the verse depends on how the last word (*bmotm*) is vocalized. The alternative is: "the corpses of their kings on their high places."
28. For discussion of the issues, see Walther Zimmerli, *Ezekiel 2,* Hermeneia (Philadelphia: Fortress Press, 1983), 417; Daniel I. Block, *The Book of Ezekiel: Chapters 25–48* (Grand Rapids: Wm. B. Eerdmans Publishing Co., 1998), 583–85.
29. For a thorough study of issues pertaining to space, measurement, and territoriality in these chapters, see Stevenson, *Vision of Transformation,* esp. 11–36. For a wider study of the issues, see Jonathan Klawans, *Impurity and Sin in Ancient Judaism* (Oxford: Oxford University Press, 2000).
30. On this last point, see Donald H. Juel, *The Gospel of Mark,* Interpretation Biblical Texts (Nashville: Abingdon Press, 1999), 147–51.
31. Juel, *Master of Surprise,* 120 (and see above, p. 11).
32. Julie Galambush, *Jerusalem in the Book of Ezekiel: The City as Yahweh's Wife,* Society of Biblical Literature Dissertation Series 130 (Atlanta: Scholars Press, 1992), 148–57. Galambush has shown, however, that the city-as-woman has disappeared in the final temple vision because she poses too great a threat to purity. Thus, the marriage metaphor does not appear in the same way that it does earlier in Ezekiel.
33. An example may be instructive here: One of the most unconventional heroines to emerge from George Eliot's novels, Maggie Tulliver (*The Mill on the Floss*), wholly defies gender roles and dies in a flood at the end. In a sense, the ending punishes her for failing to comply with social convention, but at the same time the heroine's defiant character is displaced onto nature in the form of the flood, the fierce waters representing "Maggie's passion unrecognized, repressed, roiling up to bear them down; this is her dammed-up selfhood and her passionate desire for life, which cannot be repressed" (Blau Du Plessis, *Writing beyond the Ending,* 18).
34. Water imagery connects to other literature in several directions (cf. Ezek. 1:24; 43:2; Ps. 36:8–10; Joel 3:18 [Heb. 4:18]; Zech. 13:1; 14:8; Rev. 22:1–2); see Block, *Book of Ezekiel,* 696–703. On the strong connections to other ancient Near Eastern cultures (miraculous rivers flowing from the cosmic mountain) and beyond, see Jon D. Levenson, *Sinai and Zion: An Entry into the Jewish Bible* (San Francisco: HarperSanFrancisco, 1985), 111–37. On the connections to the garden of Eden traditions, see esp. Levenson's earlier work, *Theology of the Program of Restoration,* 25–36; and Steven Tuell, "The Rivers of Paradise: Ezekiel 47:1–12 and Genesis 2:10–14," in *The God Who Creates: Essays in Honor of W. Sibley Towner,* ed. W. Brown and S. McBride (Grand Rapids: Wm. B. Eerdmans Publishing Co., 2000), 171–89.

35. As Zimmerli dryly observes, "[T]here is reported, with great lack of concern, that the water, which is empowered in the innermost sanctum by the abundance of holiness on the part of the most holy one, flows out from the sanctuary into the dried up, salty region of mysterious curses without there being given the least hint of ritual protection from the stream which emerges from the realm of the holy" (*Ezekiel 2*, 509).
36. The water is described by three verbs; *yṣ*, *yrd*, and the hapax *legomenon pkh*.
37. Zimmerli, *Ezekiel 2*, 512.
38. Elsa Tamez observes that though the end of Ezekiel returns to the language of measurement (47:13–48:35), after the river has flowed the measurements describe agrarian reforms—in her view a sign of jubilee ("Dreaming from Exile: A Rereading of Ezekiel 47:1–12," in *Liberating Eschatology: Essays in Honor of Letty M. Russell*, ed. M. A. Farley and S. Jones [Louisville, KY: Westminster John Knox Press, 1999], 68–74).
39. MT reads "two rivers."
40. Steven Tuell sees the river as the source of both fertility and material blessing ("The Rivers of Paradise: Ezekiel 47:1–12 and Genesis 2:10–14," 182–86).
41. Juel, *Master of Surprise*, 120 (and see above, p. 11).
42. *Pace* Kathryn Pfisterer Darr, who argues that Ezekiel's vision for healing is limited to Israel alone ("The Wall around Paradise: Ezekielian Ideas about the Future," *Vetus Testamentum* 37 [1987]: 271–79).
43. For a fascinating and brilliant exploration of the meaningfulness of genre, see Carol A. Newsom, *The Book of Job: A Contest of Moral Imaginations* (Oxford: Oxford University Press, 2003).
44. The partnership between literary and biblical studies cannot be taken for granted. Petri Merenlahti, for example, takes issue with the way poetics has been practiced on the Gospels, especially Mark (*Poetics for the Gospels? Rethinking Narrative Criticism* [London and New York : T. & T. Clark, 2002]).

Chapter 12

Following an Unfollowable God

Ellen T. Charry

The abrupt end to Mark's Gospel fascinated Don Juel. The fact that the Gospel lacks an account of Jesus' postresurrection appearances spoke to Juel of a God on the loose in contrast to a God whom we can anticipate. He interprets the difference between Mark and the other evangelists as a testimony to the freedom of God and insists on this freedom, I suspect, in order to remind us of our place in the scheme of things. Juel takes up the ambiguity created by the fact that this Gospel fails to mention events included in the others in order to urge us to treat the elusiveness of loose ends as indicating something of the spontaneous character of God. In comparison with the other Gospels, Mark's text leaves us hanging. Juel believes that this indicates that all our attempts to impose clarity on events that do not end as we expect, or perhaps fail to conclude at all, are doomed. God will insistently surprise us, perhaps to remind us of who really is in control of things. The future is open and we do not know how it will go. Both cynicism and naiveté are schemes for avoiding ambiguity, but, Juel insists, it will not be defeated. The biblical God, he concludes, offers no closure, no resolution of tension, and no refuge from the ambiguity of life. "The deeper into the narrative we delve, the less control we are promised."[1] With less control, we hope more in the promises of God.

This essay takes Juel's fascination with the ambiguity of Mark's ending as an opportunity to explore the theological implications of ambiguity more deeply. It is not only Mark's ending that dangles; much of life does too. Juel picks up Frank Kermode's phrase, "an unfollowable world," to describe how it seems to us. That the world may be, or at least at times may be, unfollowable raises questions not just about our ability to control or anticipate events. It raises questions about the character of God as well, because an unfollowable world suggests either that God is not present to us, not in control of events, not benevolent, or plainly confused. That is to say, it may be not only that the more ambiguity the less control *we* are promised, but more pointedly, the less control *God* appears to have. An unfollowable world suggests an unfollowable God, if we assume that God is able to preside over a followable world. If God is erratic, as suggested by a passage such as Exodus 6:24–26, we are in big trouble.

That God might not be able to have a followable world is a bewildering thought. An unfollowable God discomfits most people. If God were unfollowable, we would need to rethink our understanding of the divine character. On the tradition's view that God is powerful, wise, and good, things should be followable even if they do not always work out as we hope. Further, we should be able to anticipate, at least roughly, what God will "do," assuming God can do anything at all and we have reasonable intelligence. Life would be much easier to bear if this were so. A God who catches us off-guard or sets us off-balance in order to show who is boss is unreliable and suspect. We will never relinquish the desire to have moral and technical control over our world enough to satisfy God that he does not have to keep us hanging. We take our chances with such a God, for we could get hurt. When we are hurting, we are at a loss as far as God is concerned. Is unfollowability punishment? Are we being used, like Christ, for some other end? Is suffering pointless? Erratic parents drive children crazy.

Ambiguity like that with which Mark's Gospel ends can lead to agnostic conclusions for those who believe that God makes everything work out right in the end. An open future bodes both well and ill. Ambiguity suggests that light and darkness are inextricably entwined. The unclarity of not having someone neatly tie up the ends of the story for us means that we have some work to do. All our powers of discernment are needed to find meaning.

Despite the urgings of some to celebrate irresolvable ambiguity, which would render all attempts at making meaning equally arbitrary and perhaps malevolent, enduring unclarity is confusing and enervating. It must eventually give way to some meaning, even if that meaning is only temporarily satisfying and must later be revised.

Prolonged unclarity is not only exhausting; it is paralyzing because we do not know what to say or do in its presence. Even well-meant gestures or patterns of meaning that we apply may prove harmful. We crave epistemic order so that we can resolve mental and emotional distress and move on. We want to be free of plaguing questions and doubts about what has happened, and be able to plan for what could happen. We need to be able to read environmental clues to get closure—or at least direction—and not be distracted by "what ifs" and "if only's." Deconstruction will necessarily give way to reconstruction. Exhaustion and paralysis are simply too high a price to pay for throwing over the traces. Such freedom may be exhilarating at first but is debilitating in the end. An unfollowable world is terrifying.

If God is truly a God of surprise and is not just faking it to promote his own power, he is unreliable. God's hold over the world might be tenuous, and the world unstable and resistant to meaning. An unreliable God may be worse than no God at all, since in the latter case we would at least know where things stand. This has important implications for theodicy, the struggle to find the world meaningful and orderly in the face of misery, suffering, and evil. Untimely death, unprovoked injury, accidents, natural catastrophes, random violence, and so on, create anguish and engender helpless anger. In the face of an unfollowable world, we must either revise our understanding of the divine character or discern fresh patterns of meaning that render it followable. Simply ordering us to follow the unfollowable will not do. The tension between an unfollowable world and a followable God must be resolved in one direction or the other.

Don Juel celebrated the lack of closure in Mark in order to wean us away from needing to impose ourselves on events and to surrender our wills to God instead, even in the face of unclarity or perhaps—to take the argument one step further—evil. Juel's is a rigorous theological standard apparently based on such a high doctrine of divine control that we are to relinquish even attempts to interpret our world in meaningful terms and make our peace with whatever happens. Encouraging Christians to throw themselves on God's mercy instead of their own strength to save themselves here strains credibility, even good psychological judgment. It is impossible for us not to interpret the world as meaningful. Reliance on divine grace should not drive us to despair of knowing but to rest secure in God's goodness. In an unfollowable world, that goodness threatens to become a formal, empty category that offers scant comfort. Julian of Norwich taught us that "all shall be well, and all shall be well, and all manner of thing shall be well," but we must make sense of the world through which we peregrinate until that comes clear.

We do not need to experience horrendous evil in order to worry about an unfollowable world and an unfollowable God; everyday suffering and evil will do. Even though we cannot control meaning and outcomes, we are, I think, able to find resting places amid unclarity and confusion.

THE ART OF FOLLOWING THE AMBIGUOUS

Although I am concerned about the psychological effects of insisting on an unfollowable world that implies an unfollowable God, the word "unfollowable" itself has something to commend it. It offers a fresh way of framing the theodicy problem by offering a middle ground against the psychological temptation to polarize. By this I mean that the notion of followability is less extreme than the more traditional terms "good" and "bad" or "evil" to describe our experience of the world. Shifting the ground from "good" and "bad" to "followability" and "unfollowability" enables us to step back from the emotion called up by the words "good" and "bad" and permits us to focus on whether we can discern meaning in events, even if they turn out to go contrary to our interest. Events can be meaningful even if they go against us. Accepting meaningful defeat graciously can help us grow into sadness and disappointment with maturity. Further, finding meaning, even goodness, in events that go against us softens the blow.

The opposite of "unfollowable" may not be "predictable," as Juel may have thought, but simply "followable," even just to some degree. This is a rather neutral word, and that commends it to us. To be able to predict is to be in control. To be able to follow is simply to walk behind, integrating but not directing what is happening as we go along. To be bearable, things need not be predictable or controllable, but minimally graspable or followable. Followability suggests that for something to be meaningful it need not go our way, but that it go someone's way; it must come to a conclusion, although that conclusion need not please us. Thus, for the world (and God) to be followable it must be understandable, but not necessarily favorable toward us. Meaningfulness enables us to gain perspective on our own interests. It helps us find succor even when the advantage goes to someone else.

The concept of followability, then, offers us a calm seat from which we may be able to observe events as meaningful, even if their outcome is negative for us. It gives us a little breathing space between the justice of God and our own concerns. This space is exceedingly important, as our judgment of God often turns on the degree to which we believe that he has satisfied our own needs or desires.

With the notion of followability in mind, we may look for the goodness of God that believers have hoped to see work on their behalf. Beyond that, it may enable us to see God as good, even when that goodness is not pointed toward us but toward our enemies! That we need to adopt this posture in order to find the world followable is evident from Luke 4. In this famous passage, Jesus visits his home synagogue on his tour through Galilee. The friends and neighbors who presumably knew him as a child are delighted to see him until he preaches to them. Instead of telling them that God will rescue them from the Roman occupiers, he tells them that God will save their pagan neighbors, the Sidonians and their old enemies, the Assyrians. His friends and neighbors are so outraged that Jesus would first manipulate them by telling them that he will fulfill the Isaianic prophecy of release to captives only to then betray them by identifying those captives as their enemies that they move to lynch him on the spot. Even though the attempt fails, their point stands. Jesus escaped lynching in order to redeem Israel's enemies. Nothing could appear more unfollowable to the Nazareth worshipers.

The story of the prodigal son in Luke 15 offers another version of the same scene. The older son who has worked hard and been obedient all his life is sidelined by his no-good younger brother who wastes their father's good money and, on the brink of disaster, comes home to great rejoicing, and quite possibly—

given his father's joy—to being given part of his brother's remaining inheritance! What could be more infuriating? It is utterly unfair.

Matthew's story of the laborers in the vineyard is no different. Paying the workers the same whether they worked one hour or a full day in the hot sun is maddening. What would students enrolled in a four-year course of study do if students who only spent two years in study received the same degree that they did?

If we take all these stories as stories about God and us—as I believe they are meant to be—it is not clear that this is a God who is reliable and fair and not erratic and capricious. Worshiping devoutly, honoring parents, and working hard are all rendered pointless by the seemingly capricious moves of the various actors who stand in for God in each case. God does not take care of those who love him, but those who scoff at him or who show up just under the wire! Who is easily persuaded to be devoted to this God, especially when disciples are told that they should abandon their families and their means of livelihood to do so? Who would abandon a stable life to follow a God who is consistently unfair to his devotees? When Jesus says the first shall be last, he is not saying that the poor and the weak will displace the high and mighty. He is saying that little people who are not self-righteous but simply loyal, hard-working, and honest will be ignored and the truly undeserving will be rewarded. The world of the New Testament is surely unfollowable because it is unfair.

With these illustrations before us, the questions asked earlier take on flesh. How are we to make sense of the traditional vision that claims that God controls history and is good? These stories confirm that God is in control of events yet intentionally and repeatedly hurts or tests the simple faithful, as he tested Abraham. Yet there the story ends well, with a ram sacrificed in Isaac's stead. Here no angel or *deus ex machina* emerges at the last minute to tell the worshipers, the elder son, or the laborers that this is just a test, or even that they too will be cared for along with their enemies. They are simply left out in the cold as God turns to others. Is the God of the New Testament cruel to those who love him, manipulating them to stretch them beyond where they think they can go, while the God of the Old Testament rescues people even from tests that he sets for them?

STRATEGIES FOR FOLLOWING

Indeed, while Juel found ambiguity in Mark's ending, our brief look at other central New Testament passages suggests that beyond being unclear God is downright unfair! One understandable reaction to this unfair God is to leave him. If one cannot depend on him for rescue, why bother with him? Perhaps this God is only for the stouthearted who can tolerate being treated unfairly. Perhaps we should not expect a fair and just world under God's providence. Perhaps God is not good to those who love him, as the Abraham story suggests, but arbitrary, as the New Testament stories imply. Exodus puts it sternly: God says,

"I will be gracious to whom I will be gracious, and will show mercy on whom I will show mercy" (33:19).

This harsh warning may help those of brittle faith, but it will not help the simple faithful, those who worship God in season and out, who care for their parents, in poverty and in wealth, and who work and play by the rules, even if it is only because they lack the imagination not to. Some of the victims in Jesus' stories are likely to storm out of their devout way of life in protest, but most will probably not be able to change their way of life radically enough to eliminate God from it. The lives of the devout are simply too habituated to God to permit that much change. Pointing out that God's ways are ambiguous, arbitrary, and even outright unfair is devastating, but the truly faithful have no other foundation for their lives; they have nowhere else to go. Even in the face of unfairness and disappointment, they will be unable to flee from God. In short, most of the simple faithful are stuck with God even when they cannot like or trust him. They deserve help to keep them from despair, not only about the fate of their own souls but perhaps even more for the sake of the world.

RENDERING PAIN FOLLOWABLE

There are skills that we can practice to try to render the unfollowable more followable in the face of the seeming capriciousness of God. By training ourselves to follow better we will not only calm ourselves but perhaps come to appreciate and sometimes even benefit from what at first seems to be God's shutting a door in our faces, as was the case in the Kafka parable that Don Juel discussed, or the experience of the left-out characters in the infuriating New Testament stories.

Rendering something painful followable requires first getting some distance on it and then internalizing another vantage point entirely. To do this, it will help to distinguish various ways in which, or reasons that, some things are painful. For example, something may be unfollowable because it is sadistically cruel to a degree that seems irrational, while something else may be unfollowable not because it is illogical or irrational but because it is emotionally painful on a personal level—it assaults our self-image, for example. Increasing our ability to follow, then, requires the ability to control our emotional reactions enough to analyze the event from a wider perspective.

Here are a few ways of analyzing situations so that they become more followable and thereby less demoralizing:

1. Something may be unfollowable at one time but followable later.

- A high school student is not accepted at her first-choice college and she ends up attending a school nearby. In her second year, her mother is diagnosed with cancer and she and her mother are both deeply grateful that she is near home. With hindsight, one can see that it was all for the best.

- A fourteen-year-old comes to school heavily armed, kills the school principal in the cafeteria, and then turns his weapon on himself. This horror is rendered followable, that is, redemptive in some small measure, if the community comes to see that teenage males are emotionally vulnerable and need better social and emotional guidance to cope with dangerous and untoward impulses.

2. Something may be unfollowable in one respect but followable in another. One is passed over for a promotion she believes she deserves, yet slowly is able to see that the person who got the job brings other resources that she could not have provided, as in the case of affirmative action decisions. One can even be comforted by knowing that one has contributed something to the greater good by not being selected.

3. Something may be emotionally repugnant, tragic, and morally culpable, but on reflection logically followable, even valuable. This is the case with public transit accidents or soldiers or civilians killed by friendly fire in combat situations because of inattention to safety precautions when using dangerous equipment or disregarding weather or other warning signs. If awareness of these problems causes bystanders or those who learn of such tragedies to reflect seriously on them and they then take the knowledge to heart and live more carefully, other lives may be saved.

- Racial, tribal, and ethnic rivalries and vendettas that grip one culture in bloody violence may appear unsupportable or unwarranted to those who are unfamiliar with the cultural and historical context. Yet that very fact may have a positive effect on faraway observers if they can see their own hotly held desire to avenge past hurts or atrocities at a similar remove.
- One of the most unfollowable horrors is parental homicide, the murder of children by their parents. In Texas, a father who had Sunday visiting rights with his four-year-old son was watching a football game, but the child was whining and constantly interrupting him, seeking his father's attention. In a fit of rage, the father bludgeoned his son to death with his bare hands. In South Carolina, a mother, estranged from her husband, who had custody of her two children, was having an affair, but the lover did not want her children. She locked them in her car and rolled it into a lake, drowning them. The problem here is not that the events are unfollowable, but that they are all-too-followable. In rage in one case and panic in the other, these parents completely lost sight of their defenseless children. The danger for us is that we might see such violence as so abnormal as to be unable to imagine ourselves in such straits. Such events are only unfollowable if we think that these parents are unusually weak and that we are emotionally stronger than they are.

- Suicide and accidental death of young males in momentary fits of jealousy, despair, or daring is another painfully unfollowable event. Yet if it enables other young men to see their own vulnerability through the bravado of extended adolescence, it may give others pause before acting foolishly.

4. Something may be unfollowable at one level but followable at another. This interpretive strategy may be the most strenuous. Perhaps this is the point that Jesus, through the pens of the evangelists in the three stories mentioned above, had in mind. The faithful worshipers, the devoted son, and the hard workers all expect to make out well by living rightly. When they do not, they are all thrown into a tizzy because they lack the imaginative power and spiritual maturity to benefit from their misfortunes. The events they are caught in become followable only when their very understandable sense of fairness and justice is undone and a radically different sensibility put in its place. That is, only when their offended sense of entitlement reveals to them the depth of their own jealousy can they focus on the truly important issue for them. If they can turn from their expectation of fairness and grasp the depth of their jealousy, the events may become followable in the sense that they and their competitors begin to benefit from them. The offended pious will benefit from seeing the unloveliness of jealousy and begin to experience it as a problem to be overcome. Those who have taken their place will further benefit because if the offended party begins to control his jealousy and experience the wideness of undeserving grace, he will not have to fear retaliation and recrimination from the offended party who stood first in line. If one clings by one's fingernails to the notion that God really is in control and is good, God's interest seems to be to press the simple faithful to spiritual maturity as a result of self-confrontation wrought by experiences such as being shoved aside by lesser worthies.

None of these interpretive strategies is strong enough to take away the sting of disappointment at having not gotten what one wanted or deserved in the first place. The advantage of the notion of followability is not that it takes the pain or suffering away, but that it sets it in a larger context in which benefits to self and others become real. Followability does not restore justice or fairness, but it can provide comfort that enables the injustice to be born with grace and dignity.

The upshot of this approach is that to ask, "Why did God let this happen (to me)?" avails little if God's world is ambiguous. Those who believe take on the responsibility of figuring out whether God's redeeming hand can be glimpsed amid pain, suffering, and evil.

SPIRITUAL MATURITY

Rendering the world followable requires emotional and intellectual maturity, a reflective bent of mind, emotional depth, and a philosophical or theological orientation to ground and guide one's judgments. We will conclude this reflection on following with a short discussion of why all four of the above mentioned strategies are needed and why they are best cultivated together.

One of the most important skills for rendering the ambiguous or unfollowable followable is an ability to pierce the surface and look at things more than once and from more than one vantage point. That is, it requires a willingness to analyze one's experiences, motivations, and behavior, even in the midst of pain. A reflective mind will not content itself with first reactions or first appearances, but will press ahead to see things from different perspectives, including positions that question one's own instincts that are often self-serving. Especially important is the ability to take a point of view other than the one that first springs to mind or is most comforting. A reflective bent of mind requires self-discipline and the fortitude to tolerate and not flee from emotional discomfort. It calls one to sit in other people's seats and experience the world as they do. While our place in things looms large to us, from another perspective we may be of minimal import, although it may take time to see or admit that.

By engaging subsequent perspectives, the reflective mind will also need to be flexible enough to let go of first impressions and adopt more weighty or compelling ones as time goes on. This flexibility is a contemporary replacement for the older affection for humility because flexibility implies the possibility of being wrong and adopting another view in place of one's own. Most of the time, we think outward from ourselves. This undoubtedly distorts our ability to follow well, since self-preservation/self-love is our most ready, though not most reliable, affection.

In short, the most important skill needed for rendering the world followable is the ability to move beyond self-service. As long as we relate all events and circumstances to our own case, we will not be able to see them clearly and adjust ourselves to them appropriately. Disappointment, confusion, dismay, frustration, even outrage seem to be built into the scheme of things. If we are to sustain our faith in a good and powerful God, we will have to work hard to mature beyond self-service and to rejoice in the possibility that God has come to rescue others.

NOTE

1. Donald H. Juel, *A Master of Surprise: Mark Interpreted* (Minneapolis: Fortress Press, 1994), 121 (see above, p. 12).

Chapter 13

The Bible and Theological Education: A Report and Reflections on a Journey
Patrick R. Keifert

And they said nothing to anyone, for they were afraid.

(Mark 16:8)

I am the way, and the truth, and the life.

(John 14:6)

THE PROBLEMATIC: WHY IS THE BIBLE SO OFTEN ABSENT IN PUBLIC CONVERSATIONS IN CHURCH AND WORLD?

These two passages, the Markan description of the faithful remnant of women running from the tomb in terror and amazement and the Johannine Jesus' confident self-identification as the way, the truth, and the life, capture the dynamic polarities of the conversation and inquiry that drove the life and work of Donald H. Juel. The exploring and managing of these polarities rather than resolving them to one side or the other generated tremendous energy in the same way that the strength of electrical poles, positive and negative, generate electricity in a battery. The silence of the Bible in much contemporary public conversation and the continuing presence of the universal truth claims regarding Jesus empowered his scholarship, teaching, and preaching.

For over twenty years, my good friend and colleague Donald H. Juel and I reflected together within this polarity on the place of the Bible in modern theological education and public conversation. This essay sketches why we set out together on that journey and how we engage others, and offers some brief reflections about why these travels are so necessary, not only to the life of the church but to the flourishing of our postmodern world.

Though we found a plentitude of ways to describe what we were trying to learn, one question, in two parts, serves to capture our inquiry: "When we say the Bible is true, what do we mean? And what methods of interpretation appreciate its truthfulness?" We came to this question as we explored two locations in which the Bible is commonly thought to be central, indeed critical, to theological discourse: the academy, especially theological institutions and departments of religion, and the Christian congregation.

As we ventured out for answers, we began by reflecting upon how various centers of learning within the academy understood the Bible as true, and what methods of interpretation they used to appreciate its truthfulness. We were curious not only about how particular methods of interpretation and application were justified but also how those methods actually are used in practical situations by those who espouse them. As time went on and the significant conflict among scholars and disciplines on these questions became more apparent, we became more and more interested in how our colleagues in the academy actually persuaded each other to change their minds regarding these questions.

As another part of our journey, we focused on how people encountered the Bible in moral conversations in the congregations, and particularly how scholars, teachers, and congregational leaders used the Bible to convince those diverse audiences of a moral or interpretive position. The congregational practices we found were, in a few instances, quite encouraging, but more often than not, what we saw was discouraging.

The realities of these practices in both the academy and church caused us to reexamine the use of the Bible in theological education. To begin with, we found that our own previous academic training was, at least in part, disturbingly inadequate in preparing us to pursue these questions of truth, and that various individuals and structures within the academy employed practices of critique and persuasion that were equally inadequate. Our academic training had caused us to wonder about the relationship between traditional claims that the Bible is true and the methods we used and taught for interpreting the Bible.

For us, as for other modern students of the Bible, history was the primary "mode of intelligibility,"[1] the key methodology we had learned for understanding the truth claims of the Bible. However, we joined many students of the Bible who have found that such a method has led to an unhappy and dysfunctional divide between what we, following Martin Buss, have called "critical description and capricious faith"[2]; that is, between empirical or rationalist engagement with the text as a historical document and nonrational commitments to the Bible as the word of God.

This complete separation between two approaches to the role of the Bible— critical description and capricious faith—proved to be present in the thought and practice of the academy as well as the congregation. Indeed, the divide was especially noticeable in conversations and decisions of Christian congregations on morally controversial issues.

Our research on congregations in deep conflict over morally disputed topics such as sexuality, war, and worship uncovered ironic and disturbing patterns in the ways the Bible was used. The higher the anxiety was on a moral issue in a congregation, the *less* likely it was that leaders would turn to the Bible in hope of even aiding, much less transforming, the conversation.[3] This pattern of avoiding discussion of the Bible altogether in these circumstances was as typical of congregational leaders who made very strong claims for the authority and truthfulness of the Bible as for those who made much more modest claims. In short, whatever theory and doctrine of the Bible as authority and source of truth these leaders and their congregations avowed, there was a clear correlation between heightened anxiety and the practice of avoiding the Bible. To make matters worse, as anxiety increased, leaders expressed fear that the Bible would contribute to, if not cause, dysfunctional conflict in their congregations.

In these crises of congregational conflict, we identified two dominant congregational habits in the use of the Bible, named for their seeming effects on civil conversation within the congregation: "Bible bullets" and "pious syrup."

In a majority of cases in which the Bible was used to consider morally disputed topics, parties to the dispute tended to perceive the Bible as a source of ammunition to fire at the opposition in an ongoing war whose purpose was to obliterate the adverse position from the community. Unsurprisingly, rather than informing or persuading any conversation partners to change their minds or even to come to a peaceful agreement to disagree in love, these uses of the Bible invariably ended conversation, no matter whether the text was employed by so-called conservatives or liberals. After all, bullets are intended to end a conversation with an opponent, not to foster it.

Others, especially those who hated conflict or saw it as unchristian, responded to increasing anxiety in the congregational system by avoiding a sustained engagement with the Bible, instead pronouncing broad and saccharine judgments to "resolve" the conflict. The language used—for example, "The Bible's message is love, and so we should do the loving thing"—showed up often in these moments of high anxiety. Pouring such pious syrup upon the conversation smothered the life out of it, ironically demanding that those in conflict simply stop the conversation. The result, though perhaps less invasively violent, was nonetheless as deadly to honest moral conversation as the Bible bullet approach.[4]

When researchers shared these observations with theological leaders, especially those with degrees from established schools of theology, we found that few were surprised by our findings. In fact, they were surprised we found them remarkable at all![5]

When we probed for the reason that congregations avoided the Bible in these conflicts, congregational leaders, especially those with MDiv degrees, admitted that they withdrew from engaging the Bible in morally disputed topics precisely because they found the use of the Bible so dysfunctional to genuine conversation. Furthermore, even when they led Bible studies during times of congregational conflict, they tended to keep to a purely descriptive and factual engagement with the text. Indeed, they found that the process of making a move from the Bible to judgments on the questions at hand was threatening to their very role as leader.[6]

To be sure, a small number of congregational leaders took these opportunities for engagement of the biblical text to move toward strong advocacy of their own moral positions. However, we found that the results of this engaged advocacy were minimal; their advocacy attracted those in agreement with them, but it seldom expanded the number of those who shared each leader's position or deepened a particular congregation's engagement with the issue at hand. We concluded that unless we were prepared to accept this sort of thinly instrumental notion of the role of the congregation and its conversations in public life, we needed to discover another set of practices for the use of the Bible in theological conversation.[7]

Conversely, and perhaps more interestingly, we identified numerous congregational leaders who admitted that their own study of the Bible remained focused on the search for the original meaning of the Bible within its own context,[8] but it was hardly ever employed in practical reflection on contemporary morally disputed topics. In fact, many congregational leaders believed that their theological education had only succeeded in helping them to see the vast cultural and historical distance between the Bible and the present culture. The practical outcome of this lesson in what Paul Ricoeur aptly names "distanciation,"[9] however, was that such leaders avoided normative discourse within their congregations at all costs. In short, their education had helped them to see what the Bible was *not* good for, but it had not helped them see what it *was* good for. Theological education had not helped them find a way of engaging the Bible even in disputes in their own congregation, among people who presumably shared much in the way of commitments, much less outside their congregation among those who did not share Christian faith.

This behavior that we observed among research subjects follows a pattern we have seen in most of our students over the past twenty years.[10] When our students were asked to write about the truth of the Bible and methods of interpretation, they spent most of their time arguing for a rejection of a "literalist" or "fundamentalist" position. However, they were genuinely unable to imagine or articulate a positive argument for the truth of the Bible and the appropriate methods of interpretation, to describe how the Bible might help us see what we should do in contemporary life. Although these seminarians have varied by age, ethnicity, gender, political stance, and biblical literacy over this time period, we have observed very little variation in this "strange silence"[11] about the role of the Bible in our common life in the church.[12]

TOWARD A NEW MOMENT: RHETORICAL
RATIONALITY ENCOUNTERS THE BIBLE

As we reflected on the set of problems associated with use of the Bible in our own scholarship and teaching, and in the practices of congregational leaders, Donald and I found strong consonance between the disturbing patterns we were witnessing and the analysis of several scholars who have called for a postmodern retrieval of the ancient rhetorical tradition to shape secular public discourse. Donald joined me in studying how the work of three of my teachers at the University of Chicago—Wayne C. Booth, Stephen Toulmin, and Paul Ricoeur (who had informed my early itinerary of reflection on rhetorical approaches)—might teach the church about its own conversations.

We were aware that the term's "rhetoric" and "rhetorical rationality" were not going to seem immediately inviting to potential sojourners. Indeed, "rhetoric" suffers from a crisis in public relations.[13] In public life, we often hear the expression "mere rhetoric." Those who employ it do so with some suspicion that their audience is being manipulated rather than convinced. Their use of the term suggests that to them, "rhetoric" refers to the means of communication, the outward form rather than the inner substance of a message. Or, again, we commonly refer to "rhetorical questions" as questions to which the answer is already assumed, which need no discussion.

Though this is not what we mean by rhetoric, this common usage of the word "rhetorical" captures something at the core of proposals for rhetorical rationality—namely, that rhetoric actually pays attention to the audience and what it assumes to be the case in the world in which the audience lives. Rather than presuming to create a universal, pure, rational, neutral discourse, rhetorical rationality humbly confesses to its particularity to audience, place, time, and so forth.

Aristotle, in developing his theory of rhetorical rationality, notes that all speeches reveal three characters: the character of the speaker (ethos), the character of the speech (logos), and the character of the audience (pathos).[14] Thus, rhetorical rationality understands that all discourse takes place within a particular setting, that it is aimed at a particular audience and is delivered by particular speakers who employ assumed warrants and backing for their claims within a moral field.[15] It is about character. We might say that it is this moral embeddedness of all discourse, indeed of all knowledge, in implicit values or human interests of particular times and places[16] that much of the intellectual project of modernity has sought to escape.[17]

Modernity has been skeptical of the rhetorical project, pointing to the history of human violence and oppression as its fruits; the chief project of modernity was to imagine a kind of pure reason and pure language (e.g., mathematics) based upon objective facts that would be so indisputable as to avoid at least violent conflict in the modern world. Of course, we need to acknowledge that rhetoric was suspect in the ancient world as well. Its ancient opponents, including Plato, attacked rhetoric as a rejection of the search for truth in favor of the morally suspect act of persuasion. Especially in its Latin forms, the rhetorical tradition, which attended extensively to style and aimed at the passions, seemed to confirm the suspicions of its opponents.[18]

We were quite aware of this public relations crisis with our chosen approach when we turned to these three scholars. Even though they represent three different strains of Western philosophy, these scholars concur in rather significant ways with the analysis of this problematic on the use of the Bible and on the promise of the rhetorical approach in responding to it. Our conversation with these three thinkers deepened our analysis and funded our growing sense that a rhetorical approach to theological education in general, and especially for deploying the Bible in that setting, held some hope for the church.

Perhaps Booth's early work, *The Modern Dogma and the Rhetoric of Assent,*[19] clarified our initial diagnosis of the situation best. This volume, which published lectures he delivered to undergraduates of the University of Notre Dame in the spring of 1970, reflects the realities of that turbulent time in American society. Then dean at the University of Chicago, Booth had been granted leave by student protesters, who had placed him under "house arrest" in the University's administration building, in order to travel and deliver the lectures at Notre Dame.

Nevertheless, Booth's telling lectures about the collapse of public discourse on the college campuses found less fault with the students and more with the failure of his colleagues in the elite circles of the academy. In Booth's view, they had failed to engage in sustained reflection with one another on the questions of the day because they uncritically accepted a set of deep assumptions about the relationship of truth seeking and the good of the community in public conversation. He called this dysfunctional set of assumptions the "modern dogma." These assumptions revealed a deep divide in modernity, built around the fact/value split. Booth's analysis exactly fit the patterns we found in the use of the Bible within the academy and the church, that is, they displayed a vast gulf between the activities of "critical description" and "capricious faith."

In response to the fact/value split, Booth called for a "rhetoric of assent," his own retrieval of the premodern practice of rhetoric. The rhetoric of assent is intended to move the essence of critical intellectual inquiry beyond the practices of systemic doubt established by Descartes and Hume. Taking aim directly at the thought and life of one of the reigning philosophers of the twentieth century, Bertrand Russell, Booth demonstrated how Russell's adoption of the rhetoric of systemic doubt and the other contours of the modern dogma led Russell to incoherence, immorality, and failed leadership as a public intellectual.

Stephen Toulmin, a student of Ludwig Wittgenstein, had already developed his own itinerary for what, in his most popular work, *Cosmopolis,*[20] he terms "rhetorical rationality." Toulmin had explored modern human understanding and discovered some of the same patterns at which Booth had taken aim. However, Toulmin deepened Booth's analysis and response to the modern condition by exploring, in ever wider and deeper circles, the historical and cultural developments that brought about the modern dogma[21] and effective ways of arguing or engaging in discourse that made possible sustained public understanding and truth seeking.[22] His exploration of the use of the practical syllogism[23] and the ancient tradition of casuistry[24] has profoundly influenced our exploration of the place of the Bible in both the academy and the church.

Most importantly, Paul Ricoeur's phenomenology of the will, employed within the framework of a rhetorical rationality,[25] has shaped our understanding of the actual interpretation of the Bible in academy and church, funding our sustained work toward innovating new theories of interpretation and truth. Ricoeur's dedication to engaging the greatest *aporia* of modernity and, at the same time, investigating common practices of biblical interpretation, an investigation he has undertaken with great patience, subtlety, and complexity, has literally made such innovation possible.

Donald's own work on the Gospel of Mark became a shared task in our invention of new theories of interpretation and the truth of the Bible. Beginning with his dissertation, *Messiah and Temple,* he had sought to move beyond the impulse of the historical-critical method to dissect the text in order to seek its truth.[26] Initially, he sought to understand the whole of Mark using the then adventurous work of redaction criticism, especially the work of Willi Marxsen.[27] At the same time, he wanted to engage the historical work of his teacher Nils Dahl on the crucifixion.[28] In terms of our joint work, he often said that he sought to understand the book of Mark as a whole without losing its historical referentiality.[29]

In seeking to keep together our engagement with both the Bible as a whole and its referentiality, we sought to move beyond the fact/value split, especially beyond the modern habit of reducing truth to historical fact, a move that relegates theological meaning and significance to the category of a capricious enterprise.[30]

Ricoeur's careful phenomenology of time and narrative furthered this enterprise.[31] His multifaceted descriptive phenomenology made visible the interaction of emplotment, narrative, and diverse forms of temporality that uncovered the rhetorical character of historical consciousness. The space between fact and value, once considered by modern scholars an infinite crevice, becomes in his analysis a multifaceted set of relationships, rendering the split obsolete, indeed, silly. In place of reductive schemes of referentiality, we began to see multiple referentiality and polyvalence as the most intellectually persuasive and morally adequate approach to the interpretation of the Bible in the academy and the church as a whole. The use of a rhetorical rationality helped us move, in Richard Bernstein's terms, "beyond objectivism and relativism,"[32] and established a rich intellectual and teaching agenda.

RESHAPING THEOLOGICAL INSTITUTIONS AND REINVENTING TEACHING PRACTICES

The congregational or intellectual leader's capacity to innovate in using rhetorical rationality with the Bible in public discourse must be shaped first by developing seminarians' practices in using the Bible in classes that focus on other subject matters besides the Bible itself. We believed that the paradigm for the use of the Bible in classes could be changed by two major shifts in the way we approached the Bible: first, providing students and faculty with practice using the Bible to provide rhetorical warrants and backing for one's position, not just data in a practical syllogism; and second, reshaping our practice of inquiry to consider God as first and always an agent, not simply a subject matter, in the educational process.[33]

This twofold shift led us to teaching interdisciplinary courses that focused on different subject matters but always used the Bible in the work of the class. However, we wanted to explore this intellectual and teaching agenda in the real world of theological education as a whole. We wrote a proposal to Craig Dykstra[34] at the Lilly Endowment that led to a grant to Luther Seminary. Along with our colleague in practical theology, Roland Martinson, we functioned as the research and development team for the creation of a curriculum that took this double-premised rhetorical approach to the engagement with the Bible in theological education quite seriously.

Firstly, the rhetorical approach became a critical ingredient in the interpretation of texts in the entire curriculum. We moved beyond studying the Bible rhetorically throughout the curriculum to studying other classic texts of the Lutheran tradition, the ecumenical creeds, and sixteenth-century confessions. Similarly, classes based upon continuing living practices of the church, such as worship, integrated a rhetorical approach[35] and were themselves integrated into the traditional "text study" courses.

Secondly, we and our colleagues at Luther Seminary literally structured a new division of the curriculum on the rhetorical rationality approach, which we called "interpreting and confessing." Each student, whatever his or her degree plan, must take required courses that teach rhetorical rationality in each year that the student is resident.[36] The courses focus upon the mediating human faculties of practical reasoning (*phronesis*) and creative, productive activity (*poesis*) gathered together as Christian wisdom and witness.

Thirdly, the rhetorical approach required situational reflection as a central learning activity in the new curriculum. Certain courses and times in the student's journey were taken as critical moments for helping students move beyond the modern dogma to practicing leadership out of Christian wisdom and witness. This move to situational reflection pressed a more integrated connection between personal student formation and formation as public leader. It called also for a move from the modernist construction of text and context, theory and applied theory (the dominant models of contextual education) to a more situationalist understanding of learning.

Fourthly, the rhetorical approach continues to serve as the vision and guiding principle in our practices for creating, introducing, and critiquing courses Luther Seminary offers, resulting in two major overhauls in the curriculum in the past decade.

As Donald moved to Princeton, our project and our conversation partners broadened and became more diverse. With the generous assistance of the Lilly Endowment, we were able to involve a number of colleagues from other schools of theology in conversation and critique of our rhetorical approach. This conversation over the last decade has involved scholars, administrators, and teachers from all the disciplines within contemporary schools of theology.

This conversation, which has continued under the name "The Bible and Theological Education," has been furthered by the conversations of a steering committee[37] and three project teams. The first team, whose initial study volume was completed first, explored the nature of the study of theology within the rubric of rhetorical rationality.[38] Their work has uncovered the profoundly important role of rhetorical rationality in the preparation and practices of Christian leaders in the first four centuries of the church.[39] Indeed, these researchers have concluded that unless we view their work with an understanding of rhetorical practice, our understanding of their vision and practices is greatly flattened and diminished. Using a rhetorical approach, this team also examined how moral and doctrinal questions have been examined throughout the history of the church. Among other things, we have learned how profound are the differences in how we now understand the basic teachings of the Trinity when we start with a rhetorical approach.

A second team in this conversation has focused on the use of the rhetorical approach within the classroom.[40] Interdisciplinary teams of faculty have attempted to rethink their classes using a rhetorical imagination, considering how rhetorical rationality might affect the structure of the curriculum as a whole as well as the character of the classroom itself, and outlining how they might deploy learning activities appropriate to teach these necessary capacities of Christian leadership. Much of the group's time has been spent reviewing these proposed courses created by teams from the various schools of theology.[41]

RHETORIC AND THE BIBLE: FOR OR AGAINST TRUTH?

Within the conversation we have sustained about the Bible and theological education, we have encountered both surface concerns and deeper doubts and questions about the limits of rhetorical rationality and the potential flaws in a rhetorical approach to theological education. The third team in the Bible and Theological Education project, long anticipated but only recently formed, is composed of philosophers, theologians, and Bible scholars, who want to respond to both ancient and modern suspicion that rhetoric is too often employed as a way to avoid or confuse questions of truth.[42]

The Truth and the Bible team[43] took on the question of truth directly. The team deliberately put philosophers, theologians, and biblical scholars together with the express purpose of exploring the question of truth from the point of view of these philosophical questions in such a way as they could serve our goal of deepening the study and use of the Bible in classroom and local congregation.

Our study team gathered philosophers from across the spectrum of theories of truth. Some philosophers proposed that we should update the traditional correspondence theory of truth, the one assumed in most common conversation.[44] Others wanted to revise and apply a coherence model of truth; two of us followed Ricoeur's work in a conversation with an Anglo-American linguistic turn.[45] Finally, some members of the group proposed further development of the American pragmatist theory of truth as a vehicle for the church to consider in the use of the Bible in education and moral conversation.[46]

Despite their diverse perspectives on what constitutes the most adequate theories of truth, all members of this team have participated in the study of the Bible and reflected upon their proposals in light of their actual reading of the Bible. Philosophers and theologians have sought to interpret the Bible, both in the presence of biblical scholars and also in partnership with these scholars, all in the service of the use of the Bible in classroom and congregation.

Michael Welker represented one of the most deeply held convictions of this study team best when he pressed for the continued vocation of the church as a truth-seeking community.[47] As he so well articulated it, for the church to forsake this vocation is for the church to forsake a core characteristic of its identity and to threaten its own missional character.[48]

WHAT IS AT STAKE—THE CHURCH AND THE WORLD

On the surface, most Christians would not question that the church has a vocation as a truth-seeking community. Of course, the church seeks truth—after all, Jesus is "the way, and the truth, and the life" (John 14:6). However, these same Christians continue to imagine the search for truth within these troubling conditions of modernity that profoundly threaten the life of the church and the civil community.

Indeed, they are not alone. Despite the cul-de-sac created by the modern dogma that Booth and others have made visible, many public intellectuals are calling for a return to the dead hand of the modern project. Nowhere is this reactionary proposal more fierce (and more significant) than in the conversation resulting from the contemporary ideological conflicts throughout the world, which for some scholars goes by the rubric "the clash of civilizations."[49]

Faced with a resurgence of increasingly vocal religious communities throughout the world, including within Judaism, Islam, and Christianity, these reactionary modernists are proposing the same solutions that have proven only half successful. Specifically, they propose that public communities should cordon off values, especially religious values, into the private space and recreate (or preserve) a value-free public space, where moral and practical decisions are made based only on "objective facts."

An inherent consequence—indeed, a hoped-for consequence of these proposals of reaction—would be that religious and moral communities would lose their place in the shaping of civil moral life. Religions would be required to forsake making truth claims, at least in public, thus avoiding irrational and unnecessary conflict, and to confine their activities to their own private spaces. Even some of the most subtle interpreters of modernity have been lulled into the belief that public civilization must necessarily be limited to matters of economic and political life and that religion functions only as a nurturing, safe, private home for people to escape the travails of the public world on occasion. These interpreters fail to see the dangers to civil life should their view become dominant and faith communities cease to be public meeting places, bridges between the private and public dimensions of our lives.[50]

One example of this sort of reactionary proposal is Jonathan Rauch's recent piece in *The Atlantic*. Rauch delights in a particular form of secular tolerance he calls "apatheism," which is built on his own experience that "it has been years since I really cared one way or another" about religion. He suggests that "apatheism—a disinclination to care all that much about one's own religion, and an even stronger disinclination to care about other people's . . . is worth getting excited about."[51] He praises his Christian and Jewish friends who "organize their lives around an intense and personal relationship with God, but who betray no sign of caring that I am an unrepentantly atheistic Jewish homosexual. They are exponents, at least, of the second, more important part of apatheism: the part that doesn't mind what *other* people think about God."[52] Rauch cites with enthusiasm the opinion of philosopher Richard Rorty that "a world of pragmatic atheists would be a better, happier world than our present one." Rauch, however, prefers apatheism to pragmatic atheism, clearly believing that both are "preferable to fanatical religiosity (al Qaeda) and tyrannical secularism (China)."[53]

History has shown, however, that a retreat by persons of faith from making public truth claims will not empty the public square of values but fill it with the very fundamentalists modernists like Rauch fear most. If persons of faith who seek truth forsake the faith-based public practice of making truth claims, only those who disdain the careful search for truth and instead offer only "capricious faith" will enter the public space. In such a system, tolerance will become repressive rather than engendering of civil discourse.

More ironically, a public space emptied of persons of faith searching for truth is the best place for fanaticism to flourish. Perhaps no better current example comes to mind than the truncated public conversation from both secular and religious intellectual communities in responding to Sayyid Qutb, Al Qaeda's favorite philosopher. Qutb, a martyr under the Nasser regime in Egypt, gathered an audience of young men who, like himself, were raised in traditional Muslim communities and educated in Europe and the United States.[54] These are not the poor or ill-educated of the Muslim world; quite the contrary, they are representatives of a growing upper middle class Islamic culture.

Yet this audience is profoundly disturbed by what they observe in contemporary Western culture. They perceive the same dysfunctional divide between fact and values and spirit and body that make up the modern dogma. Some, like

Qutb, return to their religious tradition, especially the Koran, to analyze modern Christendom, and they have gathered an audience. Paul Berman suggests that Qutb's most influential works, extended commentaries upon the Koran, have not attracted the public attention of American public intellectuals that they merit. According to Paul Berman, Qutb's

> analysis was soulful and heartfelt. It was a theological analysis, but in its cultural emphases, it reflected the style of 20th-century philosophy. The analysis asked some genuinely perplexing questions—about the division between mind and body in Western thought; about the difficulties in striking a balance between sensual experience and spiritual elevation; about the impersonality of modern power and technological innovation; about social injustice. But, though Qutb plainly followed some main trends of 20th-century Western social criticism and philosophy, he poured his ideas through a filter of Koranic commentary, and the filter gave his commentary a grainy new texture, authentically Muslim, which allowed him to make a series of points that no Western thinker was likely to propose.[55]

Berman sees persuasive power in such commentaries. He notes how Qutb makes truth claims on the basis of the Koran, truth claims that clearly convince intelligent and technologically sophisticated Muslims of the life and death character of his interpretation. He underlines the power of rendering public such truth claims about a religious text, the Koran, for the contemporary Muslim world but also for the contemporary secular and religious American public intellectual who would be a world citizen. Failing to respond to Qutb's truth claims with a full, rich, religious, and secular public conversation threatens civil community.

He also notes how dangerous and ill-advised it would be to have Western politicians meddling in a discussion of these sacred matters. Indeed, to have our politicians take up this response would both obviate the hard-won successes of uncoupling religious practice from state sanctions and limit the diversity of secular and religious responses to such challenges to Western democratic society and culture. Instead, Berman asks, "Who will speak of the sacred and the secular, of the physical world and the spiritual world? Who will defend liberal ideas against the enemies of liberal ideas?" He answers, "Philosophers and religious leaders will have to do this on their own. Are they doing so? Armies are in motion, but are the philosophers and religious leaders, the liberal thinkers, likewise in motion?"[56] Berman sees that when religious leaders and philosophers take up the apatheism proposed by Jonathan Rauch, we leave the civil space to those who advocate terrorism.

CONGREGATIONAL MORAL CONVERSATION AND TRUTH SEEKING

Of course, there are varied publics to which Christians need to make the truth claims within civil space. If we are to learn something useful from the challenge of Sayyid Qutb, for example, we need to make those claims through extended and thoughtful commentary on the Bible in conversation with Islam and its holy book.

At a bare minimum, we need to forsake the modernist habit of interpreting the Bible only for the faithful or reducing our notion of the "public" interpretation of the Bible to historical studies. Instead, we must imagine commentaries on the Bible, or parts of the Bible, aimed to teach, delight, even persuade diverse audiences. Regular commentary on the Bible in relation to contemporary topics and issues would better serve the civil space, especially if they were written by persons highly competent in the topic under discussion and thoughtfully aware of a critical understanding of the Bible.

Of course, this is not likely if we take seriously Rauch's observations that "even regular churchgoers can, and often do, rank quite high on the apatheism scale."[57] He refers to these happy Christian communities as the "softer denominations" who are "packed with apatheists."[58] Although he does not want to identify them, I would suspect those he praises are the same mainline denominations that are in decline, for, as he notes, "there are a lot of reasons to attend religious services: to connect with a culture or a community, to socialize, to expose children to religions, to find the warming comfort of familiar ritual."[59] Notice that his reasons for attending religious services fall far short of seeking truth and justice, beauty and peace.

In Rauch's mind, as in the view of many thinkers hearkening for a return to modernism, the only alternative to these apatheist denominations is fundamentalism. In Rauch's understanding, religion is "the most divisive and volatile of social forces. To be in the grip of religious zeal is the natural state of human beings, or at least of a great many human beings; that is how much of the species seems to be wired"[60]—a decidedly reductionistic, yet quite common view.

In response to these reactive turns, Donald Juel and I tried with our colleagues to imagine and work out a practice for a very different Christian community that could thrive between the extremes of apatheism and religious zeal, a community capable of considered, intense, conflicted truth seeking within itself and in conversation with its neighbors.[61] Such a community must move beyond either a propositional or even a narrative approach to the Bible into a rhetorical practice of truth seeking. Although the narrative approach profoundly influences our reflection on the Bible in theological education, its focus upon only one genre of the Bible[62] and its inattentiveness to the questions of ethos, logos, and pathos in diverse publics make it relatively inadequate when compared to the rhetorical approach. Indeed, the finest practitioners of the narrative approach often end up moving beyond simply telling the Christian story to engaging in all the classical rhetorical inventions we call for in our proposal.

In diverse face-to-face communities, from the academy to the local congregation, from Alaska to Texas to South Africa, we have sought to engender and regularly practice the rhetorical innovations that take seriously how human beings seem "wired" and how difficult it is to form civil space where moral and religious wisdom can find a place. Drawing on critical social theory, our colleague Gary Simpson calls these congregations "prophetic public companions."[63]

Happily, such communities do exist, even among congregations. They approach the Bible more as beggars than soldiers in search of ammunition; they risk the pain of disagreement, even conflict, rather than smothering conversation in pious syrup. They desire to seek truth with others and witness to the truth they find, rather than simply repeating the Christian story to themselves while waiting for others to be attracted to it. Their continued work of seeking the truth in an increasingly diverse and dangerous world is a cutting edge of contemporary theological education. Their practices of using the Bible are opening new opportunities for theological education. They are the primal location of such education, and our schools of theology would do well to learn from them.[64]

Notes

1. "History as a mode of intelligibility" came into my vocabulary in a class by the same title at Chicago taught by Charles Wegener. See his *Liberal Education and the Modern University* (Chicago: University of Chicago Press, 1978); and *The Discipline of Taste and Feeling* (Chicago: University of Chicago Press, 1992).

2. Martin J. Buss, ed., *Encounter with the Text: Form and History in the Hebrew Bible* (Philadephia: Fortress Press, 1979), 5. Describing quite different phenomena, twentieth-century literature on parents, Stacy Schiff notes a pattern of either "scientific or sermonic" discourse with little in between in *The New York Times Book Review,* April 27, 2003, 9.

3. These findings are described in greater length in Patrick R. Keifert, "The Bible, Congregational Leaders, and Moral Conversation," in *Word and World* 13, no. 4 (1993): 392–97.

4. Ronald W. Duty, "The Use of Scripture in Moral Conversation," in *Testing the Spirits: An Interdisciplinary Approach to Congregational Studies,* ed. Patrick R. Keifert and Patricia Taylor Ellison (Grand Rapids: Wm. B. Eerdmans Publishing Co., 2005), 145–67.

5. Patricia Taylor Ellison, *Pioneer, Prophet, Servant-Leader: Metaphors for Leading Public Moral Conversation in Congregations* (PhD diss., University of Minnesota, July 1995).

6. Ronald W. Duty, Patricia Taylor Ellison, and Patrick R. Keifert, *Growing Healthier Congregations: How to Talk Together When Nobody Is Listening* (Minneapolis: Church Innovations Institute, Inc., 1997).

7. A denominational consultation of over twenty organizations with processes and products designed to help congregations attend to morally disputed topics showed a "Bible bullets" type pattern; all but one was designed around the advocacy format.

8. Of course, this pattern among pastors educated in the last decades simply follows the wisdom of the leadership of the biblical studies guild. Cf. Krister Stendahl, *Meanings: The Bible as Document and as Guide* (Philadelphia: Fortress Press, 1984).

9. Paul Ricoeur, "Philosophy and Religious Language," *Journal of Religion* 54 (1975): 75. Ricoeur offers "distanciation" in contrast to objectivity. The interpreter can create some distance but not objective or neutral ground.

10. Donald and I taught a course entitled "Truth and Meaning: Uses of the Bible"

for fourteen years, and both of us continued teaching the course when he moved to Princeton Seminary. I was joined by two colleagues, Sarah Henrichs and James Boyce; with them I studied Galatians rather than Mark.

11. Cf. Donald Juel, "The Strange Silence of the Bible," *Interpretation* 51, no. 1 (January 1997): 5–19. Juel is, of course, playing off the much-noted book by James D. Smart, *The Strange Silence of the Bible in the Church: A Study in Hermeneutics* (Philadelphia: Westminster Press, 1970).

12. Interestingly enough, in my experience, former lawyers proved the exception to this general rule. My hypothesis is that they have received training and practice in one of the few intellectual disciplines where rhetorical rationality has survived the Enlightenment.

13. The irony that a position that puts such a strong focus upon connecting with the audience should have a crisis in public relations simply is too delicious. We could not pass up the use of this "offensive" term to press our case. Other terms, while less offensive to modern ears, only serve to reinforce the dominant paradigm about public discourse. The irritation is itself part of the argument.

14. Aristole, *Rhetoric*, 2.1.

15. Stephen Toulmin's layout of an argument consists of six elements. The first element is the *claim*. The claim of the argument is the conclusion that someone is trying to justify in the argument. The second element is the *grounds*. The grounds of an argument are the facts on which the argument is based. The third element of the argument is the *warrant*. The warrant of the argument assesses whether or not the claim is legitimate based on the grounds. The fourth element is the *backing*. The backing of the argument gives additional support for a warrant by answering different questions. The modal *qualifier* is the fifth element of the argument. The modal qualifier indicates the strength of the leap from the data to the warrant. The sixth and final element of the argument is the *rebuttal*. The rebuttal occurs when the leap from grounds to claim does not appear to be legitimate. See Toulmin, *The Uses of Argument* (Cambridge: Cambridge University Press, 1958).

16. Jürgen Habermas, *Knowledge and Human Interests*, trans. Jeremy J. Shapiro (Boston : Beacon Press, 1971), 17–18.

17. Stephen Toulmin, *Return to Reason* (Cambridge, MA: Harvard University Press, 2001), 67–82.

18. Albert R. Jonsen and Stephen Toulmin, *The Abuse of Casuistry: A History of Moral Reasoning* (Berkeley: University of California Press, 1988), 75–88. For a description of a rhetorical approach to theology that takes seriously the Latin tradition, see Donald Compiers, *What Is Rhetorical Theology? Textual Practice and Public Discourse* (Harrisburg, PA: Trinity Press International, 1999).

19. Wayne C. Booth, *The Modern Dogma and the Rhetoric of Assent* (Notre Dame: University of Notre Dame Press, 1974).

20. Stephen Toulmin, *Cosmopolis: The Hidden Agenda of Modernity* (New York: Free Press, 1990).

21. See Toulmin, *Return to Reason*.

22. See Stephen Toulmin, Richard Rieke, and Allan Janik, *An Introduction to Reasoning* (New York: Macmillan, 1979).

23. See Toulmin, *The Uses of Argument*.

24. Jonsen and Toulmin, *The Abuse of Casuistry.*

25. Ricoeur and Toulmin offered a seminar in which each took his own tradition of thought (Anglo-American and Continental) and reflected on the same topics (e.g., practice and action).

26. Donald H. Juel, *Messiah and Temple: The Trial of Jesus in the Gospel of Mark*, SBL Dissertation Series 31 (Missoula, MT: Scholars Press, 1977).

27. Willi Marxsen, *Mark the Evangelist: Studies on the Redaction History of the Gospel according to Mark,* trans. Donald H. Juel, James Boyce, William Poehlmann (Juel's seminary classmates), and (their teacher) Roy A. Harrisville (Nashville: Abingdon Press, 1969).

28. Nils Alstrup Dahl, *Crucified Messiah, and Other Essays,* ed. Donald H. Juel (Minneapolis: Augsburg, 1974).

29. My own dissertation had argued that a relatively adequate theory of interpretation understood the text as a whole without losing a full range of referentiality. Of course, part of this full range included historical references. Patrick R. Keifert, "Meaning and Reference: The Interpretation of Verisimilitude in the Gospel according to Mark," (PhD diss., University of Chicago, 1982).

30. One cannot here employ the phrase "meaning and significance" in relationship to this time period without recognizing that this desire was directed at the work of Eric Donald Hirsch Jr. in *Validity in Interpretation* (New Haven, CT: Yale University Press, 1967) and *The Aims of Interpretation* (Chicago: University of Chicago Press, 1976).

31. Paul Ricoeur, *Time and Narrative,* 3 vols. (Chicago: University of Chicago Press, 1984, 1985, 1988).

32. Richard Bernstein, *Beyond Objectivism and Relativism: Science, Hermeneutics, and Praxis* (Philadelphia: University of Pennsylvania Press, 1983).

33. Eberhard Juengel, *God as the Mystery of the World: On the Foundation of the Theology of the Crucified One in the Dispute between Theism and Atheism* (Grand Rapids: Wm. B. Eerdmans Publishing Co., 1983); David Kelsey, *To Understand God Truly: What's Theological about a Theological School* (Louisville, KY: Westminster/John Knox Press, 1992); idem, *Between Athens and Berlin: The Theological Education Debate* (Grand Rapids: Wm. B. Eerdmans Publishing Co., 1993).

34. Our debt to Craig Dykstra and James Wind and the Lilly Endowment goes well beyond the Endowment's financial support to include their genuine interest, engagement, critique, and trust in our enterprise.

35. See Patrick R. Keifert, *Welcoming the Stranger: A Public Theology of Worship and Evangelism* (Minneapolis: Fortress Press, 1992).

36. Such courses include: "Reading the Audiences" (a first-year required course in the practices of understanding the immediate environment of a congregation, its demographics, psychographics, cultures, and social systems), "Worship," "Exercises in Biblical Theology" (a senior course using case studies from the students' internships in congregations during the previous year—a requirement in Lutheran seminary education), and a series of electives generated by teams of faculty drawn from diverse disciplines around shared neuralgic themes, such as "God, Evil, and Suffering," taught by a systematician and Old Testament scholar; "Creation and Environment," taught by a Bible scholar and an ethicist specializing in agronomy and sustainable agriculture; "Law and Justice," taught by a Bible scholar and professor of law; "Paul, Power, and Polis," taught by a New Testament scholar and systematics professor; and "Truth and Meaning: Uses of the Biblical Narrative," focusing on either Mark or Galatians and taught by a New Testament scholar and systematician.

37. This committee includes David L. Bartlett, Beverly Roberts Gaventa, Richard B. Hays, Stephen J. Kraftchick, Dennis T. Olson, Alan Padgett, Donald Juel,[†] and myself.

38. This team includes A. K. M. Adam, Wesley Avram, James Boyce, Donald

Compiers, David W. Cunningham, Susan K.Heydahl, Frederick W. Norris, Richard R. Osmer, Janet Weathers, Stephen H. Webb, Donald Juel,[†] and myself.

39. See, for example, the work of team member Frederick Norris, "Nazianzus," in *To Teach, Delight, and To Move: An Integrated Vision for Theological Education*, ed. David Cunningham and Patrick R. Keifert (Harrisburg, PA: Trinity Press International, forthcoming); also, with Lionel Wickham and Frederick Williams, *Faith Gives Fullness to Reasoning: The Five Theological Orations of Gregory of Nasiansen,* Vigiliae Christianae Supplements 13 (Leiden: E. J. Brill, 1991).

40. This team included A. K. M. Adam, James Boyce, Ellen T. Charry, Sarah Henrichs, Stephen J. Kraftchick, Dennis T. Olson, Marianne Meye Thompson, John Thompson, and Miroslav Volf.

41. Perkins School of Theology, Azusa Pacific University, Candler School of Theology, Duke Divinity School, Yale Divinity School, Princeton Theological Seminary, Fuller Theological Seminary, St. Paul Seminary at the University of St. Thomas, Lutheran School of Theology in Chicago, Philadelphia, and Gettysburg, and Luther Seminary.

42. This team includes David L. Bartlett, Ellen T. Charry, Stephen T. Davis, Dennis T. Olson, Alan Padgett, Marianne Meye Thompson, Mark Wallace, Nicholas Woltersdorff, Donald Juel,[†] and myself.

43. This team includes Alan Padgett, Marianne Meye Thompson, Steven Davies, Nicholas Woltersdorff, Mark Wallace, David Bartlett, Donald Juel,[†] Ellen T. Charry, Michael Welker, and myself.

44. See William P. Alston, *A Realist Conception of Truth* (Ithaca, NY: Cornell University Press, 1996).

45. Mark Wallace and myself.

46. Perhaps the most clear source of this approach is the work of the Chicago pragmaticists, especially John Dewey, and the Aristotelian pragmatists Richard McKeon and Wayne C. Booth.

47. See Michael Welker, "Truth Seeking Community," in *Truth and the Bible,* ed. Alan Padgett and Patrick R. Keifert (Grand Rapids: Wm. B. Eerdmans Publishing Co., forthcoming).

48. Cf. the discussion of "missional" in Darrell Guder, ed., *Missional Church* (Grand Rapids: Wm. B. Eerdmans Publishing Co., 2001).

49. By using this phrase, I am not endorsing the view of Samuel P. Huntington (*The Clash of Civilizations and the Remaking of World Order* [New York: Simon & Schuster, 1996]). Still, major questions of the sort raised by Bernard Lewis (*What Went Wrong? Western Impact and Middle Eastern Response* [Oxford: Oxford University Press, 2002]) seem vital to me.

50. Our debt to Martin E. Marty in this enterprise is clearest in these "Marty monikers" for the public church. See esp. Marty, "Public and Private: Congregation as Meeting Place," in *American Congregations,* vol. 2, ed. James Lewis and James Wind (Chicago: University of Chicago Press, 1994), 133–68.

51. Jonathan Rauch, "Let It Be," *Atlantic* 291, no. 4 (May 2003): 34.

52. Ibid.

53. Ibid.

54. Paul Berman, "The Philosopher of Islamic Terror," *The New York Times Magazine*, March 23, 2003, 29.

55. Ibid.

56. Ibid.

57. Rauch, "Let It Be," 34.

58. Ibid.

59. Ibid.

60. Ibid.
61. Members of the Congregational Studies Research Team at Church Innovations Institute are: Ann Hill Duin, Ronald W. Duty, Patricia Taylor Ellison, David Frederickson, Nancy Hess, Donald Juel,† Cynthia Ann Jurisson, Craig J. Lewis, Mark MacDonald, Anne Marie Neuchterlein, Jose David Rodriguez, Gary Simpson, David Stark, Arlynne Turnquist, and myself; in addition, the following are guests of the team: Mary Ann Zimmer, C. Kirk Hadaway, Lois Y. Barrett, Anita L. Bradshaw, Jonathan Case, Nathan Frambach, Scott Frederickson, Gail Riina, Michael Welker.
62. See Mark Wallace, *The Second Naiveté: Barth, Ricoeur, and the New Yale Theology* (Macon, GA: Mercer University Press, 1995), for an insightful discussion of these issues.
63. Gary Simpson, *Critical Social Theory: Prophetic Reason, Civil Society, and Christian Imagination* (Minneapolis: Fortress Press, 2002), 125–45; see also his chapter in *Testing the Spirits,* 175–89. Simpson is a member of the Congregational Studies Research Team at Church Innovations Institute.
64. Recognizing congregations as the primal location of theological education remains one of the greatest opportunities for theological education in a post-Christendom North America.

Contributors

C. CLIFTON BLACK, Otto A. Piper Professor of Biblical Theology, Princeton Theological Seminary, Princeton, New Jersey.

BRIAN K. BLOUNT, Richard J. Dearborn Professor of New Testament Interpretation, Princeton Theological Seminary, Princeton, New Jersey.

ELLEN T. CHARRY, Margaret W. Harmon Associate Professor of Systematic Theology, Princeton Theological Seminary, Princeton, New Jersey.

BEVERLY ROBERTS GAVENTA, Helen H. P. Manson Professor of New Testament Literature and Exegesis, Princeton Theological Seminary, Princeton, New Jersey.

THOMAS W. GILLESPIE, President and Professor of New Testament, Princeton Theological Seminary, Princeton, New Jersey.

PATRICK R. KEIFERT, Professor of Systematic Theology, Luther Seminary; President and Director of Research, Church Innovations Institute, St. Paul, Minnesota.

JACQUELINE LAPSLEY, Associate Professor of Old Testament, Princeton Theological Seminary, Princeton, New Jersey.

PATRICK D. MILLER, Charles T. Haley Professor of Old Testament Theology, Princeton Theological Seminary, Princeton, New Jersey.

D. CAMERON MURCHISON, Dean of Faculty and Executive Vice President and Professor of Ministry, Columbia Theological Seminary, Decatur, Georgia.

DENNIS T. OLSON, Professor of Old Testament, Princeton Theological Seminary, Princeton, New Jersey.

MARIANNE MEYE THOMPSON, Professor of New Testament Interpretation, Fuller Theological Seminary, Pasadena, California.

MICHAEL WELKER, Professor of Systematic Theology, University of Heidelberg, Heidelberg, Germany.